Advance praise for

Hawking Hits *on the* Information Highway

"While it is common knowledge that the Internet has opened new areas of communication and commerce in the drug trade, no one has put this phenomenon into criminological perspective until now. Laura L. Finley has opened the proverbial 'Pandora's Box' and given us much to think about regarding the role of the Internet in creating and addressing the current drug problem in the U.S. ...This book offers an initial review of the relationship between common criminology theories and the Internet drug trade, and provides the reader with informative history and details of the trade—purchasing, tools to avoid detection, and information—making the many complex social and legal issues created by the Internet accessible to all interested parties. This well-organized and well-written book is a timely launch of an informed and intelligent discussion of this new dimension of addictions."

Craig Love, Senior Study Director, Westat

"The Internet has revolutionized the way society operates and conducts business in previously unimaginable ways; yet there is a darker, more sinister side of the Internet that has given birth to the cybercriminal, particularly the cyber drug trafficker. The transnational aspect of cybercrimes, particularly relating to the challenges of investigating, prosecuting, and deterring unlawful cyber drug sales and operations, is a central theme woven throughout this book. *Hawking Hits on the Information Highway* is a valuable contribution to the field, which will undoubtedly appeal to and attract the interests of criminal justice scholars, practitioners, and students."

Michael Pittaro, Assistant Professor of Criminal Justice, Lehigh Valley College

"Absolutely riveting. *Hawking Hits on the Information Highway* is a beautifully clear and thoroughly researched account of exactly how both illegal drug dealers and the government's drug warriors exploit the Internet."

Jeffrey A. Schaler, School of Public Affairs, American University;
Author of Addiction Is a Choice

Hawking Hits *on the* Information Highway

Jeffrey Ian Ross
General Editor

Vol. 1

PETER LANG
New York • Washington, D.C./Baltimore • Bern
Frankfurt am Main • Berlin • Brussels • Vienna • Oxford

Laura L. Finley

Hawking Hits *on the* Information Highway

The Challenge of Online Drug Sales for Law Enforcement

PETER LANG
New York • Washington, D.C./Baltimore • Bern
Frankfurt am Main • Berlin • Brussels • Vienna • Oxford

Library of Congress Cataloging-in-Publication Data
Finley, Laura L.
Hawking hits on the information highway: the challenge of online drug sales
for law enforcement / Laura L. Finley.
p. cm. — (New perspectives in criminology and criminal justice; vol. 1)
Includes bibliographical references and index.
1. Computer crimes—Investigation. 2. Drug traffic. I. Title.
HV8079.C65F56 363.25'977—dc22 2007026946
ISBN 978-0-8204-8600-0
ISSN 1555-3418

Bibliographic information published by **Die Deutsche Bibliothek**.
Die Deutsche Bibliothek lists this publication in the "Deutsche
Nationalbibliografie"; detailed bibliographic data is available
on the Internet at http://dnb.ddb.de/.

© 2008 Peter Lang Publishing, Inc., New York
29 Broadway, 18th floor, New York, NY 10006
www.peterlang.com

All rights reserved.
Reprint or reproduction, even partially, in all forms such as microfilm,
xerography, microfiche, microcard, and offset strictly prohibited.

CONTENTS

	Series Preface	vii
	Preface	ix
	Acknowledgments	xiii
	Introduction	1
Chapter 1	The War on Drugs	23
Chapter 2	Online Drug Sales and Information	51
Chapter 3	Policing the Web	81
Chapter 4	The Rise of Drug Testing	99
Chapter 5	Marketing Cheating on the Web	119
Chapter 6	Understanding and Predicting the Future of Online Drug Sales	131
	References	163
	Index	177

SERIES PREFACE

Thanks to the global expansion of e-commerce, the average consumer, armed with nothing more than a credit card and a post office box, can purchase items from almost anywhere in the world to be shipped almost anywhere in the world. This type of transaction was almost unimaginable a decade ago. This phenomenon has transformed not only the ideas of economics, merchandising, and entertainment but also the buying and selling of legal and illegal drugs. People seeking easy access to prescription drugs, whether because of legitimate need or nefarious purposes, do not even need to shop for a doctor—they can simply click a button to "buy now." Those looking for illicit substances can find them online with the same ease.

This development makes the job of law enforcement and regulators that much more difficult. We cannot be sure that the legitimate drug products sold online are made to the same exacting standards as those we normally purchase from the corner pharmacy. Online sales also means that drug users need not lurk in the dark back alleys of our inner cities or visit open-air drug markets in less desirable parts of town to make their purchases. In addition to serving as a simple, convenient means of buying and selling online, the World Wide Web is a tremendous marketplace for information about drugs, including tips on how to get high, make specific substances, or beat drug tests. More than just an area of interest, the world of online drug sales, purchases, and information may literally be altering the shape of the war on drugs. Media treatments aside, there is little scholarly research on this topic. Online drug sales and purchases are misunderstood and underexplored issues in the scholarly fields of drug use, abuse, and trafficking.

As editor of Peter Lang's series "New Perspectives in Criminology and Criminal Justice," I'm proud to introduce you to Laura Finley's groundbreaking book *Hawking Hits on the Information Highway*. As the first book in the series, it is truly a piece of cutting-edge scholarship that pushes the boundaries of the disciplines of criminology and criminal justice.

Finley analyzes a number of important issues for the reader, including cybercrimes, methods of selling drugs online, the online consumers/purchasers, the dealers, and the law enforcement officers and agencies responsible for monitoring this kind of activity. She also looks at the industry that has cropped up that promises drug users quick fixes to enable them to beat the pervasive piss tests. Not content to simply report on this phenomenon, Finley identifies the problem of online drug sales as an element of criminological theory.

I'm sure that scholars, instructors, practitioners, and students in many fields—not just criminology, criminal justice, anthropology, and sociology—will be intrigued by Finley's book.

Jeffrey Ian Ross, Ph.D.

PREFACE

Why "Hawking Hits"?

A play on words, "hawking hits" emphasizes that drug peddlers of all sorts have increasingly selected the Web as their entrepreneurial vehicle. Hits, of course, is a colloquial way to describe a substance that gets one high. It is also common lexicon to describe the number of Web pages that emerge from a specific search. Hawking is a way to describe those who have something for sale. The term clearly conjures up a certain image—that of an innocent victim falling prey to a dark and dangerous predator that has been lurking in the shadows for the appropriate moment to attack. Yet, as this book argues, Internet-based drug sellers often do not fit this predatory image. This book explores the changing nature of drug dealing and buying, as well as the challenges for police and other bodies involved in enforcing the War on Drugs, when the Web is the source of the transaction.

Hopefully this book will make it clear that Internet drug sales are worthy not only of media and public policy attention, but of academic attention as well. It may come as a surprise, then, that little scholarly work has addressed this issue. Although there is a growing body of work on cyber forms of crime, and even materials developed for cyber investigations, few criminologists have given any focused attention on cyber drug dealing. The texts available that discuss the challenges in and protocol for investigating cyber crimes devote very little space to the specific topic of online drug sales. This book is intended to fill that gap.

Not all computer-based drug issues addressed in this book are crimes. Many could be considered computer-based deviance, a topic that also has had little examination. For instance, the book addresses a vast array of online behavior related to drugs, running the gamut from sales of controlled substances to fraudulent claims about pharmaceuticals to video clips of oddballs getting high. For example, Kenneth S. Tunnell recently authored a book about drug testing and drug masking that included some valuable information about the Web. Tunnell's work, however, did not focus on drug sales or prodrug information specifically.

Because this is, in essence, the first book-length examination of the topic, it provides a generally descriptive look at the phenomenon of online drug sales and drug information. That is, the book synthesizes relevant literature then provides descriptions of what is available on the Web. Clearly, further research will need to go beyond descriptive data. Additionally, this book is intended to be the beginning of a sociological examination of how Internet sales are changing the nature of the War on Drugs. Not only do Internet sales challenge the "what" and the "how" of drug buying and dealing, but they are changing the "who" and the "why" as well.

Organization of the Book

The Introduction offers an overview of all the topics that will be addressed in this book. It highlights the rapid growth in use of the Web in general, as well as use for a variety of criminal or deviant acts. It also indicates the scope and extent of cyber crime, the associated costs, and an introduction to the difficulties posed by cyber crime for law enforcement.

The Introduction then breaks down each of the types of online drug sales—prescription drugs, steroids, and illicit drugs and introduces the scope and extent of this type of drug sale. The Introduction also sets the stage for later discussion of online drug and drug-testing information, tips, and recipes, and sale of drug masking or adulterating items. The final portion of the Introduction introduces readers to the difficulties in policing the Web for cyber drug dealing specifically.

Chapter One offers a brief overview of the War on Drugs, emphasizing the origins, scope, expenses, as well as successes and failures to date. By no means a "complete" history, the material offered here is intended to provide a frame for the reader to see how the drug war has morphed, as well as the commonalities over time. Additionally, the Introduction includes a discussion of policing international drug trafficking, as so much of the Web-based sales involve multiple nations and states. It is also useful in highlighting who is considered a drug user and dealer, as this helps to understand the challenges law enforcement will face as they attempt to police the Web.

Chapter Two provides more detailed information about prescription drug, illegal drug, and steroid sales on the Web. It builds on the Introduction by providing descriptive data on the number of sites offering these substances, as well as description of some of the main features of the sites. Drugs included in the examination are: Darvon, hydrocodone, Vicodin, Percocet, Ativan, tamazepam, Viagra, Ritalin, Adderall, steroids and testosterone, marijuana, hallucinogens, crack and cocaine, heroin, *Salvia divinorum*, phenethylamines, and tryptamines. In addition, the chapter discusses the array of sites that provide "pro-use" information about illegal drugs and the many sites offering recipes for making drugs or including drugs in baked goods and the like.

Chapter Three builds on the material in the Introduction to discuss in greater detail the challenges faced by law enforcement in "policing" the Web. Included are challenges in law, jurisdiction, apprehension of offenders, training for law enforcement, as well as concerns about prosecuting online drug offenders.

The focus in Chapter Four is on drug testing, including its origin as part of the War on Drugs, its expansion into various industries and institutions, and a detailed critique. This leads into Chapter Five, which explains how the rise in drug testing has spawned a parallel rise in adulterants and detoxification products. Although some companies sell these products from their storefronts, the Web has become the mall of drug test evasion. A whole Web subculture exists that helps users evade drug tests. The chapter features a description of some of the Web sites offering these products for sale, as well as a discussion of the legal issues surrounding these sales. In addition, it provides analyses of information about evading drug tests provided on the Web.

Chapter Six provides the connection to criminological and sociological theory. It also sums up the scope and extent of online drug sales and the challenges for law enforcement, as well as predictions and recommendations for the future of Internet-based drug dealing. Included as well are the significant privacy and speech concerns involved in any type of censoring of the Web to curtail drug dealing.

ACKNOWLEDGMENTS

Everyone has met one of those people who over-commits. Beyond simply saying yes to everything that comes their way, these people even seek out additional activity. Confession time: I am one of those people, Whether this is a tremendous personality flaw or some crazy sign of brilliance is yet to be determined. Likely, the answer lies somewhere between. Regardless, because I wrote this book while I was writing another one and working two full-time jobs, there are many people who I absolutely must thank, as they were impacted in many ways by my crazy schedule.

First, my husband and daughter. Always quick with a smile and a hug— Peter and Anya (4 years old), I thank you for your love and support. I appreciate you more than you will ever know.

Second, my students and employers. I wrote this book while I taught sociology and worked in prevention at a domestic violence agency. My students and peers had to cope with my attempts to appear perky after long nights of writing, and didn't groan too loudly when they had to repeatedly hear about the next thing I planned to include in the book.

In addition, a huge thanks to Jeff Ross for creating this series and for all his valuable assistance in editing this book. Thanks also to Ken Tunnel, Craig Love, and Jeff Schaler for reviewing the text and adding their valuable insight. To all of those who heard parts of this book at various academic conferences, thanks for the tips. In addition, thanks to Phyllis Korper and Sophie Appel at Peter Lang for making the production phase of this so easy.

At this point, everyone has done what they can to ensure the facts in this book are as accurate as possible. Any remaining errors are mine.

Peace.

INTRODUCTION

The Internet Explosion

"I'll just Google it." Virtually all of America is familiar with the phrase, and many do Google (or Yahoo, or the like) at least one thing most days. As a professor, I know the Internet has dramatically changed higher education, in both good and bad ways. Students can easily do research on the Web, and e-mail has made professors far more accessible to students. Some students, however, do more than research—they just use the Web to access other people's research and pass it off as their own. And some students pester their professors with inane questions and silly requests (Dear professor ... I wanted an A. Can you please change my grade? Thanks so much—loved the class ☺). Clearly, it is not just higher education that has been revolutionized by the new technologies. And obviously, as Marshall McLuhan maintained, we are not only impacted by the messages—that is, the content available—but by the medium as well. One example of how the medium changes us can be seen in research about heavy users of BlackBerrys. Not only are some heavy users experiencing what has been dubbed "BlackBerry thumb," (BlackBerrys can do damage ..., 2005), but other research has found that the IQ of heavy users drops more than if they were to smoke marijuana (Pimentel, 2005)! Although some, like me, find perverse amusement in that research, it is indeed important to examine the ways new technologies are both used and, as Postman (1996) and Mander (1992), discuss, use us.

Since its conceptual birth in 1962 by scholars at MIT, the Internet has exploded as a method of worldwide broadcasting, information dissemination, and as a medium for collaboration without regard for geography (Lenhart, Madden, & Hitlin, 2005). In 2006, *Time* magazine selected all of us (you, as they called it) as the people of the year based on our ability to create our world with new technologies. In March 1989, a British scientist working at a Swiss physics laboratory came up with the idea of the Web, which is the Internet's multimedia component (Staples, 2000). A year later, software to support viewing, editing, and sending hypertext was developed, and by the mid-1990s, the first primitive Web browser was created (Staples, 2000). In this relatively short history, use has expanded rapidly. In 2002, an estimated 3 million users were online at any time (Gillen & Garrity, 2002). Although Asia is the most connected continent, the U.S. provides the most Internet users (21.6%). In the U.S., 68.5% of people are said to use the Internet (Internet domain survey, 2001). Similar rates are true in Canada where 64% of households had at least one member who regularly used the Internet (Internet domain survey, 2001). As of January 2001, there were almost 171 million named hosts, or sites, on the Internet, with each host representing a network of up to 254 million computers (Internet domain survey, 2001).

Who Uses the Web?

People of all ages use the Internet. Children and teens continue to use the Internet in growing numbers. Since 2001, teen Internet use has grown 24% (Lenhart, et al., 2005). It is estimated that over 40 million people under the age of 18 use the Internet on a regular basis, with approximately 87% of the 12- to 17-year-olds in the U.S. being online (Lenhart, et al., 2005). Teens average 16.7 hours per week online—more than they do watching television (Office of National Drug Control Policy, 2002). *Detroit Free Press* research in 2006 found that 90% of 12- to 17-year-olds use the Internet, and half do so daily. Approximately 19 million teens in that age range send and receive text messages regularly (Kershaw, 2005). One-third of 13- to 15-year-olds and almost half of 16- to 17-year-olds said their parents know "very little" or "nothing" about what they do on the Internet, whereas 64% reported they did things online they wouldn't want their parents to know about (Khatri, 2006). The next age group, college-aged students, is even more likely to be online—one study found that 93% of college students have Internet access (Davis, 2003).

Not only do people use the Internet to gain information, they also use it to communicate with others. Almost 80% of Americans who use the Internet do so to send and receive e-mail. Aside from the Internet, a popular way to communicate is by blogging (a blog is a Web site that contains an online personal journal with reflections, comments, and often hyperlinks provided by the writer). A recent Pew Internet and American Life Project report found that at least 8 million U.S. adults have created blogs, and 27% have read them. Readership of blogs grew 58% in 2004 (Hudson, 2006). Another popular form of expression is the biography-style Web site, like MySpace. Students tell me they will share some of their most personal life experiences, both in writing as well as in pictures, on their MySpace site. In a lot of ways this is a scary thing, which I describe in Chapter Two.

Internet use is not equal across all demographic groups. The digital divide, as it has been called, refers to gaps in the access and use of digital technologies between the haves and have-nots in society. The gap might be in regular access to a quality computer with all the bells and whistles, or in skills and abilities to use computer technologies. Although it is now possible to access computers and use the Internet from a variety of public locales, people are far more likely to regularly use an Internet connection from home. Daley (n.d.) reported that people with a college degree are eight times more likely to have a computer at home, and sixteen times more likely to have Internet access at home than those with lower levels of education. Geography, socioeconomics, and race are other correlates of the digital divide. For instance, a low-income person living in a rural area is twenty times less likely to have Internet access than a more affluent person in an urban area (Daley, n.d.). Low-income whites are three times more likely to have home Internet access than low-income blacks, and four times as likely as a comparable Hispanic child (Daley, n.d.). Whites are more likely to have Internet access at home than blacks and Hispanics are from any location (Daley, n.d.). The only racial minority to use the Internet at rates comparable to whites is Asians/Pacific Islanders (Daley, n.d.).

The Web Is Changing Everything

Certainly the Internet has numerous important and beneficial functions. It has, by all accounts, changed the way that people live, learn, work, and shop.

Perhaps one of the most important claims made about the Internet is that it is an inherently democratic tool. That is, anyone can be both consumer and producer of online knowledge. This may be best exemplified by the online encyclopedia Wikipedia. Any person is free to add to the entries about incredibly diverse topics, and I can attest to the fact that many consult it regularly as a starting point for research. Yet, as with any technology, the Internet can be used in more insidious ways. As one Customs agent put it, "The Internet is changing the way everybody does business, including the bad guys." Schmalleger (2005) explained, "The dark side of new technologies, as far as the justice system is concerned, is the potential they create for committing old crimes in new ways or for committing new crimes never before imagined" (p. 762).

New Forms of Crime

Computer offenses are a relatively new category of crimes. It encompasses crimes committed with a computer and those occurring in cyberspace. Some computer crimes are new with the technology, whereas others are older offenses that simply use new technology as a tool (De Angelis, 2000). Although computer crime is not entirely new—the first federal prosecution for an offense was in 1966—it has taken on new forms and greater frequency (Judson, 2000). In particular, as computer use in general, and Internet use specifically, increased in the 1990s, more serious forms of computer crime became apparent, especially as the global world becomes more and more dependent on computers (Judson, 2000). De Angelis (2000) explained that the Internet has democratized white-collar crime, as anyone with some access to the technology and some minimal skills has the potential to become a white-collar criminal in our computer-reliant society.

Even prior to the tremendous surge in Internet use in the 1990s, so-called amateurs were finding creative ways to commit what were then called "technocrimes." A 27-year-old housewife from Maryland with no computer training figured out how to steal more than $36,000 from People's Security Bank from watching the popular television show *60 Minutes* (Bequai, 1987). According to Bequai (1987), "Criminals are trading in their guns for computers, since the chances of being caught are miniscule" (p. 50). Estimates suggest less than one in 20,000 will be caught.

So-called deviants and criminals use the Internet for gambling on sports, for stealing people's credit cards or even their entire identity, for sex crimes against both children and adults, and for perpetuating racism and hate. Some Web sites peddle pornography, and some teach willing visitors how to make bombs or other terrorist tools (Judson, 2000). The Internet is used for everything from simple extortion to complex transnational money laundering (Barrett, 1997). School-aged kids even use the Internet to taunt others, a phenomenon known as cyber-bullying, and people of all ages have been found stalking others in cyberspace. Some hackers illegally copy software programs from the Internet, called software piracy (Schmalleger, 2005). Crackers, or malicious hackers, break into systems to vandalize, plant viruses and worms, embezzle, defraud, or steal corporate secrets (De Angelis, 2000). "Salami Slicers" make computer transfers of funds from multiple accounts (De Angelis, 2000).

Of great concern after the terrorist attacks on September 11, 2001 is the threat of cyberterrorism. One U.S. intelligence official has claimed he could shut down America with $1 billion and twenty capable hackers (De Angelis, 2000). Cyberterrorism would be far more devastating to huge numbers of people than would other forms of terrorism, according to experts (De Angelis, 2000; Schmalleger, 2005).

The "New" Cybercriminals

Clearly, the Internet can facilitate a vast array of crimes, from the personal to property, from local to international. Yet, perhaps more importantly, the Internet has helped "democratize" perpetrators and victims. Rather than an overweight kid being bullied by a high school jock, for instance, we can now see loners bullying popular kids via Instant Messaging (IM). Instead of searching for a crack dealer in a red-light district, users can locate the individual by searching Google while they snack on cheesepuffs. They can make their drug order safely from their bedroom and cozy in their pajamas by "clicking now."

Scope and Extent of Cybercrime

Computer crimes are not rare. On the contrary, cyber-related crimes are on the rise. De Angelis (2000) reported that nearly all white-collar crimes now involve the use of computers or telecommunications. Few organized efforts have been made to tally the incidence of cybercrime, however. The Computer Intrusion Squad/Federal Bureau of Investigations (CSI/FBI) Computer Crime and Security survey, conducted annually, is the most widely cited source on the extent and scope of cybercrime. It generally tallies attacks on corporations, both by insiders and outsiders (Power, 2000). Most of the efforts to measure the extent and scope of cybercrime have been conducted by commercial organizations and use somewhat limited methodologies (Wall, 2001a).

Regardless of the flaws in measurement, we know that the number of computer crimes is big and growing. The Los Angeles District Attorney's Office estimated that 20% of the 600 cases handled by their Stalking and Threat Assessment Unit in 1999 involved e-mail or some other form of electronic crime. The Manhattan District Attorney's Sex Crime unit has also said approximately 20% of their cases involve the Web in some way (De Angelis, 2000). The Computer Investigation and Technology Unit of the New York City Police estimated that 40% of their cases involve electronic threats and harassment, with almost all of the cases occurring in the last three or four years (Taylor, et al., 2006). Carter and Katz (1998) found that 98.5% of their respondents had been victimized with some having been victimized more than twenty-five times. With respect to child pornography, a Time/CNN poll of 409 teenagers between the ages of 13 and 17 found that 66% of girls and 54% of boys had experienced someone saying offensive things to them online (Taylor, et al., 2006). Twenty percent of teens in the U.S. who regularly use the Internet have received an unwanted sexual solicitation on the Web, according to the agency Protect Kids.

The Costs of Cybercrimes

Cybercrimes are also costly. A project conducted in 1987 by the American Bar Association found that of 300 corporations and governmental agencies surveyed, 24% had been the victim of some type of computer-related crime in the previous twelve months, with estimated losses of between $145 million and $730 million (American Bar Association, 1987). More recently, the Department of Justice estimated computer fraud alone cost U.S. businesses more than $10 billion annually in 1998 (Judson, 2000). Although exact figures are not always available, a look at some specific cases highlights the cost of cybercrime. When the "Phonemasters," a group of cyberhackers, gained access to AT & T, British Telecommunications, GTE, MCI, Southwestern Bell, and Sprint telephone networks, the FBI estimated the losses to the above businesses at $1.85 million. Four high school students, ages 14 to 16, hacked into a Bay Area Internet server in San Francisco, California, and used stolen credit card numbers to go on a shopping spree at an online auction site. They ordered $200,000 worth of computers and had them delivered by UPS to vacant homes, where they would later pick them up (Power, 2000).

Difficulties for Law Enforcement

Crimes on or related to the Web present a number of challenges for law enforcement. First, offenders are difficult to apprehend because there are many ways to become virtually anonymous on the Web. Encryption software and anonymous remailers (e-mail forwarding sites that resend electronic mail from false addresses, making it untraceable) make it difficult for law enforcement to find computer criminals (De Angelis, 2000).

Second, some types of cyber-related crimes may be less likely to be reported than traditional crimes. It may be that the average citizen does not understand the frequency, impact, or seriousness of such crimes. Furthermore, because these crimes rarely involve direct physical threats, even victims may be hesitant to report them (Bequai, 1987).

Third, although efforts are in place in some major cities and at the federal level, training for law enforcement in investigating cyber-related crimes is woefully poor (Moore, 2005). The St. Louis police department was the first to create a computer fraud squad in 1983 (Bequai, 1987), but many agencies today, especially rural ones, still have virtually no ability to investigate computer-based crime.

Fourth, identifying just who has jurisdiction for crimes involving the Internet is often difficult. Local officials investigating cybercrimes such as cyberstalking have found that offenders are often located in different cities, states, or even countries (Moore, 2005). State laws also may vary about specific offenses and may not be readily applied to Web-related crimes. For instance, only sixteen states have stalking laws that clearly cover stalking committed electronically. It is left to courts and juries to determine if general stalking legislation can be applied to incidents occurring over the Web (Akdeniz, 2001).

Fifth, involvement by federal officials often requires collaboration between a number of agencies, which is difficult to arrange, implement, and fund. The time and money involved in a collaborative effort of this sort might prohibit investigation of all but the most serious cases (Grabosky & Smith, 2001).

Sixth, "policing" the Internet requires some level of cooperation with Internet Service Providers (ISPs). Although many ISPs have offered their complete cooperation with investigators, others are more hesitant.

Seventh, prosecuting someone for a computer crime, or using computer-based evidence, has proven difficult to date. Not only are most investigators poorly trained to deal with computer evidence, but so are many prosecutors, both in the U.S. and across Europe (Barrett, 1997). In addition, as the 1995 trial of O. J. Simpson made clear, jurors are likely to be unprepared to sift through complex technological data.

Eighth, material on the Web has been protected as an important component of free speech in such cases as *Reno v. ACLU*, 521 U.S. 844, 850-52, 870 (1997) and *ACLU v. Reno*, 31 F. Supp. 2d 473, 476, 493 (E.D. Pa 1999), although it is still unclear what, precisely, is protected. More detail on each of these challenges is provided in Chapter Three.

Policing Cyberspace to Date

U.S. Agencies

In the U.S., federal agencies have done the most to date in terms of policing criminal Web activity (De Angelis, 2000). This has included a number of undercover operations, coordinated efforts among multiple agencies, training, providing information, establishing special cybercrime units, and collaborating with industry. The FBI and the U.S. Secret Service are the agencies most directly charged with enforcing computer crime laws. The FBI deals with espionage, terrorism, banking, organized crime, and threats to national security. The FBI's primary tool for addressing cybercrime is the National Computer Crime Squad (De Angelis, 2000). The Bureau has also created a guide for parents to help them ensure that their children will be safe in their online activity, available at fbi.gov. It is unlikely these have much impact, however, as most parents do not actively search the Web for this information. They have several computer crime squads as well as an Intellectual Property Center in Washington, DC (De Angelis, 2000).

The Secret Service is charged with investigating crimes against Treasury Department computers and against computers that contain information protected by the Financial Privacy Act, such as credit care information (Judson, 2000). The Secret Service also has jurisdiction over "access device fraud," or any card, code, account number of other means of account access that provide access to things of value or that can be used to transfer funds (De Angelis, 2000).

U.S. Nonpolicing Agencies

Nongovernmental agencies have also worked to address cyber-related crimes. For instance, the National Center for Missing and Exploited Children created a Cyber Tipline in March 1998 (De Angelis, 2000). The International Association of Computer Investigation Specialists (IACIS) and the Computer Emergency Response Team Coordinating Center (CERT/CC) are other nongovernmental organizations that offer assistance, especially to law enforcement agencies without their own computer crime specialists (De Angelis, 2000; Wall, 2001b). The High Technology Crime Investigators Association offers assistance, training, and information for individuals investigating this type of crime. The National Center for Victims of Crime (NCVC) is handling more online cases than ever. In 2000, the NCVC opened the Stalking Resource Center in 2000 to address the needs of online victims (Hitchcock, 2002).

Drug Dealing as a Form Of Cybercrime

Given the tremendous growth in cybercrime, it is no surprise that enterprising drug dealers have found ways to sell their products online. An increasing number of Web sites are devoted to drug sales of all sorts. Sellers also utilize chat rooms, e-mail, auction sites like e-Bay, and private Web rings to peddle their wares. In addition, greater use of drug testing has created an entire industry of detoxification and test-cheating information. This industry has largely found its home on the Web where people share information and peddle their potions. An official with the Philadelphia-based Treatment Research Institute claims it is as easy to purchase drugs on the Web as it is to purchase a book or a compact disk. These includes pseudo-pharmaceutical sites offering prescription drugs, sites where consumers can purchase steroids, and sites devoted to the sale of marijuana and other illegal nonprescription drugs.

Prescription Drug Deals

Lawful Online Sales

Certainly there are many benefits of being able to purchase prescription medicines on the Web. Health-related research is the sixth most common reason cited for using the Internet (Hubbard, 2004). Almost 50% of all online users do Web research on health-related issues on a monthly basis, and another 39% do so every few months (Dorschner, 2006). The poll found 42% of these users are looking for drug information (Dorschner, 2006). Research has shown most people support online sales of pharmaceuticals. In Germany, for instance, 89% of 1000 people polled in 2001 believe Web sales should remain legal, about 10% had already made an Internet prescription drug purchase, and another 21% planned to do so in the upcoming year.

Those living in areas far from a pharmacy can easily order their prescriptions. People with disabilities or those otherwise homebound no longer need to struggle to find transportation to and from a pharmacy. Furthermore, the Internet never closes, so those needing to fill prescriptions do not have to meet a nine to five workday. In addition, many find the anonymity of the Internet appealing. Rather than be physically associated with filling a prescription for an antidepressant, for example, and fearing a possible stigma from the neighbors, someone can now order their Prozac from the comforts of their own home, stigma free (at least theoretically). Many people prefer ordering from the Internet for simple reasons, because it eliminates the hassle of finding a parking spot, finding what they need, and waiting for a cashier to check them out.

Illegal Sales

Some entrepreneurs have seized the opportunity to dabble in the online prescription drug arena in a number of illegal ways. Amphetamines, benzodiazepine tranquilizers, and potentially lethal drugs like fentanyl and secobarbital are among the drugs sold most commonly online. Understanding the scope and extent of unlawful Internet-based drug sales is especially important at a time when prescription drug abuse has been named the number one drug problem in some states, such as Florida. For the third year, the Partnership for a Drug-Free America study found that 20% of American teens had tried prescription painkillers. Teens identify prescription drugs as easy to obtain, not illegal, and less dangerous than other drugs (McShane, 2006). More emergency room visits are for misuse and overdose of prescription drugs than by all illicit drugs combined (Misuse of pharmaceuticals ..., 2006).

There are two major types of illegal prescription drug sales. A site can provide illegal, doctored-up, or fake versions of approved medicines, or it can provide legitimate prescription drugs but without the required prescription (Hubbard, 2004).

Dangerous Drugs

An investigation conducted by the National Association of Boards of Pharmacy (NABP), prompted by drug company Eli Lilly, found that a vast majority of pills available online contain dangerous levels of impurities. When people ordered Lilly's top-selling antipsychotic drug Zyprexa, they received a drug called Telorzan. The NABP then sent the drugs on for screening by the FD, and found that some pills contained 17 times the level of impurities expected in Zyprexa (Herper, 2005). In a similar investigation conducted solely by the Food and Drug Administration (FDA), copies of Viagra and Lipitor purchased online had, respectively, only 65% and 81%, respectively, of the active ingredients required of both drugs. Not a single pill met U.S. manufacturing standards (Herper, 2005).

Veronin and Youan (2004) reported that approximately 10% of the world's drug trade involves counterfeits. In the United Kingdom, the Medicines and Healthcare Products Regulatory Agency (MHRA) seized stolen or faked Viagra worth more than 3 million pounds each year (Frith, 2006). Although some online pharmaceutical products are not effective because they barely contain the required active components, the reverse is also true. Ambient knockoffs purchased online were as much as twice as strong (Herper, 2005).

No Prescription Required

One of the biggest concerns with Web-based prescription drug sales is the ease in which someone can purchase potent, even lethal, drugs without a prescription. One study found 495 Web sites selling prescription drugs in just one week of analysis, and verification of an actual prescription was only required on 6% of those sites (Sullivan, 2004). Many sites offered highly addictive drugs like OxyContin, Percocet, and Darvon (Sullivan, 2004). The United Nations' International Narcotics Board (INCB) has said that approximately 90% of pharmaceutical sales made online do not have a prescription (School starts random drug testing, 2005). Even if a prescription is required, many sites boast online consultations to provide the appearance of meeting the requirement (Sullivan, 2004). A Google search for "buy fentanyl," a drug legally used in hospitals as an anesthetic but illegally as an alternative to heroin, will produce a number of links. Fentanyl is easy to purchase with any major credit card (Zirin, 2005). Although a prescription is required to purchase fentanyl legally, online sellers are often happy to provide a brief "consultation" (Zirin, 2005).

Prescription drugs more commonly used by children and teens are also easy to obtain. A simple Google or Yahoo search for buying Ritalin online reveals a number of sites where one can do so. Never mind the required prescription, at pediatrics.about.com, consumers are provided a simple checklist that will lead to a diagnosis and prescription.

As noted above, the "lifestyle" drugs, like Viagra, are the easiest to purchase online. A national survey of 676 men aged 35 and older found 20% had purchased Viagra online, and two-thirds of those men did not check to see if the Web site was legitimate. Few saw any problem with the ease at which they could purchase Viagra—only 38% felt it should be necessary to have a prescription for the substance (Breen, 2007).

A Global Issue

Although the U.S. is the largest market in the world for illegal drugs, the problem does not belong solely to the U.S., either on the demand or supply side. In the United Kingdom, methadone and antidepressant drugs are readily available on the Web (Illicit internet prescription drug sales…, 2003). When British officials created a list of prescription drugs to try to purchase via the Internet, they found sites easily accessible to children offering a variety of substances. The search was conducted using the search engine most frequently used by children (Littlejohn, Baldacchio, Schifano, & Deluca, 2005).

A particular difficulty is that many sites offering prescription medications originate outside the U.S., where large drug firms may make copycat pills that would be illegal here but are not overseas due to dramatically different safety and production standards (Herper, 2005). For instance, in Brazil the law provides for three classes of drugs: the brand names sold by big-time firms; the generics; and the similares, medicines that supposedly have the same amount of active ingredients but have not been tested on humans (Herper, 2005). Mexico's system is similar to Brazil's, whereas in Argentina there are only the brand names and similares, no generics (Herper, 2005). Even in the U.S., online prescription drug sales is a "very fuzzy area of the law," according to Dr. Frank Palumbo, director of the University of Maryland's Center on Drugs and Public Policy (Reaves, 2002).

Who Is Purchasing Prescription Drugs on the Web?

There is some evidence that people with existing substance abuse problems are using the Internet to further their addictions. Gordon, Forman, and Siatkowski

(2006) found that 11% of drug-addicted patients in a private residential treatment facility had used the Internet to purchase drugs or locate dealers. Officials are very concerned about the lack of age restrictions needed for purchasing any kind of drug on the Web, considering Internet access and use rates by young people. The INCB claims, "The illicit trade over the Internet has been identified as one of the major sources for prescription medications abused by children and adolescents in certain countries such as the U.S." More detail on who is buying and selling on the Web is provided in subsequent chapters, as an important point of this book is that Web-based drug exchanges are contributing to a shift in both "who" and "how" the drug war should be policed.

Web-Based Steroid Sales

Anabolic steroids, illegal for purchase in the U.S. without a prescription, are also relatively easy to obtain on the Web. Anabolic steroids are Schedule III controlled substances (the Controlled Substances Schedules are discussed in greater detail in Chapter One) and are in the same class as barbiturates, LSD, and Vicodin. Simple possession of a Schedule III substance without a prescription is punishable by up to one year in prison and/or a minimum fine of $1000 (Schmalleger, 2005). An investigation by the U.S. House of Representative Committee on Government Reform found hundreds of Web sites offering anabolic steroids. They placed twenty-two online orders and received ten shipments, all from outside the U.S. In most other countries, steroids can be sold without a prescription (Davis, 2005). In January 2005, law enforcement officials discovered anabolic steroids for auction on e-Bay, the popular online auction site (Brunker, 2005) NABP investigators purchased four items they thought to be steroids in October and November of 2004, ranging in price from $90 to $140 (Brunker, 2005). Like prescription drugs, steroids purchased online may contain more (or less) than the buyer wanted. Counterfeit steroids purchased online have sometimes contained cooking oil and motor oil (Brunker, 2005).

Who Is Buying Steroids on the Web?

Some bodybuilders have identified the Web as the best way to get steroids, once they got past the notion that the Web is "for geeks" (Blake, 2005). Bodybuilders can ask peers for advice about using, can get information about where to purchase steroids and can even order them online without concern about being judged by nonusing peers and little fear of being caught (Blake, 2005).

Illicit Drug Deals on the Web

A vast array of illegal drugs is also available online. In one study, a Google search for drugs revealed 100 links, with fifty-three offering opiates for sale without a prescription, and thirty-five selling assorted illegal drugs, including barbiturates, steroids, and date rape drugs.

Marijuana

Marijuana remains the most easy to obtain (Reaves, 2002), and it seems many are trying. In 2003, "marijuana" was one of the top 100 words used in search engines. Searching for "marijuana" in a commonly used search engine will obtain over one million listings (Office of National Drug Control Policy, 2002). Most sites even offer one-click shopping and secure digital payment via PayPal (an e-commerce business that allows payments and money transfers to be made through the Internet) or a similar organization (McCandless, 2004). In addition to purchasing grown marijuana, consumers can easily buy marijuana seeds, as well as access or purchase information on how to grow marijuana at home. There is even a Zagat-style rating (restaurant rating) of online seed banks at suresite.com (Goldberg, 1999). Officials from the National Organization for the Reform of Marijuana Laws (NORML) estimated there are over 400 varieties of marijuana seeds available on the Web. Those interested in growing can also use the Web to communicate with "experts," exchanging how-to tips (Goldberg, 1999).

Many marijuana sellers, and most of the sellers of hardcore drugs, are hidden from search engines like Google (McCandless, 2004). A 2004 for study by researchers at Columbia University's (New York) Center on Addiction and Substance Abuse found 337 "portal" sites that offered opiates, central nervous system depressants, and stimulants—basically, all varieties of substances listed as federally controlled banned substances (Zirin, 2005). Once a consumer reaches the portal site, they are passed on to anchor sites, of which the Columbia study found 158. These sites are where the actual selling takes place. This distances the marketers from the sellers (Zirin, 2005).

Other Hard Drugs

Reaves (2002) found it possible, but not easy, to purchase cocaine and heroin online but was shocked to find a number of sites describing how to make these substances at home or selling pamphlets with instructions for home preparation. Some sites offer precursor substances, or substances needed to synthesize a specific drug. A casual Internet search for furanone, verve, and gamma hydroxy butrate conducted by Winnicoff, Houck, Rothman, and Bauchner (2000) revealed more than 100 sites selling this GHB precursor (often called Verve or Jolt by teens). In September 2005, e-Bay agreed to ban sales of pseudoephedrine and other substances used to make methamphetamines, following state laws to control the spread of precursor chemicals (*The Oregonian*, 2005). The corporation removed at least forty-one auctions selling over 507 grams of pseudoephedrine (*The Oregonian*, 2005).

A Global Issue

Online sale of illegal drugs is also not just a U.S. problem. In Japan, drug use is typically far less than in the U.S. and other industrialized nations but has increased rapidly in the last decade, in large part due to Internet sales (McCandless, 2004). In 2000, authorities in Great Britain and Ireland found over 1000 sites offering illicit drugs, including marijuana, methylenedioxymethamphetamine (MDMA), cocaine, and heroin. It is estimated that there are at least five large-scale online vendors in Great Britain (McCandless, 2004). In 2000, Mike Freccia launched his "pan-European pot portal" which he called iToke.co.uk. He and partner Mike Tucker want to "be the FedEx of pot delivery" (Bawden, 2000). Switzerland and the Netherlands were home to the greatest proportion of sites. Even in China, well known for their far-reaching Internet filtering systems, Web surfers can make illegal drug purchases. Interestingly, although phrases like "free speech" and "human rights" are blocked because of the country's concern about dissenters, sites offering illegal drugs, stolen goods, and sex are widely available (Barboza, 2006). A Canadian drug seller claims to have sold 4 million marijuana seeds online, demonstrating the Canadian connection. Korean customs seized 14 kilograms of drugs in 2005 from fifty-four cases, fourteen of which involved Internet orders (Ja-Young, 2006). The study of 100 Google links found that half the sites were registered to owners outside the U.S.

Similar to the issue with prescription drugs, some countries outside the U.S., like the Netherlands, have more liberal drug laws. Great Britain downgraded cannabis to a Class C drug, which carries a far lesser maximum penalty, in 2003. Experts suggest this might increase sales, both on the streets and on the Web (McCandless, 2004). Although law enforcement says the downgraded status will not impact their pursuit of buyers and sellers, many feel it will (McCandless, 2004).

Online Information and Tips

Drug Recipes

In addition to actual sales of illicit substances, interested consumers can find out how to make their own illegal drugs. The U.S. Department of Justice (DOJ) is aware of the wealth of information about illegal drug manufacturing and use available on the Web. In a 2002 report, the DOJ acknowledged that many sites not only offer recipes and instructions for producing illegal drugs, they also include directions for finding precursor chemicals and equipment required, all under the radar of law enforcement. As early as 1997, the United Nations International Drug Control Programme announced that speed and Ecstasy had become more popular than their precursors, cocaine and heroin, in large part due to the tremendous array of recipes for synthetic drugs on the Internet (Spinney, 1997).

Drug Paraphernalia

Paraphernalia for drug consumption is widely available as well, as are tips on how to best consume certain drugs. Marketed in many amusing ways, often paraphernalia is sold under the shell of an ordinary product, such as lip balm containers, highlighters, and key chains.

Cheating Drug Tests

In addition, Web sites offer a vast array of products designed to adulterate urine or to mask the effects of a drug test. Since drug testing has become so common for all types of populations (the topic of Chapter Four), an increase in the number of products designed to help people pass drug tests was inevitable. A vast array of detoxification products is available online. For some businesses, these products represent the bulk of their sales (Tunnell, 2004). Most of the public has heard of "The Original Whizzinator," a prosthetic penis and urinating device that comes with dehydrated human urine. Not only that, but the device includes heating pads so that the urine sample is normal temperature, and it comes in a variety of skin colors, lest the testee be observed when providing the sample. It retails for $150, whereas additional urine packages cost $12 each or a bargain price of three for $30 on the site, www.whizzinator.com.

Most prodrug sites feature information about passing drug tests. Ureasample.com, available in eleven languages in addition to English, offers information on over 250 medications that can cause false positives in drug tests. Alwaytestclean.com provides users with advice, detection times, and information on how to beat each type of drug test. Also featured is a discussion of "when to get a lawyer." Cleartest.com not only provides information about how to beat a variety of drug tests, it also features a Frequently Asked Questions link and the Pot Smoker of the Month profile, which describes pot use by celebrities. How-to-pass-a-drug-test.net includes a 24-hour hotline.

Information and Ideas on the Web

Not only does the Web offer a variety of illegal or questionable items for purchase, but it is fast becoming one of the primary methods for exchanging information about illegal drugs. The Web offers a wealth of prodrug information about illegal substances in a number of formats. Web sites provide users information about what "tripping" on certain substances feels like, how and where to find dealers, the market price for some drugs, how to pass a drug test, and how to make specific drugs and drug paraphernalia. Discussion, message, and bulletin boards allow users to exchange this information, as do chat rooms.

Some sites also describe how to use legal substances, such as cold medications, to obtain euphoric effects. The largest and most extensive site of this nature, Erowid, offers information about and sales of an array of substances, from marijuana to obscure drugs used for research. The site is home to more than 20,000 documents about assorted drugs and drug-related topics. In 1995, the site had 28,000 visitors per day, with far more today (Erard, 2004). Some people even use Web cams to share their experiences with illegal drugs. Yahooka.com, a promarijuana site, not only provides a wealth of information about growing, using, and selling marijuana, but it also boasts 5947 links to other sites, including 1203 in languages besides English (Erard, 2004). Cannabisnews.com, marijuana.com, marijuananews.com, hightimes.com, Yahooka.com, and marijuanaworld.com are all easy-to-find sites featuring information about making, using, and covering up marijuana use, as well as offering readers opportunities to chat or blog. Hightimes.com, sponsored by the promarijuana magazine, *High Times*, even has a special "high on the air" feature, which involves readers sending in pod casts, or "pot casts," as they are called, of themselves or friends high on marijuana.

The Web and Club Drugs

Wax (2002) maintains that the tremendous growth in use of the Internet, by young people in particular, has paralleled the "club drug revolution." Throughout the 1990s, youth began experimenting more with new types of illicit drugs, including Ecstasy, GHB, and Ketamine. In 2000, 8.2% of high school seniors admitted to using club drugs, up from 5.6% in 1999 (Johnson, O'Malley, & Bachman, 2000). In 2001, the National Drug Intelligence Center reported they found 25 sites providing information on producing, selling, and using Ecstasy, GHB, and LSD (Erard, 2004). Students claim it is easy to obtain, both on and off the Web (Wax, 2002). Numerous sites discuss recreational use of these new club drugs—some do so in a precautionary manner, but many others condone use (Wax, 2002). Still others provide detailed directions for synthesizing GHB (Wax, 2002). For instance, Erard (2004) reported that, by February 26, 2004, nine people from around the U.S. and Canada had posted reports about seven different varieties of Ecstasy, including specifics on the effects of each, on pillreports.com. On Bluelight.com, interested persons can use a message board to discuss buying, using, selling, and masking drugs. Bluelight's users have been known to warn others of fraudulent sales, and to share information on where to purchase drugs like LSD in specific cities (Erard, 2004). According to Erard (2004), these interactive sites, "serve as the memory of the drug culture." Online instructions are available for converting powdered cocaine to crack, and one site even features a "Crack dealer locator service," which identifies dealers in major cities. Readers can easily find charts about cocaine purity and price in most states.

Law Enforcement and Online Drug Dealing

The sale of illegal drugs online is so big it has overwhelmed law enforcement. Government agencies claim they can do little to control these sales without significantly more resources and funding. "The system we have in place has been overrun by the volume of illegal Internet drug sales," according to Richard Stana, director of the homeland security and justice team in the General Accounting Office, which is the investigative arm of Congress

(Sullivan, 2004). Jon Katz, author and former journalist for *Wired* magazine, asserted, "The government is going to learn what the music industry is learning. The net is a wall buster. It's not policeable. There are not enough cops in the world to monitor all the communication and digital commerce that's going on" (McCandless, 2004).

How to Police the Web

Drozdova (2001) explained there are two approaches to cyber security: protective and reactive. The protective style generally involves making a target less vulnerable—for instance, making access more difficult. The reactive approach is deterrence based. Investigation, prosecution, and punishment of those who violate computer crime laws is, in theory, supposed to deter those individuals from offending again (specific deterrence) and the rest of us from doing it at all (general deterrence). This approach then involves greater surveillance and increasing power to law enforcement to investigate and apprehend cyber criminals. Clearly, there are problems with each approach. The following section offers a brief overview of these difficulties, which are discussed in greater detail in Chapter Three.

Difficulties in the Approach to Policing

Most people purchasing drugs online do not purchase large volumes, making it even less likely they, or their seller, will be caught. According to Dr. Punyamurtula Kishore, who works at Preventive Medicine Associates in Chestnut Hill, MA, people, "see it like they are getting a small enough quantity that they fly under the radar. People feel safe. They get a nice UPS box in the mail." Furthermore, many wonder if these small-time sales *are* worth the bother to police. As trafficking of large quantities of drugs occurs on a daily basis, some maintain any efforts to go after small-time users is time, money, and effort misspent. This concern is not exclusive to Web-based sales. It is a concept that small-time use should not be a major focus for law enforcement that has led, in part, to specific localities decriminalizing marijuana joints.

Others maintain that Web-based sales offer yet another example of why policing victimless crimes like drug use is illogical. As Jon Katz explained, "That's the power of the Net—it's really not for the government to be telling people whether they should be using marijuana or not, and the Internet makes it possible for people to make those judgments on their own. The Internet has killed off traditional notions of moral policing" (Goldberg, 1999).

Legal Issues

Another difficulty is the absence or lack of clarity in laws that could be used to prosecute online dealers. This is true of all types of drugs—prescription as well as controlled substances. Although there have been efforts to address this concern, there are still many legal issues that remain unclear. These are outlined in Chapter Three. Legal issues are especially difficult in the crackdown on information, on paraphernalia, and the detoxification industry. In 1999, the Senate passed the Methamphetamine Anti-Proliferation Act that would have made it illegal to distribute any information, in print or online, about manufacturing or selling controlled substances. The bill was killed by the House, yet was later reintroduced as part of the Bankruptcy Reform Act, only the latest version dropped the Internet portion (Erard, 2004). Officials are trying to police the sale of paraphernalia and adulterants but are making little progress. State laws vary in regard to drug-related paraphernalia. Both New York and Maine very specifically define and prohibit paraphernalia, but other state laws are less clear.

Regarding items used to cheat drug tests, Congress considered a bill in spring 2005 outlawing the sale and use of products designed to mask drug use (Young, 2004). Fourteen states already have similar legislation. Additional information is provided about this issue in Chapter Three.

Global Issues

As noted, one of the most significant challenges is the global nature of the sales. According to John Taylor, the FDA's associate commissioner for regulatory affairs, his agency is doing all that it can but is daunted by the task. "Each day thousands of individual packages containing prescription drugs are imported illegally into the U.S. simply because the sheer volume has grown to exceed the capability of FDA field personnel to properly process it" (Sullivan, 2004). Karen Tandy of the Drug Enforcement Agency (DEA) concurred, and maintained that her agency needs greater global jurisdiction to truly pursue online drug sellers (Sullivan, 2004). Although the FDA, DEA, Customs, and other federal agencies have apprehended some online sellers through coordinated efforts, these are merely the tip of the iceberg. They must still rely heavily on foreign law enforcement agents to collaborate (Sofaer & Goodman, 2001). Although some countries have been cooperative, others are not. The INCB has singled out Pakistan, asserting officials there failed to prosecute companies sending illegal shipments of psychotropic drugs to Switzerland and the Netherlands.

Catching the Offenders

Adding to the challenge for law enforcement, the Web allows people to easily change identity and location (Reaves, 2002). Furthermore, lawmakers are concerned with censoring the Web. The public in general seems to want the Web to remain a free forum. In 2000, the FDA, General Accounting Office, and several members of the House of Representatives called for a requirement that all online pharmacies be required to disclose their owners, their location, the doctors involved, their affiliated pharmacies, and their telephone numbers, but the legislation went nowhere as there was little support in Congress. According to William Hubbard of the FDA, "getting a bill regulating the Internet is about as hard as it gets" (Gaul & Flaherty, 2003). Web-based material is generally protected as free speech (De Angelis, 2000).

· 1 ·

THE WAR ON DRUGS

"If this is a war, we're all soldiers"

Tom Brokaw

Introduction

Interestingly, there has not always been a War on Drugs in the U.S. It wasn't until the start of the 20th century that any organized drug control efforts were put in place. The huge scope and expenditures on drug control emerged even more recently, after the 1970s. The focus of the War on Drugs has changed somewhat over time, vacillating between more rehabilitative efforts to incarceration as the primary vehicle of policing drug users. One constant, however, is that the drug control policies that have been enacted were rarely simple. That is, they were and still are often connected to racial, political, and economic motives. It remains to be determined how Internet-based sales will alter the War on Drugs.

This chapter presents a brief summary of the War on Drugs to date, then outlines its current versions. It also provides a discussion of the effectiveness of the War on Drugs to date. The chapter provides a framework for understanding how Internet-based sales fit into the existing scheme of the drug wars.

A War Mentality

A "war" mentality has become ubiquitous in the U.S. No longer reserved for actual military engagements, the U.S. wages war on a vast array of social problems (both real and socially constructed). Starting with the War on Poverty in the 1960s, the U.S. has increasingly approached social issues like drunk driving, teen pregnancy, and school violence with an "us versus them" mentality (Caulfield, 2000). Whether this is the most effective way to alleviate a social problem is the subject of much academic debate. Regardless of the discussions held in the hallowed halls of academe and the critiques offered in scholarly books and journals, a war-making approach to social problems has persisted and even expanded in recent years. The War on Drugs, then, is one of the earliest and most ongoing manifestations of this mentality.

In 1971, Richard Nixon was the first president to officially declare a War on Drugs, stating, "America's public enemy number one in the United States is drug abuse. In order to fight and defeat this enemy, it is necessary to wage a new, all-out offensive" (Levine, 1998, p. 27). The War on Drugs has escalated tremendously since Nixon's declaration, in scope, expenditures, and tactics.

Key Themes in the War on Drugs

Looking back at the history of drug legislation and the War on Drugs in America, a few key themes emerge. First, regulations and prohibitions have not necessarily been tied to the harm(s) of the substance. Second, drug laws have long failed to fairly distinguish between use and abuse. Third, legislation and enforcement of it is very much influenced by race and socioeconomics (Gerber & Jensen, 2001). Prior to the 20th century, drug use was not viewed as a social problem per se, and few laws prohibited drug manufacture, use, or sales. Laws in place were directed largely at what would today be prescription or pharmaceutical drugs. Even this early legislation dealt with purity, not whether the substance in question was addictive, dangerous, or even effective. (Swann, 2004). In general, no substances were prohibited for personal consumption until the 20th century. As Szasz (1992) explained, "From the time the Pilgrims first landed until 1914, the American people had the freedom as well as the obligation, the right as well as the duty, to care for and control their bodies, manifested by legally unrestricted access to the medical care and the medicines of their choice" (p. 6).

Racism and Drug Laws

The earliest legislation that covered what we call illicit drugs today was also not truly directed at eradicating harm. Instead, it was heavily influenced by racist attitudes and race-based assumptions. For example, following the Civil War, Chinese workers were used for a number of projects, most notably to build the rapidly expanding railroad system in the U.S. They brought with them the habit of smoking opium, which caught on with some Americans as well. Opiates were easy to obtain, and, although no tracking mechanism existed gauging how widespread their use was, some sources suggest that doctors gave babies born to addicted mothers opium in their formula (Schmalleger, 2005)."There were plenty of patent medicines for children, including Mistress Winslow's Soothing Syrup, Mother Bailey's Quieting Syrup, and Kopp's Baby Friend. All of these contained opiates" (Hoffman, 1987, p. 25).

Hoffman explained that the "typical" user was different than today's conception of the average drug addict.

> ...they were largely female, mostly white, and mostly in their forties. Women users, outnumbering men by nearly three to one, were an easy target for addiction—first because opiates were prescribed for menstrual and menopausal discomforts; and second, because it was thought unwomanly to be seen drinking liquor in public, or to have lingering on your breath (Hoffman, 1987, p. 25).

When the Chinese workers were finished working on the railroads, their use to the country was generally complete. Legislation allowing only American citizens to import or to manufacture opium quickly followed (Hyde, 1990; Ksir, et al., 2006). The first of these was a San Francisco, California ordinance, which was followed by federal legislation in 1880 and 1887 (Hyde, 1990; Ksir, et al., 2006. Robinson & Scherlen, 2007). Outside the U.S., concern about opium prompted the first international discussion about drug use in 1909. The British, who profited from the opium trade, resisted prohibitions on the substance (Hyde, 1990).

In the early 1900s, a similar phenomenon occurred with cocaine. Until drug reformers linked cocaine to "Negroes" and violence, it was used widely in medicines and tonics, was part of the original recipe for Coca-Cola, and was readily available at pharmacies or by mail order (Ksir, et al., 2006). The racism of drug legislation and enforcement continues, with concerns today about what substances are prohibited, who is prescribed specific drugs, as well as who is stopped, searched, arrested, and punished for drug violations. To offer one example, the fact that a person must possess 100 times the amount of cocaine to receive the same sentence as someone possessing crack has been described as racist.

Early Laws Regulating Drugs

The Pure Food and Drug Act of 1906

The first major piece of drug legislation in the U.S., the 1906 Pure Food and Drugs Act, prohibited interstate commerce of adulterated or misbranded food or drugs, requiring that drug packages state how much of particular substances were included. As the name suggests, it was intended to regulate the purity of food and drugs sold in the U.S. It did not, however, make any specific substances illegal (Ksir, et al., 2006). Prior to this legislation, what would today be considered prescription drugs were widely available, as was today's "paraphernalia." For instance, in 1896, coca leaves were included in Coca-Cola, Bayer and Company sold heroin as a sedative for coughs in 1898, and the 1897 edition of the Sears Roebuck catalog included hypodermic kits, syringes, needles, vials, and even a carrying case for morphine (Robinson & Scherlen, 2007).

The Harrison Act

In 1914, the Harrison Act required dealers and dispensers of opiates to register and pay a fee of $1.00 per year to the federal government (Schmalleger, 2005). Again, the law did not make any drugs illegal, but required that users purchase or possess any of the taxed drugs based on a prescription from a registered physician (Ksir, et al., 2006). Non-registered traffickers could face a $2,000 penalty and up to five years in prison. Users were not the primary focus of the legislation—sellers were (Schmalleger, 2005). Marijuana was not included, as it was not considered to be a dangerous drug at the time (Schmalleger, 2005). There is definitely evidence that drug use was widespread at the time. It is estimated that approximately 1 in 400, or 200,000 Americans, were dependent on opium or some opium derivative when the Harrison Act was passed (Ksir, et al., 2006).

The first significant arrest for a Harrison Act violation came just prior to the 1920s. Similar to a concern today with Internet sales, a Dr. Webb was prescribing opiates after brief telephone conversations with consumers.

The Supreme Court held in 1919 that these phone conferences did not qualify as a proper examination (Ksir, et al., 2006). The Narcotics Division of the Treasury Department was charged with enforcing the Harrison Act and interpreted the Supreme Court's decision to mean that even a valid prescription for a habit-forming drug was not a "legitimate medical purpose," helping to cement the idea that use and abuse of some substances are one and the same (Ksir, et al., 2006).

The Roaring Twenties and the Prohibition Era

In 1922, Congress passed the Jones-Miller Act, which more than doubled the maximum penalties for dealing illegally imported drugs. Also critical was the Act's stipulation that possession of illegally obtained opiates was sufficient for conviction. This established users as criminals, rather than just the sellers (Ksir, et al., 2006). The U.S. experiment with prohibition between 1917 and 1933 also impacted the direction of the fledgling War on Drugs. It established the notion that the best way to curtail drug use and abuse was to prohibit potential users from having legal access to the substances, rather than to address why they wanted it in the first place. This is in contrast to assessing and addressing the reasons why people might use drugs and seeking to prevent drug use via education (Ksir, et al., 2006; Robinson & Scherlen, 2007).

Harry Anslinger and the Bureau of Narcotics

In 1932, Congress created a separate Bureau of Narcotics, and named Harry Anslinger to head the Bureau. Anslinger had almost complete control over federal drug-related efforts, including education, prevention, treatment, and enforcement between 1932 and 1962. Perhaps Anslinger's most important achievement was the passing of the 1937 Marijuana Tax Act, requiring those wishing to import, buy, or sell the substance to register and pay a tax of $100 per ounce (Ksir, et al., 2006; Schmalleger, 2005). Anslinger's success can be largely attributed to the media deluge tying marijuana to violence and crime, despite no evidence to support this tie. Most notably, the film *Reefer Madness* demonstrated the depraved lengths to which a marijuana "addict" would go when they craved a high. Again, the movie showed how violent criminals were more often than not people of color, and Anslinger's slur campaign not only has a legacy in drug legislation, but in the public's (mis)understanding of who is a drug user. These laws were clearly influenced by racism (Jensen & Gerber, 1998; Robinson & Scherlen, 2007. Schmalleger, 2005). Anslinger once said,

> Most marijuana smokers are Negroes, Hispanics, jazz musicians, and entertainers. Their satanic music is driven by marijuana, and marijuana smoking by white women makes them want to seek sexual relations with Negroes, entertainers, and others. It is a drug that causes insanity, criminality, and death—the most violence-causing drug in the history of mankind (O'Connor, 2006).

In addition, as with many drug laws today, the law appears to have been authored by individuals who themselves dabble in prohibited substances. Miller (1996) noted,

> Federal narcotics commissioner Harry Anslinger admitted he discreetly supplied illegal drugs to a wealthy and beautiful woman he admired, to a U.S. Navy officer, and to a powerful member of Congress (later identified as Senator Joseph McCarthy); Anslinger moreover threatened to prosecute a reporter who discovered the practice (p. 15).

As was and continues to be true, legislators refused to acknowledge the legitimate medical purposes of the drugs they were banning. In 1937, the American Medical Association urged Congress to vote against prohibiting marijuana because of its medicinal uses, to no avail (Robinson & Scherlen, 2007).

Under Anslinger's watch, Congress also passed the 1951 Boggs Act, which quadrupled penalties for marijuana offenses and authorized the death penalty for selling marijuana to minors. It was the first legislation that included marijuana with cocaine and heroin (Robinson & Scherlen, 2007). The 1956 Narcotic Drug Control Act, which mandated a jail sentence without probation or parole for any drug offenses except first ones, allowed for death sentences for anyone selling heroin to people under the age of 18 (Ksir, et al., 2007; Robinson & Scherlen, 2007).

Anslinger left a legacy that remains today. He was instrumental in crafting the connection between drug control and foreign policy (Ryan, 2001). "By tying drug policy into foreign policy, by making it appear to citizens and politicians that foreign foes bore the responsibility for American drug problems, that foreign enemies were using drugs to destroy the American people, antidrug crusaders succeeded in embedding punitive drug policy deep in the minds of Americans, thereby helping to ensure its persistence" (Ryan. 2001, p. 20).

The 1960s: Drugs and Crime as Political Issues

The late 1960s saw a dramatic escalation in the War on Drugs, and even greater attention paid to illicit drugs. Drug use and abuse had been fairly insignificant political issues until the later 1960s, as had crime. In the 1968 election, Richard Nixon brought crime to the forefront and in doing so, expanded the role of law enforcement and corrections in the U.S. Nixon also declared drug use to be a national emergency, saying, "The abuse of drugs has grown from essentially a local police problem into a serious national threat to the personal health and safety of millions of Americans" (Beiser, 2001). At the same time, states responded to outcry from liberals that judges had too much discretion and were using it in racially biased ways, and to conservatives, who claimed the discretionary sentencing was too lenient. States began reducing the flexibility that judges had when dealing with all types of offenders, resulting in fixed, mandatory sentences for a number of offenses, and drug offenses in particular (Beiser, 2001). Mandatory sentencing was not new; on the contrary, it was attempted in 1953 with the passage of the Boggs Act, which had only three years prior been repealed due to overcrowded prisons and outcry among judges (Terkel, 1997).

Much of the new attention to drugs was fueled by concern over the approximately 20% of Vietnam War soldiers who returned dependent on some chemical. In addition, politicians were alarmed at the increasing use of drugs among young people (Terkel, 1997). In response to increased drug use, and to experimentation with different types of drugs, a number of drugs were reclassified (Musto, 2002). Amphetamines and barbiturates, which were legal at the time, were added to the list of "dangerous drugs," which also included LSD and other hallucinogens, the opiates, cocaine, and marijuana (Ksir, Hart, & Ray, 2006). This reclassification was a precursor to the 1970 Comprehensive Drug Abuse Prevention and Control Act, commonly called the Controlled Substances Act. The law mandates that the controlled substances be under federal jurisdiction, specifically, under the newly formed Drug Enforcement Agency.

The law delineates five schedules or lists of drugs with varying penalties for sales. Penalties for possession remain the same across all schedules, and are dependent on the amount of drug a person has. Szasz (1992) commented, "Prior to 1914, the main ingredients of American patent medicines, in addition to alcohol, were cocaine and morphine. Now, these drugs are our favorite scapegoats" (p. 62). Schedule I drugs are those deemed to have a high potential for abuse and no acceptable medical use. Schedule I drugs include marijuana, heroin, LSD, mescaline, peyote, Quaaludes, and MDMA (Ecstasy) (Schmalleger, 2005). A first-time offender possessing or intending to sell Schedule I drugs may face life imprisonment and a $10 million fine (Schmalleger, 2005). Schedule II drugs are those with a high potential for abuse but with some accepted medical use, and include morphine, cocaine, and methamphetamine. The commonly used ADHD medication methylphenidate (Ritalin) is also a Schedule II drug (Schmalleger, 2005). Schedule III drugs have less potential for abuse than Schedule I or II, when abuse occurs it is more moderate physically and psychologically, and they have accepted medical uses. Anabolic steroids and most barbiturates are Schedule III drugs. Schedule IV drugs have a low potential for abuse and, when abuse happens, it leads to only limited physical or psychological effects. These drugs are also accepted for medical use. Xanax, Barbital, Cloral hydrate, and Fenfluramine are Schedule IV drugs. Schedule V drugs are characterized by even lesser effects of abuse than Schedule IV drugs, but are similar in all other ways. Substances having small amounts of codeine or opium are listed as Schedule V drugs (Ksir, Hart, & Ray, 2006). The Act also allowed the Attorney General to include any raw materials that can be made into a controlled substance in one step, called "immediate precursors" (Ksir, Hart, & Ray, 2006).

The 1970s: Drug War Escalation

Following the Controlled Substances Act, the 1970s really ushered in the era of harsh, punitive remedies to the drug "problem." The drug war was in full swing. Lik e the Anslinger era, demonization via the media set the stage for the passage of various legislation, and solidified in the public mind the image of the drug pusher and the loser-user (Musto, 2002). President Nixon was proud to have arranged with producers of more than 48 television shows to get them to introduce antidrug themes, a practice that continued into the 1990s (Miller, 1996). One Nixon aide reported that the plan was, "If we hyped the drug problem into a national crisis, we knew that Congress would give us anything we asked for" (Miller, 1996, p. 157).

In 1973, New York led the way with the nation's harshest drug sentences. The Rockefeller laws, named for then-governor Nelson Rockefeller, declared a mandatory 15 year prison term for those possessing small amounts of narcotics (Beiser, 2001). Now, every state as well as the federal government has some type of mandatory minimum sentencing. In 1973, the U.S. established a number of enforcement bodies and tracking tools for drug use and abuse.

The National Drug Control Strategy, the National Household Survey on Drug Abuse (NHSDA), and Monitoring the Future (MTF) all were inaugurated, as was the Drug Enforcement Agency (DEA) (Robinson & Scherlen, 2007).

In general, the Ford and Carter administrations were far more moderate in their approach to drug use. Carter even advocated that marijuana be decriminalized, and eleven states did this between 1973 and 1979 (Terkel, 1997). The Carter administration pushed for a demand-side, treatment-based approach to the War on Drugs (O'Connor, 2006). Still, the war mentality persisted. Under Carter, for instance, the Comprehensive Drug Abuse Prevention and Control Act was amended in 1978 to allow asset forfeiture, a controversial element of today's War on Drugs (Robinson & Scherlen, 2007).

The Reagan Era: Supply-Side Interventions

President Ronald Reagan is typically the president most associated with the War on Drugs. Similar to Nixon, Reagan's war was ideological as well as physical. Szasz (1992) identified the array of claims drug warriors in the 1980s made. These include First Lady Nancy Reagan's claim that "any user of illicit drugs is an accomplice to murder" and Drug Czar William Bennett's claim that drug abuse "is a product of the Great Deceiver ... We need to bring to these people in need the God who heals" (p. 32). Ms. Reagan's "Just Say No" campaign was all about demonizing users. Like today's war in Iraq, many assert the rhetoric was simply a tool used to obtain greater power. "President Ronald Reagan and his spouse Nancy announced that drug users were threatening America. As the perceived threat from communism dwindled, the president pumped up the perceived threat from drug users to justify authoritarian governmental actions that had earlier been justified as a response to the communist threat" (Miller, 1996, p. 26).

Reagan authorized the CIA, an agency charged with foreign surveillance and law enforcement, to enforce domestic drug laws (Miller, 1996). Reagan involved all the major federal agencies, including the DEA, the FBI, the Internal Revenue Service, the Bureau of Alcohol, Tobacco and Firearms, the Immigration and Naturalization Service, U.S. Marshals Service, U.S. Customs and Border Protection, and the Coast Guard, in combating drug trafficking (Ksir, et al., 2006). In 1981, Congress passed the Military Cooperation with Law Enforcement Officials Act, which authorized the Pentagon to assist state and local police in drug war efforts. In 1989, Reagan's successor, President George Bush furthered the involvement of the military in the drug war by creating six regional task forces within the Department of Defense. These acts are inconsistent with the 1878 Posse Comitatus Act that prohibits military involvement in domestic law enforcement (Redden, 2000 Terkel, 1997). As can be expected, the involvement of the military furthered the notion of a "war" and changed the look of the drug war. In the early 1990s, police were being supplied with the tools of the military, including machine guns, sniper rifles, helicopters, grenade launchers, and laser surveillance equipment (Redden, 2000).

The drug war escalated in the 1980s in other ways as well. Harsher penalties for specific offenses were added, and additional items were added to prohibited lists. Much of the new concern was tied to a few high-profile drug-related deaths, including comedian John Belushi and basketball star Len Bias (Terkel, 1997). In 1984, the Comprehensive Crime Control Act, among other things, expanded the government's ability to seize the property and assets from convicted and even accused drug offenders in both civil and criminal courts (Parenti, 1999). Allowing asset forfeiture to occur through civil courts is a dramatic change, as the burden of proof is so much lower than in criminal court (Parenti, 1999). States followed suit with similar asset forfeiture laws, and by 1990, forty-nine states had their own laws (Parenti, 1999). The 1986 Crime Bill imposed twenty-nine new mandatory minimum sentences (Parenti, 1999). It required a mandatory five-year prison term for anyone caught with 5 grams of crack, and 5.1 grams or more increases it to a mandatory ten years. At the same time, a person can have 100 times the amount of cocaine, or 500 grams, before they will receive an equal sentence (Terkel, 1997). Those convicted from the new laws were denied probation and suspended sentences (Parenti, 1999). Many have critiqued this legislation and its' discriminatory impact, including the U.S. Sentencing Commission, but Congress has refuse to alter it (Dyer, 2000). Study after study has made it clear that this legislation, and enforcement of it, disproportionately impacts people of color (Mauer & Keys, 2007).

The 1988 Omnibus Drug Act expanded drug offenses to include substances used to make drugs (precursor substances), and also authorized the death penalty for murder committed in conjunction with a drug-related felony. The Omnibus Drug Act also established the position of Director of National Drug Control Policy, called the drug czar, as a cabinet-level position. The drug czar is charged with preparing a national drug control strategy and budget (Ksir, et al., 2006). Furthermore, the 1988 Act continued to expand military involvement in the War on Drugs, providing $2 million to the DEA for training of law enforcement and another $3.5 million to equip them with military gear (Parenti, 1999).

The drug war expanded in scope in the 1980s as well. The 1988 legislation authorized the eviction of public housing tenants who engaged in criminal activity of any sort in or around housing projects (Parenti, 1999). The law also targeted users by denying them certain benefits after they have been convicted, most notably, student loans (Schmalleger, 2005). The crack epidemic in the mid-1980s prompted increased police narcotic units that mostly focused on arresting street-level users and dealers. Hot-spot policing, which involves targeting areas thought to be high-drug areas, also became popular (Parenti, 1999). Sherman (1990) maintained that crackdowns, the sudden increase in officer presence in a specific region, were a widely used form of narcotics policing. Also in 1988, Congress further addressed the issue of precursor substances in the Chemical Diversion and Trafficking Act. This Act allows the DEA to monitor chemicals that are not immediate precursors but are needed for production of a scheduled drug (Ksir, et al., 2006). In addition, President Reagan initiated the use of drug testing as a tactic of the War on Drugs (discussed in Chapter Four).

The 1990s: And on It Goes

Both the ideological and actual attacks on drug users and sellers continued under the first president Bush. Almost immediately after taking office, President Bush sent troops to Panama to overthrow the Noriega regime and bring General Manuel Noriega to trial as a drug trafficker (O'Connor, 2006). President Bush also authorized the withholding of federal aid to states unless they appointed their own drug czars and sent more offenders to prison (O'Connor, 2006). Bush's drug czar, William Bennett, who was later discovered to have a serious gambling addiction, advocated a zero-tolerance approach to drug use, emphasizing that any use, even casual experimentation, should be a punishable offense. He once agreed with a caller on a talk show who proclaimed that drug dealers should be beheaded (O'Connor, 2006). According to Szasz (1992), "The Bush administration endorsed and intensified the effort to enlist 'kids' in the War on Drugs. Betraying one's own parents was not enough; better to betray one's friends as well" (p. 79). Furthermore, the Bush administration continued the Reagan era drug education programs, which Szasz (1992) critiqued. He writes, "drug education is a campaign of pharmacological disinformation in the service of justifying the government's

War on Drugs" (p. 82). Everyone, it seems, was a potential drug addict. In 1990, a Georgia newspaper printed "drug coupons" and asked readers to write on them the names of possible drug users before submitting them to the sheriff's department (Miller, 1996).

The Crime Control Act of 1990 doubled appropriations for state and local drug-enforcement grants, expanded the regulation of precursor drugs, and included anabolic steroids as a controlled substance, among other things (Schmalleger, 2005). Harsh punishments continued, and users and abusers continued to be treated as one and the same. The Supreme Court upheld the reasonableness of mandatory life imprisonment for simple possession of drugs in 1991. Miller (1996) noted, "The average federal sentence for homicide is less than seven years, [while] a nineteen-year-old with a clean record received 10 years for carrying crack for a dealer" (Miller, 1996, p. 73). In 1994, the death penalty was extended to drug kingpins, or leaders of large-scale drug production and distribution organizations (Ksir, et al., 2006). The Clinton administration's drug bill also increased penalties for manufacture and dealing of drugs in "drug-free zones," most notably, schools and playgrounds (Parenti, 1999).

International Drug Controls

As drug trafficking is a global issue, there have been a number of efforts to attain greater cooperation among nations. Some of these have come from international agreements, and some are from U.S. hegemony. The first effort was the 1912 Hague Convention, which attempted to "suppress the nonmedical use of drugs" (Terkel, 1997, p. 128) This was followed by the Opium Convention of 1925, but there was still not tremendous support for international narcotics controls (Albrecht, 2001).

A number of other treaties were consolidated into the Single Convention on Narcotic Drugs in 1961, intended to limit worldwide drug production to only that needed for scientific, medical, and industrial use. The treaty has been signed and ratified by 166 countries and was the first international agreement to represent the Prohibitionist approach to drug policy (Albrecht, 2001). A decade later, the Psychotropic Convention provided for international control of amphetamines, barbiturates, and hallucinogens. The 1971 convention authorized member parties to provide treatment instead of legal interventions (Albrecht, 2001). In 1988 the Vienna Convention sought to address drug trafficking and money laundering (Albrecht, 1997; Terkel, 1997).

The 1988 convention was distinct from the earlier two, according to Albrecht (2001), in that it clearly echoed the U.S. War on Drugs. Rather than focusing on drugs as a health and administrative issue, this was a convention on criminal law that emphasized specific strategies, including forfeiture, controlling money laundering, limiting availability of precursor drugs, and cooperation between police agencies. The Vienna Convention, through Article 3, Paragraph II, stressed that member countries should criminalize cultivation, possession, and purchase of drugs for personal consumption. Other countries, most notably the Netherlands, did not and still do not completely adhere to this recommendation (Albrecht, 2001). A major focus of the 1988 convention was on reducing drug trafficking, yet Article 2 specifies that member parties must refrain from law enforcement activities outside their national territory without consent (Albrecht, 2001). The idea was to promote global cooperation, but the reality is that deep divisions in member nations' approach to drug control made this type of consent unlikely.

The U.S. has attempted to mandate that other countries cooperate with our War on Drugs. According to Gerber and Jensen (2001), there are three reasons why the U.S. has exported our War on Drugs: our need for enemies; the decline of the Red Scare; and our role as the world's police force. More recently, the 1986 and 1988 Anti-Drug Abuse Acts make foreign aid and access to the U.S. market contingent on the development of narcotics control efforts. In 1989, the U.S. launched "Operation Just Cause," an invasion of Panama, in part to pursue the War on Drugs and arrest General Manuel Noriega (Robinson & Scherlen, 2007).

Opponents maintain our global efforts are ineffective at best, and have resulted in greater violence and poverty in countries like Columbia. It has dispersed the drug industry to countries like Venezuela, Argentina, and Brazil (Robinson & Scherlen, 2007). In other cases, U.S-led drug war initiatives in other countries have wrought overt damage. For instance, in 1978, the U.S. used Agent Orange, the toxic exfoliant, in an attempt to eradicate poppy fields in Mexico (Robinson & Scherlen, 2007). Ryan (2001) commented, "In general, American policy toward Mexico has reflected an uncomfortable balancing of foreign policy with drug policy concerns. Similar balancing has had to occur in regard to Peru, Bolivia, and Columbia" (p. 39).

The North American Free Trade Agreement (NAFTA) expanded trade between the U.S., Canada, and Mexico in the 1990s. It also exacerbated drug trade between those countries (Robinson & Scherlen, 2007). The invasion of Afghanistan and toppling of the Taliban, although positive in many ways, increased the production of opium, as the Taliban had been very effective at eradicating poppy fields (Robinson & Scherlen, 2007). U.S.-based international efforts in that area continue to expand today. The DEA has agents in more than forty countries, and the State Department's Bureau of International Narcotics and Law Enforcement Affairs had a budget of $914 million in 2004 (Ksir, et al., 2006).

Today, the International Narcotics Control Board (INCB), headquartered in Vienna, is the primary international body dealing with drug-related issues. They have announced that methamphetamines are the world's greatest drug problem, with more users worldwide than users of heroin and cocaine combined (World Drug Report, 2007).

One of the big challenges for the U.S. has been that other countries have not always followed suit with the same drug prohibitions we have. In particular, other states rely far less on incarceration of offenders than does the U.S. For instance, Gaylord (2001) noted, "Hong Kong's police and prison statistics do not suggest a society hell-bent on criminalizing drug users" (p. 65). Hong Kong practices what has been called, "Enlightened Prohibition," whereby treatment and rehabilitation, education and participation, and research are all important components (Gaylord, 2001).

Although the U.S. headed toward prohibition and criminalization in the 1920s, Great Britain went in the opposite direction. Bean (2001) explained that the 1926 Rolleston Committee Report in Britain (also known as the Report of the Ministry of Health' Departmental Committee on Morphine and Heroin Addiction) recommended that addiction be treated as a disease, not a crime. The Committee recommended providing addicts small amounts of drugs for maintenance purposes. Doctors were allowed to prescribe heroin and morphine for this purpose, and the prescription of cannabis and cocaine was not considered a major problem until the mid-1980s (Bean, 2001). The British government increasingly turned to an American model, however, even appointing a drug czar in 1998 and adopting drug testing and asset forfeiture policies (Bean, 2001). Bean (2001) commented, "The extreme nature of the American criminal justice system has been a barrier, producing a measure of distrust that limits the wholesale transfer of ideas" (p. 93).

Erickson and Haans (2001) contended that the U.S. has tried to influence Canada to adopt and maintain prohibitionist drug policies. In the 1980s, for instance, Canadian drug law was considered among the harshest of the Western democratic countries, and the Royal Canadian Mounted Police (RCMP) collaborated with American police in learning strategies to enforce drug laws.

When President Reagan pushed the War on Drugs, Canadian Prime Minister Brian Mulroney did as well (Erickson & Haans, 2001). The 1997 Controlled Drugs and Substance Act carries maximum sentences of seven for possession of cocaine, heroin, morphine and other opiates, with life sentences for trafficking those substances (Erickson & Haans, 2001). Following the U.S. model, the Canadian Supreme Court has affirmed searches of students in schools and border searches (Erickson & Haans, 2001). Yet at the same time, there are signs that Canada might take a less punitive approach. In fall 2003, Canada decriminalized possession of small amounts of marijuana. People found having less than 30 grams are punished only as harshly as a traffic ticket. The Bush administration is critical of Canada's efforts, fearing that Canada will become a major supplier of marijuana to the U.S. (Roleff, 2004). It supplies a brand of marijuana called B.C. bud (British Columbia). In another example of a possible move away from U.S. influence, Canadians have been far more resistant to drug testing in the workplace (Erickson & Haans, 2001). In 2006, the Canadian government has been criticized for their move away from harm reduction and toward a more U.S.-influenced drug policy that includes mandatory minimum sentences (U.S. involved in discussions ..., 2006).

In Latin America, U.S. drug policy has created a quagmire. In the late 1980s, according to Andreas (1995), fifty-four federal agencies and seventy-four congressional committees had some role in drug policy in Latin America. The primary tool for pressuring Latin American countries into a U.S.-style War on Drugs has been the offer of economic assistance in the form of payments as well as equipment, training, and advice. Another tool used to pressure Latin American countries to conform to the U.S. model is the annual certification process. Started in 1986, the process categorizes countries into three groups: producer, consumer, or transit states. Unless a country on the list demonstrates they have cooperated completely with counternarcotics efforts, sanctions are applied. States failing to certify receive no U.S. assistance and are known as drug-trafficking nations (Bouley, 2001).

According to Bouley (2001), "Many Latin American governmental leaders perceive U.S. drug policy as a violation of Latin American sovereignty because the United States is attempting to solve its domestic drug problem by interfering in the internal affairs of another country" (p. 179). In October 2006, Bolivian president Evo Morales, a former coca farmer, touted the legal uses of coca. Morales and other advocates maintain that coca can be used for teas, shampoos, and sodas. The U.N currently bans all coca trade (Legal uses of coca touted, 2006). Because the drug trade is a major source of income in many Latin American countries, opponents of U.S. policies denounce them as nonhumanitarian (Bouley, 2001). Given that Latin America is a major source region for the drugs most in demand—cocaine, marijuana, heroin, and increasingly, methamphetamines—it is nearly impossible to control drug use without cooperation from these countries. Perhaps the film *Cocaine Cowboys* (2006) best illustrates this. In the film, Jon Roberts and Micky Munday explain how easy it was to work with Columbians to smuggle cocaine into the U.S. in the 1970s and 1980s. When they arrived in Miami, Roberts called it a "virgin city." Still part of the Deep South, Miami was known for its beaches. In the 1950s, one police car patrolled an area the size of Rhode Island. As the nearest mainland U.S. destination, Miami was ripe for boat and air drops of drugs. In the movie, Roberts and Munday discuss stashing cocaine in their neighbors' garages and in vehicles they would tow. Police were easily corrupted and helped them move drugs in patrol cars on some occasions.

The Current War on Drugs

George W. Bush appointed John Walters as his drug czar in 2001. Walters is known for denying the existence of racial disparities in the drug war (O'Connor, 2006). He has helped escalate the drug war in Latin America. There are three key prongs of the current Bush administration's stance on drugs, outlined in March 2004. First, they have pushed for even greater attention to teenage drug use, including increased use of drug testing. Second, they have advocated expanding treatment programs. This has been done primarily through vouchers to help poorer people pay for treatment. Third, they have made more effort to address global drug use and trade via eradication and interdiction (O'Connor, 2006).

Man-Made and Prescription Drugs

More attention is being paid to methamphetamines and prescription drug abuse in the drug war's current iteration. The Office of National Drug Control Policy (ONDCP) launched their "Synthetic Drug Control Strategy" in 2006, which calls for reducing methamphetamine and prescription drug misuse 15 % by 2009. The plan also involves a global component, as drug czar John Walters explained the administration would be working with Mexico, Germany, India, and China to control methamphetamines making and trafficking (ONDCP unveils ..., 2006) Unfortunately, attempts to crackdown on U.S. methamphetamine labs have spawned more labs in Mexico. Many of these labs use precursor substances shipped from Asia (Meth labs proliferate ..., 2006). In the U.S., many states are expanding their control over nonimmediate precursors (drugs that require additional manipulation but that have the necessary chemical makeup) out of concern that regular over-the-counter drugs like ephedrine and pseudoephedrine can be made into methamphetamine (Ksir, et al., 2006).

Interestingly, some states are using the Web to counteract methamphetamine offenses. Tennessee, Montana, Illinois, and Minnesota already have online registries for offenders and claim the public has the right to know if an offender lives in their neighborhood. Bills to create methamphetamine-offender registries are being considered in Oklahoma, Washington, Kentucky, West Virginia, and Illinois and Minnesota are currently implementing registries. Others oppose the use of registries. "The problem with these registries is that we're creating a class of untouchables within our society who cannot rent apartments or secure employment. When you diminish the likelihood that ex-felons can live and work in society, you increase the chances that they will return to criminal behavior," said Jonathan Turley of George Washington University (Online registries ..., 2006, para. 6).

Control of Steroids

Furthermore, steroid use has gained a great deal of attention, in particular among high-profile professional athletes. The 2004 Anabolic Steroid Control Act added a number of anabolic steroids to the list of controlled substances Act (Davis, 2005). The National Institute of Health documented that steroid use among twelfth graders escalated dramatically in the late 1990s (Davis, 2005). Although some are using steroids to enhance their athletic performance, others are using them for purely cosmetic reasons, like appearing more muscular to attract girls. The American Academy of Pediatrics (AAP) has condemned steroid use and recommended greater adult supervision and intervention (Pediatricians call for action ..., 2005). The vast majority of the illegal anabolic steroids being used in the U.S. come from abroad, according to Davis (2005).

Marijuana Legislation and Enforcement

Some things never change. Continuing the theme that use equals abuse, the Supreme Court ruled in 2005 that the federal Controlled Substances Act still supersedes state initiatives legalizing drugs. In 1996, California approved use of marijuana for medical purposes, and ten other states have passed similar laws (Robinson & Scherlen, 2007). The court ruled, however, that federal law enforcement bodies can still arrest people who are, by state law, legally selling or legally buying medical marijuana. The Supreme Court of Michigan recently ruled that merely a trace of a controlled substance in a driver's body is enough to obtain a driving-under-the-influence conviction under the state's zero-tolerance laws. The driver in that case was pulled over for erratic driving, admitted smoking marijuana, and was given a blood test. The test did not reveal tetrahydrocannabinol (THC), but traces of THC metabolites that can be in the system for up to thirty days after smoking (Michigan court says ..., 2006). In an extreme example, in 2005, two 10-year-old girls in Florida were arrested and suspended from school for pretending a bag of parsley was pot (Girls arrested for pretending parsley ..., 2005).

Media Campaign—Moral Panic?

The media blitz from earlier decades has expanded as well. "Philip Morris, Anheuser-Busch, RJR Reynolds, American Brands, DuPont, Johnson & Johnson, SmithKline Beecham, Hoffman-LaRoche, the Procter & Gamble Fund, the Bristol-Myers Squibb Foundation, and the Merck Foundation have all been important sources of money for Partnership [for a Drug-Free America] propaganda. Those groups are manufacturers (and affiliated foundations) of tobacco, alcohol, and pharmaceuticals" (Miller, 1996, p. 27). In 2006, the DEA launched a traveling exhibit that promotes the idea that the War on Drugs and the war on terrorism are connected. The exhibit includes a mock heroin processing lab from Afghanistan but fails to note that the Taliban virtually eliminated heroin production in the area (DEA exhibit ..., 2006).

Paraphernalia Legislation and Enforcement

Little attention was paid legally to drug paraphernalia until the 1970s, when states began to add laws regulating sales of bongs, scales, torches, and assorted other items associated with drug use. In 1988, a revision of the Controlled Substances Act prohibited paraphernalia sales federally (Ksir, et al., 2006), and all but two states have antiparaphernalia laws. Federal laws, however, are rarely enforced. Lawmakers today are addressing paraphernalia, as well as looking at other things related to drug consumption and sales, including drug testing and products designed to assist someone in passing a drug test.

Drug War Expenditures

In the last two decades, expenditures for the War on Drugs have increased dramatically, from $65 million in 1969 to $1.5 billion in 1981 to $19.179 billion in 2003 (Tunnell, 2004). This represents more than a 1200% increase (Drug free workplace, 2002). Combined federal, state, and local drug war monies surpassed $30 billion in 1999, and have continued to grow. The vast majority of these monies—67%—is earmarked for supply reduction efforts, including law enforcement, interdiction, and international efforts. Only one third of the drug war monies is devoted to rehabilitation and treatment (Tunnell, 2004). For instance, in 2002 the ONDCP declared the following breakdown in federal monies: $3.587 (19.1%) for treatment with research; $2.548 billion (12.5%) for prevention with research; $9.513 billion (50.5%) for domestic law enforcement; $2.074 billion (11%) for interdiction; and $1.098 billion (5.8%) for international efforts (ONDCP, 2002). In 2000, the ONDCP calculated the costs of drug abuse in the U.S. at over $67 billion, with almost 70% of that number coming from the costs of crime associated with drug abuse. These numbers, however, are largely connected to law enforcement and incarceration—approximately 3% of the portion of crime costs was associated with victims (Study finds significant..., 2005).

Impact on Usage Rates

In 2005, the U.S. Department of Health and Human Services reported results from the 2004 National Survey on Drug Use and Health. This study found that 110 million Americans aged 12 and over admitted to using an illicit drug at least once in their lifetime, a total of 45.8% of the population in that age range, and 34.8 million Americans (14.5%) ages 12 and over had used an illicit drug in the last year (Curley, 2005). By far, the most frequently used drug is alcohol, with 198.22 million Americans (82.4%) ages 12 and over admitting to ever using it, and 50.3% using alcohol in the last month. This is followed by tobacco, another legal substance (Curley, 2005).

Although some people express great concern with the rates of drug use in the U.S., others look to the positive side. The head of the United Nations' Office on Drug Control and Crime claimed in June 2006 that "worldwide containment" of drug supply, demand, and trafficking had been largely achieved. He was referring, in part, to the World Drug Report, which showed a 22% decrease in opium poppy production in 2005 and declining usage rates for cocaine in the U.S. as well as elsewhere in North and in South America (UN gives upbeat ..., 2006). The National Survey on Drug Use and Health found few people had **ever** used most "hard" drugs. For instances, only 3.3% of those surveyed admitted to ever using crack, and only 1.3% had ever use heroin (Curley, 2005). Even more significant is the fact that the numbers of people who can be said to **abuse** these drugs, measured by use in the past month, were 0.8% for cocaine, 0.2% for crack, and 0.1% for heroin (Curley, 2005). With regard to marijuana, which remains the most frequently used illegal drug, only 6.1% of those surveyed admitted to use in the past month (Curley, 2005). Worldwide, approximately 160 million people, or 4% of the population aged 15 to 64, admitted to using cannabis (World Drug Report, 2007). Although 21% of countries saw and overall decrease in drug consumption in 2000, 25% experienced this decrease in 2003. Fewer total countries saw increased use in 2003 when compared to 2000 (44% versus 53%) (World Drug Report, 2007).

Caught in the Net

Not only has the War on Drugs escalated in cost, but it has also expanded in scope. As Tunnell (2004) noted, however, it is not just those typically regarded as "criminal" populations who are subjected to greater surveillance as part of the War on Drugs. Policymakers have also paid greater attention to potential users who might hurt the economy. "These other drug users who increasingly have come under suspicion and monitoring are otherwise law-abiding, working, and tax-paying men and women" (Tunnell, 2004, p. 2). One way this has happened is through increased use of drug testing for entire groups, as in the cases of many workplace drug testing programs and school-based drug testing (discussed in Chapter Four). Staples (2000) explained the dangers in some of these new forms of social control, arguing "as new forms of social control are localized in everyday life, they are capable of bringing wide-ranging populations, not just the official 'deviant,' under their watchful gaze" (p. 6). Furthermore, "The notion of 'innocent until proven guilty' seems like a cliché these days, when people are apt to be subjected to disciplinary rituals and surveillance ceremonies simply because statistics indicate that they have the potential for being offenders" (Staples, 2000, p. 6).

Often this surveillance leads to guilt by association, as in the legislation authorizing eviction of public housing residents for possessing or using drugs on the premises or for allowing someone else to do so (Tunnell, 2004). In 2005, the Supreme Court allowed drug dogs to sniff outside cars during routine traffic stops as well as to investigate around a house when there is no reason to suspect drug-related wrongdoing (Court gives more latitude ..., 2005). In some cases, prosecutors have looked to new interpretations of existing law to expand the drug war. In North Carolina, a mother was prosecuted for assaulting her child with a deadly weapon—her body (Miller, 1996). Women have also been charged with drug trafficking for passing drugs to their babies through the womb or via breast milk.

According to Neuspiel (1996), black women are ten times more likely than white women to be reported to child welfare agencies for their prenatal drug use. Even so-called "help" services might not be so helpful if you use drugs. Miller (1996) provided an example. "Employee Assistance Programs put workers' physical and mental records into large data bases that can be informally accessed by police. In many states health care professionals are supposed to report drug-using pregnant women to government authorities, and state social service agencies routinely repot drug-using mothers to police" (p. 13). In sum,

> Vilification of drug users is continual. That rhetoric serves to loosen inhibitions against attacks on ordinary people, excusing legal and extralegal sanctions that might otherwise seem unconscionable. Nazis who made war on Jews portrayed them as communists. The same is said of drug users. President Richard Nixon and Vice President Spiro Agnew popularized the image of marijuana as procommunist war opponents. Drug warriors go further yet, declaring that drug use itself is a communist plot (Miller, 1996, p. 16).

Tools of Drug Warriors

The property of those accused but not necessarily convicted of drug crimes can be seized under asset forfeiture laws. There are two types of forfeiture: criminal and civil. In criminal, the forfeiture occurs after someone has been convicted, and the government must follow all due process requirements during trial. Civil forfeiture affords the government far more latitude. A property owner is not always entitled to attend the hearings nor may there be a right to a jury trial. Forfeiture victims have no right to counsel. Rather than the government proving their case, the property owner must disprove the government's claims.

Tips from informants are admissible hearsay in civil forfeiture hearings (Miller, 1996). Today, past convictions are no longer in the past; instead, any evidence of former drug use can justify additional repression. For instance, the 1996 Personal Responsibility and Work Opportunity Reconciliation Act allowed states to deny food stamps and cash assistance to peoples convicted of drug felonies (Robinson & Scherlen, 2007).

Medicalizing the Problem

Another movement, starting in the 1960s and escalating into the 1990s, was to medicalize the problem of drug abuse. Again, "help" comes with a cost.

> ... defining a drug user as sick generates support for the drug war among family and friends of victims. Although consequences that befall victims can be more serious than if they were simply defined as criminal, the medical bill of attainder allows family and friends to view the person as sick rather than criminal. Instead of being outraged at injustice, they are grateful that law officers captured the victim in time to offer help (Miller, 1996, p. 12).

Szasz (1992) summarized the problems with medicalizing the War on Drugs, calling it "a moral crusade wearing a medical mask" (Szasz, 1992, p. 58).

Militarization of the War on Drugs

Building on the infrastructure created during the Reagan era, the military is now regularly involved in drug war efforts (Tunnell, 2004). In 2004, the Defense Department spent approximately $500 million on drug interdiction efforts (Ksir, et al., 2006). In the 1990s, Police paramilitary units (PPUs) were involved in some 40,000 drug raids each year, with over three-quarters of police departments in the U.S. having this type of unit by the mid-1990s (Kraska, ed., 2001). SWAT-style raids have even occurred in schools, most notably Stratford High School in Goose Creek, South Dakota, in 2003. Based on allegations from the school's principal that students were selling marijuana, the local SWAT team invaded the school. They forced kids as young as 14 on the ground, handcuffed them, and pointed guns at their heads while drug dogs sniffed their bags. No drugs were found. One student, Le'Quan Simpson, 14, had this to say about the raid: "They hit that school like it was a crack house, like they knew that there were crack dealers in there armed with guns" (Law enforcement ..., 2006, para. 3). In July 2006, a federal judge approved a

$1.6 million settlement against the police department, city, and school district for violating 150 students civil rights. Kraska et al. (2001) explained that the militarization of criminal justice has been mutually beneficial. The military is guaranteed expansion of their budget (particularly in peacetime), and law enforcement is able to utilize the military's sophisticated technology, weaponry, and personnel.

Incarceration Focus

The primary method of dealing with drug offenders is clearly centered on law enforcement, and, more specifically, incarceration. Mandatory minimum sentences for drug possession and trafficking increased, resulting in more people incarcerated for drug offenses than any other type of offense. More than 230,000 drug-law violators are in state prisons and local jails, and more than 60,000 drug offenders are in federal prisons (Ksir, et al., 2006). Thousands of others are on probation and parole, leading to over 6.3 million people under some form of correctional supervision (Redden, 2000). In 1999, a person in America was arrested for a drug violation every 20 seconds (Redden, 2000). The number of people incarcerated in the U.S. for drug violations exceeds the total number of people incarcerated in the United Kingdom, France, Germany, Italy, and Spain combined, and the U.S. has the largest prison population in the world (Walmsley, 2003).

Conducting the War on Drugs as essentially a law enforcement issue has had a disproportionate impact on people of color. Although three-quarters of drug users in the 1990s were white (non-Hispanic), blacks were far more likely (and remain so) to be arrested, convicted, and sentenced to prison than whites. According to Sklar (1995), almost 90% of people sentenced to state prisons for drug possession in 1992 were black and Latino. Between 1986 and 1991, there was an 828% increase in incarcerations of black women for drug offenses, a 328% increase for Latinas, and a 241% increase for white women (Sklar, 1995). In 2002, slightly more than 47% of state prison inmates serving time for drug offenses were black, just over 23% were Hispanic, and just over 24% were white. These rates are clearly not in synchrony with each group's representation in the population (Harrison & Beck, 2005). Haney and Zimbardo (1998) noted that the U.S. had more black men under the control of criminal justice in the 1990s than there were black men in college. A 2003 report found that black men have a 32.2% chance of going to prison, compared with 17.2% for Hispanic men and 5.9% for white men (More blacks imprisoned ..., 2003). Because whites tend to use and sell drugs inside rather than outside on the street corner, in yards, and on the streets, they are harder to catch. Concentration of police resources in black neighborhoods pretty much ensures that more blacks will be caught (More blacks imprisoned ..., 2003). Furthermore, much research has documented that blacks are far more likely to be stopped in their cars and to be searched, despite the fact that more contraband (drugs and weapons) is confiscated from cars driven by whites (Amon, 2003).

The number of drug offenders being incarcerated at both the federal and state levels continues to grow, despite a vast array of evidence indicating other methods would be more successful and less costly. The Bureau of Justice Statistics calculated that costs to keep drug law offenders incarcerated exceeded $8.6 billion in the mid-1990s (Schmalleger, 2005). Yet numerous studies have found that demand-side interventions, such as substance abuse treatment programs, can save tremendous amounts of money. Rydell and Everingham (1994) found that domestic law enforcement efforts cost fifteen times as much to achieve the same reduction in societal costs of substance abuse. A study released in 2005 by the University of California at Los Angeles (UCLA) found that every dollar spent on substance abuse treatment creates $7 in monetary benefits for society. These benefits come in the form of medical costs, mental health services, criminal activity, earnings, and other government programs like unemployment compensation (Study finds significant financial benefits..., 2005). Although some forms of drug abuse counseling are available in prisons, these have been continually depleted and underfunded. According to Terkel (1997), fewer than 2% of drug offenders receive any drug treatment as part of their sentence.

Drug Warriors Claims

Defenders of the War on Drugs are often referred to as drug warriors. Their arguments center on the "costs," both real and ideological, of drug use and of the drug trade. The U.S. government asserts we are prevailing in the War on Drugs and that it is one that can, eventually, be won. Asa Hutchinson, former director of the DEA and a former congressman, claimed that the War on Drugs is working. He argued that the U.S. has made progress, both on the supply and demand sides. Overall drug use is down, especially for harder drugs like cocaine. Hutchinson asserted that less than 5% of the population uses illegal drugs of any kind today, and that this represents tremendous progress.

Speaking in 2002, he cited a Customs seizure of more than 16,000 pounds of cocaine along the U.S.–Mexico border, as well as increased seizures of methamphetamine and heroin as signs that interdiction is working as well. The ONDCP claims that one-third of the cocaine from South America is intercepted prior to making it to the streets of the U.S. or other countries (Hutchinson, 2004).

Drug war advocates also stress that the U.S. has helped other countries control drug production and distribution and has pressured foreign governments to try drug traffickers. According to one State Department report, there were more prominent drug figures in prison in 1996 than ever before (Levine, 1998). Laws allowing the government to seize the assets of drug dealers have also been an option, and pressure for other nations to do the same has supposedly helped cut the funds of drug dealers (Levine, 1998). Hutchinson (2004) further maintained that drug treatment courts are a highly effective innovation in the War on Drugs, citing a 70% success rate.

Opponents Arguments

Others maintain that the War on Drugs is a dismal failure and can never be won. According to Pollard (2005), the global illicit drug market, measured at retail prices, is higher than the Gross Domestic Product of 88% of the world's countries. It is estimated that the size of the world illegal drug market is between $45 and $280 billion (Pollard, 2005). Interdiction, opponents argue, is successful in stopping only 10% of the illegal drugs that enter the U.S. (Levine, 1998). When one border is sealed, innovative drug dealers simply find another one. Similarly, when one country's supply is reduced, due to eradication or other efforts, another country may become the primary supplier (Terkel, 1997).

Officials cannot possibly inspect all incoming packages, so drugs can easily be shipped into the country in a number of ways. A U.S. Customs official has said only 3% of the packages that enter by sea each year are inspected (Levine, 1998). Furthermore, estimates are that up to 25% of the marijuana used in the U.S. is grown domestically (Levine, 1998).

Drug war opponents argue that the U.S. can only exert minimal influence over other countries, some of which it has contentious relationships with, at best. Even when foreign governments agree to follow U.S. advice or commands, they often do not have the resources or political ability to do so (Levine, 1998). Some countries refuse to cooperate because they disagree with U.S. policies. For instance, Mexico disagrees with the death penalty and will not extradite offenders they know might be executed. DEA agents garner resentment, as the actions they take in other countries would not be allowed in the U.S., such as executing searches without warrants (Terkel, 1997). Arresting drug traffickers may only result in a job promotion for someone else, as in the case where the Medellin cartel was replaced by the even harsher Cali cartel. The CATO Institute maintains that traffickers expect interferences with their sales, and thus plan for alternate arrangements (Carpenter & Vasquez, 2005).

Although proponents of the War on Drugs may point to a decrease in worldwide opium production in the 1990s, in reality the estimated 3000 metric tons of opium still available would provide the entire world with heroin many times over (Carpenter & Vasquez, 2005). In addition, in some areas, farmers cannot grow other crops easily, especially those that would generate significant monetary return (Carpenter & Vasquez, 2005). Plan Colombia, a $1.3 billion effort to address narcotic trafficking in Colombia, was primarily a military endeavor, assisting the Colombian military in obtaining equipment, supplies, and weapons. Only a small portion of the funds were earmarked for strengthening democracy and ensuring human rights (Robinson & Scherlen, 2006). Marez (2004) asserted that, while the U.S. claims to want an end to drug abuse, state policies have often supported drug trafficking. In the 1970s, the Nixon administration supported heroin trafficking in Southeast Asia to fund the war in Vietnam, and in the 1980s and 1990s, the U.S. government backed groups involved in the cocaine trade for political ends (Marez, 2004).

Regarding the alleged success of asset forfeiture, opponents maintain it will have minimal impact, as it represents less than 2% of America's illegal drug market (Duke & Gross, 1993). In addition, drug war opponents are concerned that asset forfeiture laws violate civil rights (Levine, 1998). Jensen and Gerber (2001) asserted that asset forfeiture can be very lucrative for law enforcement agencies. Between 1989 and 1998, law enforcement received nearly $6 billion from asset forfeiture. In 80% of the DEA's forfeitures, property owners were never charged with a crime (Terkel, 1997). It is also suggested that government inflates their "successes" to further the war.

> Another element of bureaucratic thrust is seen as drug warriors exaggerate their accomplishments. At one time federal authorities were embarrassed to announce seizures of X number of ounces or pounds of drugs because the weights were so puny.

So announcements instead began referring to seizures of "enough drugs to supply X number of doses," a measurement that could be massaged to make ten pounds of pure heroin supply as many as thousands of "cut" doses as authorities needed in order to make the seizure look impressive (Miller, 1996, p. 163).

Rather than focusing on the logistics, some critics maintain that the very notion of a War on Drugs is flawed. Jensen and Gerber (2001) maintained there was no objective data justifying a War on Drugs in the 1980s, saying that drug use was down. Instead, they maintain the drug war was a function of claims making by politicians, the media, criminal justice, and drug dealers, for example. According to Miller (1996), that a given drug is illegal tells us nothing about the harm it might bring. "Legal status is determined by its standing in a culture and by what people believe about its users. Those factors have nothing to do with chemistry" (Miller, 1996, p. 2).

Studies used to determine whether a drug is "dangerous" are not always objective. Again, Miller (1996) compared this with Nazi Germany. "In Nazi Germany top scholars, who relied on government-funded research for personal income and professional prestige, put a scientific veneer on anti-Semitic rhetoric. So, too, do scientists in the United States receive government money to make reports that drug warriors cite as proof of their hate rhetoric" (Miller, 1996, p. 24).

Another popular argument made by proponents of the drug war is that prohibitions against marijuana are necessary because marijuana is a "gateway drug," that use of a lower-classed drug can lead to the subsequent use of "harder," more dangerous drugs. Studies that purportedly confirm the gateway hypothesis are fraught with methodological problems (Sullum, 2003). Furthermore, most people who use marijuana never go on to use other drugs (Sullum, 2003).

Perhaps Szasz (1992) summed up the perspective of radical drug war critics best.

> In short, we have tried to solve our drug problem by prohibiting the "problem drugs;" by imprisoning the persons who make, sell, or use such drugs; by defining the use of such drugs as diseases; and by coercing drug users to undergo treatment (coercion being necessary because drug users want drugs, not treatment). None of these measures has worked. Some suspect these measures have aggravated the problem. I am sure of it. They have had to—because our concept of the nature of the problem is mistaken, our methods of responding to it are coercive, and the language in which we speak about it is misleading.

How Will Internet Sales Fit in the War on Drugs?

Despite critics' very legitimate concerns, it is obvious that some semblance of a War on Drugs is here to stay. Given that, it is important to consider how the changing nature of drug sales will be addressed. If it is true that we are experiencing a significant global change in the types of drugs being used and the purposes for using them then law enforcement at all levels will need to adjust their tactics. What is successful in apprehending a street-corner crack dealer is likely not very successful in catching a doctor running a pill mill. If users are able to learn about, buy, sell, and even make their own drugs from information obtained online, law enforcement have their work cut out for them. Do we continue passing laws and make them more applicable to the Web? Do we use the Web to "sting" those seeking to buy or sell online? Or do we abandon the pretense that we can police the Web and focus more on education and awareness? In addition, will we carry on in the same vein as we have—passing and enforcing legislation more unplanned than organized and often based on assumptions rather than objective data? Given the global nature of Internet drug trafficking, will cross-national cooperation work better than it has in the past? These are questions to be considered after reading more about what is available, provided in the next chapter.

· 2 ·

ONLINE DRUG SALES AND INFORMATION

Introduction: What Is Available on The Internet?

It would be simpler to list what is NOT available. The Web is, simply put, a smorgasbord of drugs and drug information. This chapter details some of the drugs available for purchase and the kind of information purveyed on prodrug sites. The first part of the chapter describes the availability of prescription drugs, steroids, and illicit drugs on the Net. It integrates the author's own descriptive study of Web sites with information from governmental and other sources. The chapter also details the type of information that is available about drugs, including drug recipes and how to alter existing drugs to get high. It is important for the reader to know that this research is descriptive. That is, the author did not attempt to purchase any of the substances advertised on the Web Sites described herein.

The chapter concludes with an assessment of who is selling and who is buying drugs online. This sets the stage to discuss one of the challenges for police—identifying the suspects.

Drugs Available

Prescription Drugs on the Web

Sale of prescription drugs is the easiest form of online drug sale (Reaves, 2002). The Web is literally a treasure trove of advertised prescription drugs. deKieffer (2006) reported a Google search for "Internet Drug Store" resulted in approximately 35 million Web sites. It is not clear how many of these sites truly provide the advertised items. Thus, the number of sites offering prescription drugs for sale forms the basis of the material in this section.

Illegal online pharmaceutical sales take a number of forms. Some people sell unapproved drugs via the Internet, some dispense drugs approved by the U.S. Food and Drug Administration (FDA) without prescriptions, others make fraudulent claims about the medications, and other sites provide illegal or doctored up versions of approved pills (Hubbard, 2004). The FDA estimated that there were over 1000 Internet pharmacies in 2004 (Veronin and Youan, 2004). International Narcotics Control Board (INCB) member Herbert Okun said, "It started as a trickle and—wham!—now it's a mushroom cloud," in reference to the growth of Internet drug sales (Pisik, 2001, p. 27). In 2005, the online prescription drug industry was estimated to be worth $23 million to $1 billion per year (I-team 10 investigates ..., 2005).

In 2006, the INCB recognized the Internet as a major conduit for questionable sales of the more than 10 million illegal shipments entering the U.S. each year (Abuse of prescription drugs seen ..., 2006). In an interview with *Nightline* reporter Chris Cuomo (2006), federal Drug Enforcement Agency (DEA) agent Tim Stover demonstrated how easy it is to find prescription drugs on the Web. A search for no-prescription hydrocodone gave 141,000 listings. In 2004, the General Accounting Office (GAO), the investigating arm of Congress, found it easy to purchase prescription drugs on the Internet and cautioned that many are mishandled, sold without proper prescriptions, or are missing important warning information. Researchers purchased eleven different drugs from sixty-eight Internet pharmacies located in twelve different countries.

The 2004 research by the GAO found pharmacies based in Canada to be the most legitimate. Although all of the eighteen Canadian pharmacies examined in the study required a valid prescription, only five of the twenty-nine U.S.-based pharmacies did. The remaining U.S. sites, as well as the other twenty-one sites from foreign countries, relied on medical questionnaires or required nothing prior to arranging a sale. The National Center on Addiction and

Substance Abuse (CASA) released their analysis of Web-based prescription drug sales in July 2006, which involved 185 Web sites. No prescription was needed on 89% of the sites. Thirty percent of the sites actually boasted that no prescription is needed, another 60% offered online consultations, and 10% simply made no mention about prescriptions (More web sites offer unfettered prescription drug sales ..., 2006). Only 2 of the 185 sites were licensed by the National Association of Boards of Pharmacy. Even those where a prescription is required allow users to fax the prescription in. It is obviously not too difficult to forge a doctor's signature and fax a fake prescription (More Web sites offer unfettered prescription drug sales ..., 2006). Prescription forgery is popular because it can be financially lucrative, offenders perceive it as a victimless offense, chances of being apprehended are small, and penalties are slight (Colvin, 1995). Additionally, some 85% of forged prescriptions are filled. The United Nations' International Narcotics Board (INCB) says approximately 90% of pharmaceutical sales made online are done without a prescription.

Even if a prescription is required, many sites boast online consultations to provide the appearance of meeting the requirement (Sullivan, 2004). Federal law prohibits purchasing controlled substances online. This includes pain relievers like OxyContin and Vicotin, sedatives like Xanax and Ambien, stimulants like phentermine, Adderall, and Ritalin, and anabolic steroids without a valid doctor's prescription. The U.S. Department of Justice does not consider cyberdoctors who use online questionnaires to be legitimate. Sites that require users to complete an online medical form, allegedly reviewed by a doctor, are prone to error. On average, deKeiffer (2006) said e-doctors look at some 300 of these forms per day, approximately one per 90 seconds. They are generally paid per application (anywhere between $5 and $80), so they have every incentive to hurry.

Web-based sellers seem to assume that users know precisely what to do with the drugs when they get them. In the GAO research, only the Canadian sites included instructions for use, and only one-third of the non-Canadian sites provided warning information. Most of the drugs did contain the proper active ingredients, although two were counterfeits and two had different chemical compositions (Some Internet drug sales ..., 2004).

As noted earlier, many prescription drugs ordered online contain impurities. The FDA has reported that almost 90% of prescription drugs coming into the U.S. and purchased via mail or ordered online are dangerous (Tinnin, 2005). This might be an understatement—in one case, pills marketed as Viagra contained cement (Lee, 2006). In 2005, a team of investigative journalists attempted to make online purchases of a number of prescription drugs and found this to be quite easy. Once the drugs arrived, they made arrangements with Pfizer to have them tested. According to Joe Theriault, Vice President of Global Security at Pfizer, "They [online pharmaceutical companies] are selling an array of junk that frankly I would be afraid to put in my system." Norvasc, a blood pressure medicine that the team ordered was fake, and the Viagra they received had only a small amount of the active ingredient (I-team 10 investigates ..., 2005). According to the *U.S. News & World Report*, the top ten most frequently counterfeited drugs in 2004, all sold regularly on the Internet, were Viagra, Lipitor, OxyContin, Procrit, Zoloft, Cipro, Celebrex, Serostim, Albuterol, and Crixivan. The GAO cautioned that the worst countries in regards to drug impurities and fakes are Argentina, Costa Rica, Fiji, India, Mexico, Pakistan, the Philippines, Spain, Thailand, and Turkey. In December 2006, *Business Week* reported the story of a Belize-based counterfeiting operation. Workers there crafted fake Viagra, Lipitor, and Ambien from raw ingredients shipped from China. The drugs were then hawked on the Web (Grow, Elgin, & Weintraub, 2006).

Stoppler (2005) warned of a number of problems with drugs purchased from illegal online pharmacies: they might be outdated or expired; manufactured in substandard facilities, contain dangerous ingredients or have been improperly stored, be too strong or too weak, may be the wrong drugs, or may be outright fakes. In 2007, *The Washington Times* reported that patients who ordered depression and insomnia drugs online received schizophrenia drugs instead. Three people were treated at emergency rooms for side effects (Lopes, 2007). The National Association of Boards of Pharmacy claimed that almost half of all online pharmacies offering prescribing services are located outside the U.S. (Stoppler, 2005).

> When investigators arrived at the back street lock-up garage, the stench of mould and rotting fruit was overpowering. Stacked in a corner were many boxes of medicines. Had these drugs not been intercepted in north London, six weeks ago, they would have been posted to patients who had been tempted by low prices and easy availability to buy prescription drugs on the Internet (Lee, 2006, p. 30).

According to the Government Medicine and Healthcare Products Regulatory Agency (MHRA) in the U.K., some of the companies selling drugs online make more than GBP £1 million per week (£485,296) £485,296 (Lee, 2006).

In addition to varying levels of ingredients and contaminants, Hickman (2006) cautioned that only one-quarter of drugs purchased online actually arrive. William Hubbard reported to the U.S. Senate that in 2003, the FDA and Customs opened 1153 shipments of pharmaceuticals coming into the U.S. Of these, 88% were unapproved drugs. They also found controlled substances and drugs that are no longer allowed in the U.S. (Hubbard, 2004).

In recent years, American consumers, upset with high prices and difficulty accessing the drugs they need, have turned to Canadian pharmacies. Even easier than going to Canada is to order those drugs online. In 2004, Health Canada, that country's equivalent to the U.S. FDA, estimated there were some 170 Internet pharmacies in the country (deKeiffer, 2006). Although many Americans purchase these drugs thinking they are produced in either the U.S. or Canada, Canada has no requirement of that nature. Thus, Canadian-based pharmacies can obtain their supply from various countries. Additionally, there are dozens of sites that use the word Canada in their name or feature something Canadian like a maple leaf in their advertising signage or Web site but have nothing to do with that country (deKeiffer, 2006).

The case of Liam Brackell highlights the global nature of online drug sales. Brackell walked under a train in the U.K. at age 24 after trying more than twenty-three types of prescription drugs he purchased online. His mother, Susan, tried desperately to stop him. She regularly checked his room, at one time finding 320 Valium pills he purchased online, and even sabotaged his computer and intercepted the packages he received from Hong Kong, China, and various African countries (Lee, 2006). Susan said her son spent hours searching the Web for different types of drugs and would spend up to GBP $80 per transaction (Lee, 2006). Ryan Haight, an honors student from La Mesa, California, died in 2001 when he mixed morphine he was taking for back and joint pain with two prescription antidepressants and the painkiller hydrocodone (Lyons, 2007).

In order to research what is available and how it is marketed, the author and her research assistants conducted Google searches of a number of the most-abused prescription drugs. Of the first ten links available in a Google search for "buy Darvon," seven clearly required no prescription. It was unclear whether two others required them. These links were to the same source, drugstore.com, which says a prescription will be required at the end of the purchase. Several of the others blatantly advertised that no prescription was needed, or provided a set of links to other online pharmacies where no prescriptions were needed. Buydarvon.net offered the following information: "Shipping and delivery is by default discreet in order to protect personal privacy and security." Losepain.com cautions users, "Before purchasing Darvon, make sure you have consulted your physician," and reminds users it is their responsibility, not that of anyone affiliated with the site, to ensure use is safe and appropriate. All the sites featured information about the drug, directions and cautions for use, side effects, and drug interactions. Pharmacyseek.com features a list of popular drugs on the left so users can link to find information and make purchases of those substances as well. It also features links to "join and save on meds," links to pharmaceutical sites requiring no prescription, and links to doctors who do phone consultations.

Another Google search, this time for "buy hydrocodone," revealed more of the same—information about the drug, links to places to buy it, and in general, no prescription required. One interesting feature of this search was the number of sites that were dead ends—that is, once you clicked to link, you were unable to go back to the previous page by clicking the back button on the computer. This could be the result of a number of things: a bug in the system, or a clever way to force users to stay on the page. No prescriptions were required in the first ten links in a search for "buy Vicodin" either. Links were either dead, offered to sell the medication without prescription, or provided links to other sites doing so. Just like the offers for knife sets and vacuum cleaners on QVC, a televised home-shopping network, some sites even offer a free 30-day trial period for purchasing assorted medications, such as USrxLeader.com and SafeUSMeds.com. Searches for "buy Percocet," "buy Ativan," and "buy Tamepam" revealed more of the same. If a person cannot buy directly from that site without a prescription, most provide links to other locations offering no-prescription-needed sales. Some provide an automatic redirect, most frequently to topmeds10.com, which offers more links to no doctor visit and no prescription sales.

Viagra, the prescription drug used to assist men with erectile dysfunction, is equally easy to obtain. The very first link that appears, the blue highlighted "sponsored link," advertises next day delivery in discreet packaging and requires no prescription. Again, only one of these top ten links did require a prescription. Several others advertised online consultations. Chances are they are all owned by the same company and one is simply a front for the next company.

Prescription drugs more commonly used by children and teens are also easy to obtain. A simple Google search for "buy Ritalin," the drug known for its use with Attention Deficit Disorder (ADD) and Attention Deficit Hyperactivity Disorder (ADHD), conducted by the author revealed numerous sites where someone could purchase the substance. The subtly named noprescriptionneeded.com features the offer, "Buy Ritalin Online through No Prescription Needed Pharmacies." Only one of the links listed on Google's first page of "hits" instructed users that Ritalin is a Schedule II substance and cannot be purchased without a valid prescription. Several of the sites specifically advertised that no prescription was needed. One site was clearly marketed to parents, as it began with this introduction: "Does your child have ADHD? Let's face it, having to go to your doctor's office each and every month for a new prescription for your child's Ritalin, Concerta, or Metadate is very inconvenient." Some sites serve as clearinghouses and link users to numerous sites where Ritalin can be obtained in a variety of dosages and amounts. Findrxonlin.com/Ritalin.htm links users to a site where the drug can be purchased. This site makes the claim, "We will provide you with info on: U.S. Doctors who will set you up with consultations over the phone and provide you with legit prescriptions for meds like Vicodin, Lortab, Lorcet, Xanax, and Valium." Most feature "Buy Now" links like those used on amazon.com to purchase books and CDs. One link, RxList.com, connected to a message board where a user had posted, "Where can I buy Ritalin without a prescription?" At the time of the search, in July 2006, the post had been viewed 1230 times, although many of the responses did caution "Anthony" about the dangers of buying Ritalin online. As evidence of the federal government's concern about the ease in which people can purchase this drug and the potential for misuse, the first link to appear is deadiversion. usdoj.gov/consumer_alert.htm. This is a U.S. Department of Justice Drug Enforcement Agency site cautioning users against purchasing drugs online. It lists several medications that are prohibited by federal law to be purchased online, features links to stories about DEA efforts to crack down on online drug sales, and offers tips on identifying rogue pharmacies and detecting pharmaceutical drug abuse.

Similarly, a search for "buy Adderall" revealed many sellers. Again, having a valid prescription does not seem to be a barrier to purchasing the amphetamine. At Drugstorescripts.com, a user is asked to complete an online questionnaire and to name a Primary Care Physician, but it is not clear that there is any follow up with the named doctor for prescription information. One site, Drugstore.com, did emphasize that Adderall is a controlled substance that should be kept out of reach of children and never shared with others for whom it was not prescribed. Buymedsquick.com serves as a clearinghouse to connect users to online pharmacies. The site explicitly states they are not selling any drugs; rather, they connect users ONLY to legally licensed pharmacies.

Steroids on the Web

In early 2005, news agencies reported that the online auction site e-Bay had steroids for sale. MSNBC, the cable channel, in collaboration with the National Association of Boards of Pharmacy, purchased some of the steroids in October and November 2004. Investigators paid between $90 and $140 each for four separate purchases. In two of the cases, the investigator received a notice from e-Bay that the auction had been closed due to a rules violation, but the purchase still went through. All four were tested and turned out to be steroids, including Dianabol, Sustanon, and testosterone propionate. All of these are Schedule III controlled substances, and simple possession of any of them without a valid prescription carries a sentence of up to one year in prison and a minimum $1000 federal fine. After an e-Bay internal investigation, company officials determined that steroid sellers had been listing their products as books about steroids. One of the sellers, a student from the University of Florida, said he had stolen the steroids from someone's bathroom at a college party before he posted them on e-Bay. In 2004, postal inspectors seized 105,948 steroid units (one unit equals 50 tablets or 10cc injectable) and arrested 127 people for mailing steroids (Brunker, 2005).

According to Lucas Blake, junior manager for www.eurobolic.com and an author for the online blog-style magazine *Ezine*, ordering online is the best way to obtain steroids. He wrote, "At first [the] Internet wasn't treated with much respect by bodybuilders, it was in fact quite overlooked. Let's face it, most bodybuilders weren't really interested in a geeky virtual network used mainly by geeks. Bodybuilders just weren't geeks. Gradually things changed, though, as people realized that by using [the] Internet, they can easily communicate with other people from all over the world" (Blake, 2005). In addition, Blake discussed the appeal of global communication from the comfort and anonymity of one's home.

In a four-part special series in 2005, *Hartford* [Connecticut] *Courant* staff writer Paul Doyle reported that a Google search for "steroids" produced more than 5 million responses, and "buy steroids" generated 762,000 references. Some of the domain names that appear are overt, such as legalsteroids.com and anabolicshop.com. The first site Doyle investigated, juiceinjoe.com, detailed for even a novice precisely how to purchase steroids on the Web. The site author, Trevor Gladstone, appealed to the "average Joe," maintaining that, "Steroids have literally changed my life" and "The wimp was replaced by a stud." Gladstone's site also promises to help users avoid being scammed by other online steroid sellers, and walks users how to create a fake domain name so they can post messages on message boards that will give them credibility when making purchases (Doyle, 2005). Steroid.com had 41,512 members at the time of Doyle's investigation. Doyle found it very easy to purchase steroids at three sites—vipershop.org, marssel4bolex.com, and alinshop.org. Simply providing an e-mail address, address, and answering a few brief questions gets one registered at these sites, and actually selecting purchases is like navigating amazon.com. He purchased what he thought a teenager might buy, given recommendations by steroid experts. Doyle wrote, "when I make the random Website purchase, I understand the allure of Internet shopping. Type your name and address, click through a few pages and your purchase arrives a few days later. It's easy and quick and anonymous. No human interaction required. It's the perfect method for buying something illegal." He then set up a post office box to receive the shipments. He received e-mail confirmations regarding the arrival of his shipments, only to discover the steroids came from Spain, Poland, and Moldova, a country he had never heard of (it is located between Romania and Ukraine).

During his experiment with online steroid purchases, no one ever asked for Doyle's age, although two of the sites listed the requirement to be at least 18 as a term and condition of making a purchase. The packages arrive safely and in a timely fashion, and the injectable substances he ordered arrived with a fictitious invoice seeming to proclaim them as a faulty part for a computer. Inside, of the computer part, he found his goodies. Doyle then ordered syringes online, which is also illegal. He was supposed to need a doctor's prescription, but merely had to wire $49.99 to the seller in Mexico and they arrived in two weeks (Doyle, 2005).

In February 2007, ESPN reported an Internet-based illicit steroid distribution network that may have provided illegal performance-enhancing substances to Los Angeles Angels outfielder Gary Matthews, Jr., former heavyweight champion Evander Holyfield, and former baseball superstar-cum-author, Jose Canseco (Fish, 2007). Online businesses Signature Pharmacy and Applied Pharmacy are said to have connected buyers to physicians who wrote illegitimate prescriptions for steroids. Gary Wadler of the World Doping Agency commented, "The Internet represents a marked area of vulnerability. There are no borders. Who knows why you're buying? ...Who is the most comfortable with the Internet? Kids, the same people who have the air of indestructibility" (Crackdown on online steroid sales, 2007).

A Google search for buy steroids revealed a plethora of sites, primarily directed at bodybuilders. Steroid.com advertises a suppliers list and has links for resources, a discussion forum, research chemicals, articles, books, and a "buy now" link. The site does feature a warning that users should know the laws in their country. This seems to suggest the site owners absolved themselves from any responsibility in the event of an unlawful sale. The site proclaims, "Do not contact steroid.com for any reason regarding products from our sponsors." The advice is to contact the sponsor directly. The site advertises that no prescription is required and that they ship worldwide. Syringes are also available for purchase. Domesticgear.com features a picture of a very buff male and female bodybuilder. Links include an anabolic forum for discussion, articles, and a bodybuilder calculator. The site also lists a variety of types of steroids for purchase, as well as shopping Frequently Asked Questions (FAQs) and shipping FAQs. Users are required to buy in bulk, as there is a $300 minimum order for shipping. Interestingly, at the bottom of the page is a message expressing sympathy for the victims of Hurricane Katrina and a link to donate to victims via the American Red Cross. Who ever said drug dealers lack compassion?

Steroidshop.net is based in Western Europe. On the right side of the page are a number of flags that users can click on to translate the Web content into other languages. It advertises that they "don't sell fakes" and do not require a prescription. Their ten best sellers are listed, as well as a number of links, including information on steroid cycles, discounts, oral steroids, injectable steroids, sexual health, steroid information, training, dieting, mistakes, side effects, and FAQs. Like domesticgear.com, users are encouraged to buy in bulk, and regular customers can save money if they refer other users to the site.

Mesomorpheses.com/buy-steroids.htm also features pictures of bodybuilders. This site seems to be devoted to the legal issues surrounding steroid sales. The home page begins with the question, "Is it legal?" It then specifies that steroids are illegal in the U.S. without a valid prescription, and warns users not to sell anabolic steroids. The site also cautions that the DEA considers online questionnaires to be an unacceptable form of physician consultation. The site also includes links to books, DVDs, contests, bodybuilder indexes and profiles, a message board, and links to other sites.

Buysteroids.org, on the other hand, is devoted to demonstrating to users that they are not "scammers" or "fakes," as are many online sellers. In addition, they offer bodybuilder profiles, information on cycles, effects, ranking of the most popular steroids, laws, injection techniques, and calculations for amounts needed, as well pictures and information on detection. The tag line for Elitefitness.com is "Buy steroids for bodybuilding here." Rather than selling steroids, the site peddles a book that details the secrets of mail order steroid success, which ranks domestic and international steroid sellers. The site features a letter from the author, which starts out, "Dear friend and fellow athlete." The letter explains that "we all" fall into three categories: those who want to buy steroids but cannot find them; those who found them but "got burned;" and those who will buy them and get burned. Allegedly, the book will help users avoid all three of those outcomes.

The eighth link from the Google search for "buy steroids" is to a Yahoo! group where someone posted the question, "Where can I buy steroids?" The person who posted the question went on to say, "Don't give me all the illegal crap and what damage you can do, etc… I know the risks and I'm willing to take them. Who can I approach to ask?" The best answer, according to the site, is to use the Internet, to buy small amounts online, and to utilize message boards.

Anabolicsteroids.org is also directed at bodybuilders and advertised "legally obtained" steroids from "fully licensed pharmacies" in Europe and Asia. The site offers links on men's health, weight loss, skin care, special offers, steroid cycles for novices, bulking, syringes, and human hormones. The final hit on the first page of the Google search was a link to a directory of online pharmacies.

Using "buy testosterone" as a Google search word proved an easy way to find sellers as well. Humangrowthhormone.com is the most professional looking of the initial hits from the Google search, with alternative pictures of various laboratory scenes conjuring up images of chemicals being used for research. Billing themselves as "the largest human growth hormone portal," the site offers testosterone in spray, pill, and injectable forms, as well as a number of supplements and enhancers. All are offered Amazon-style, with a "add to cart" shopping feature. Information available on the site includes describing human growth hormone (HGH), why hormone replacements are needed, information on the products, on weight loss, on sexual enhancement, on creatine, on fat blockers, and on herbal Viagra. No legal statements are available on the site. The second hit is for testosteroneformula.com, which advertises all natural pills. At the very bottom of the page is a very small link titled "disclaimer," which says that the site has not been evaluated by the FDA.

At anaboliceurope.com, one can check out a list of various types of testosterone products and their prices. The main page also discusses the most popular types of testosterone and how that has changed since the U.S. scheduled steroids as a controlled substance. Nextag.com features e-Bay-style sales of testosterone creams and gels.

Illicit Drugs on the Web

Between 2004 and June of 2006, the number of Internet site selling controlled substances grew from 157 to 185, according to the National Center on Addiction and Substance Abuse, although other estimates put the number closer to 1000 (Waller, 2006). The easiest drug to find online, not surprisingly, is marijuana. A simple "Google" or "Yahoo!" search for "marijuana" turns up many sites offering readers a chance to participate in some way. As noted in the Introduction, discriminating buyers can find a Zagat-style rating of online seed banks at suresite.com (Goldberg, 1999). Those interested in growing can also use the Web to communicate with "experts," exchanging how-to tips (Goldberg, 1999). Cannabisnews.com, marijuana.com, marijuananews.com, hightimes.com, yahooka.com, and marijuanaworld.com are all easy-to-find sites featuring information about making, using, and covering up marijuana use, as well as offering readers opportunities to chat or blog. Hightimes.com even has a special "high on the air" feature, which involves readers sending in pod casts, or "pot casts," as they are creatively called, of themselves or friends high on marijuana.

Yahooka and Erowid are two clearinghouse-style sites offering all kinds of information. Yahooka.com, a promarijuana site, not only provides a wealth of information about growing, using, and selling marijuana, but it also boasts 5947 links to other sites, including 1203 in languages besides English (Erard, 2004). Yahooka's "CommUnity Online" link offers visitors opportunities to get involved in chat rooms, use discussion or message boards, get on mailing lists or in news groups, join clubs or Web rings. Users can even have free e-mail. Marijuanaworld.com is one of the few sites that features a disclaimer that those under 18 are not allowed to enter. Upon entering, users find a "talkweed" forum, a "pot humor" link, and links to Hemp T.V. and Pot T.V. Users of these sites find them to be a forum for information about all kinds of drugs, however, not just marijuana. For instance, Erard (2004) reported that, by February 26, 2004, nine people from around the U.S. and Canada had posted reports about seven different varieties of Ecstasy, including specifics on the effects of each, on pillreports.com. On Bluelight.com, interested persons can use a message board to discuss buying, using, selling, and masking drugs.

The number of links that come up when one enters the search word "Buy marijuana" is too big to analyze. Of the top ten sites that came up, only one offered a disclaimer about age and legality. Because the search was conducted just a few weeks prior to Christmas, many of the sellers were in the giving spirit. They featured a special box someone could select to buy "X-mas buds" and have them shipped overnight. An interesting link was marijuanagirls.com, which offered the twin gems of girly images and pictures of various weed. Another interesting link was to greencookbook.com, where users can read the testimonial of the 71-year-old grandmother who authored the book, which features recipes for including marijuana in main dishes, side dishes, desserts, etc. This, too, can be shipped overnight.

Buying hallucinogens is not difficult, either. The first link in a Google search for "buy hallucinogens" is enthnosupply.com, which offers hallucinogens, euphoriants, and sedatives. Information is provided about the effects of each drug. Buydrugsonline even has the tag line, "Buy LSD." The only one of these sites to offer a disclaimer about legality is walpurgisnight.com. The site describes the effects and legality of many substances, including but not limited to *Salvia divinorum*, amphetamines, LSD, mescaline, and ephedra. It links, as do many of the others, to Pillsrx.net, which offers LSD as well.

In October 2006, the London *Daily Mail* reported the ease in which someone can obtain dangerous "date rape" drugs via the Web. The author, Barney Calman, reported finding a gamma-butyrolactone (GBL) dealer, Ben, in South London with a simple Internet search. Within a day he was also able to buy a huge array of pharmaceuticals banned in the U.K., including ketamine and flunitrazepam, the liquid version of tranquillizer Rohypnol. Calman reported that many sites offer GBL under the guise of being a hardware store, where they offer "liquid soap" and "glue remover." Calman also found a number of online message boards where people were exchanging tips on buying medications online (Calman, 2006).

"Buy crack" revealed informative sites, both for those wishing to prevent people from experimenting with the stimulant and for those seeking to find it. The first link that came up was parentingteens.about.com, which provided directions to parents who might suspect their teen of drug use, including a link to purchase a home test kit. The second link was to cocaine.org, which reads like a purely informational site. Users can read what crack is as well as when it is best to take it.

Heartofrichmond.com/PDF/wisecrack.pdf provides tips for crack users about buying, quantities to purchase, and advise for use before partying and while partying. "Wise crack" offers suggestions on how to ingest crack so the high lasts longer. The site also details what users can expect after they smoke crack and the risks involved in smoking. Words of wisdom offered by the site include, "Try to buy from the same person if possible so that you get to know the quality and lessen your risk of being 'vicked' (which is when you buy something that looks like crack but is not). Users are advised to wear loose clothes to a party in which they plan to smoke crack, as they will inevitably sweat. Another site offers "clever names" that can earn someone respect when they are seeking to purchase crack. These include "Rock," Ready Rock," and "RockyRock." Lonewacko.com is a blog in which someone asks the "lone wacko," who responds, where to find crack in a particular area.

"Buy heroin" is more likely to result in links where users can read about someone who bought (and used) heroin, rather than sites offering it for sale. The first link, however, does offer heroin for sale. At findrxonline.com/free_pure_heroin.html provides links where a user can purchase heroin as well as hydrocodone, Xanax, valium, and Ambien. Users can also "Enter to win a free phone consultation." About what precisely is not clear. Blacktable.com tells someone's tale of being a functional addict and, having moved on, missing that phase of life. Another link is to Erowid's experiences vault, in which "Will" posted about missing his "friend Harry," or heroin.

"New" Drugs

S. *divinorum* is a mind-altering substance that has gained popularity in some regions of the U.S. and elsewhere. The S. *divinorum* Research and Information Center describes it as being safe and gentle on the body and not addictive. It is not a stimulant, nor is it a sedative, narcotic, or tranquilizer. It is an entheogen that some have said is in a unique pharmacological class. It is a hallucinogen now being sold in smoke shops as well as on the Web. Long used in native rituals in Mexico, the substance grows wild in the Southwest. *Salvia* is not banned federally, but it is illegal in Delaware, Louisiana, Missouri, Tennessee, and Oklahoma as well as in Australia, Denmark, Belgium, Italy, and South Korea. Spain bans sales but not possession or use, and in Finland, Norway, Iceland, and Estonia, one cannot import S. *divinorum* without a valid prescription (S. *divinorum*, n.d.) Alaska, California, Illinois, Iowa, Maine, New Jersey, New York, North Dakota, Utah, and Oregon are considering bans (Oregon weighs ban …, 2007). A Google search for "buy *Salvia*" revealed a number of sites purveying the so-called "sacred sage." Iamshaman.com seems to be the preferred site, as other sites even recommended users link to it. The founders of Iamshaman.com are working the natural substance angle, rather than the drug angle. They even mentioned they donate a portion of their proceeds to various indigenous groups and their causes in a gesture indicative of a social justice mentality.

Many teens are engaging in polydrug use, or multiple drug use, especially those who might be dubbed "high risk." This includes runaways and homeless teens, those who have been in legal trouble, and youth who have mental illnesses. Some also dabble with tryptamines, some of which are illegal controlled substances and some of which are still classified as research substances in the U.S. All of these are widely available on the Web. A common combination for high-risk youth is Xanax, Ketamine, and methadone, called a "Xani Booster" by my students. Again, all three components are for sale on the Web.

Sanders' (2006) work with polydrug-using street youth found that although many were given phenethylamines in clubs, by either acquaintances or strangers, others admitted to having searched them out on the Web. 178 phenethylamines are available online (Sanders, 2006). The U.K. has a blanket ban on phenethylamines (Sanders, 2006), but in other locations the drugs are not illegal.

Tryptamines are easy to find online. Although the DEA issued an emergency classification of some tryptamines as controlled substances, others were not classified as such, leaving some gaps that both sellers and buyers can exploit. A Google search for "buy tryptamines" revealed a plethora of sites set up like e-Bay, the online auction company. Many specifically advertised "research chemicals" in their tag lines. These examples at first appear to be purely academic, describing the chemical makeup of the various tryptamines and their effects. The "offer to buy" and "offer to sell" links are more discreet than with other sites offering drugs. The Green Party Drug Group from the U.K. was the ninth link to appear on the day of the search, August 14, 2006. That site features information about drug-related books, information about a variety of substances, and a "Health on Drugs" section that details the effects of each substance, how to be safe using them, and how to use supplements to make them work better. Another link was to a blog where a user described his first experience with the tryptamine diisopropyltryptamine (DIPT). The user described how he took DIPT in his dorm room in 2000, along with propranolol, a drug for heart conditions. He describes the impact on his senses, as well as the fact that he had a slightly more intense orgasm.

Other Drug-Related Material

Pro-Drug Information

A study by Boyer, et al. (2001) found the prodrug sites are more likely to result from a Web search than are antidrug sites. In New Zealand, for instance, social service providers are expressing concern that teens are using the Internet to learn about drugs they wish to try. This most frequently involves some type of prescription drug such as Ritalin (Tiffen, 2005). In Rumbough's (2001) survey of 985 university students, 9.5% admitted visiting sites that describe how to manufacture illegal drugs. Only 2% said they had actually attempted to use that information to make drugs, with 1.7% reporting that their efforts were successful. In July 2006, drug czar John Walters, director of the White House Office of National Drug Control Policy hosted a roundtable discussion with teenagers to discuss the ways they used technology to further substance abuse. One 17-year-old told Walters "I was always searching [the Internet] for new ways to get high." He said he learned how to grow marijuana and how to crush pills and would regularly instant message his friends so they could access his favorite drug sites. And, when his parents decided to give him a drug test, he found out how to detoxify online (Teens, technology, and drugs ..., 2006).

The vaults of Erowid's site, for instance, provide answers to questions regarding which cough medicines will produce a high and what "tripping" on certain substances feels like (Wax, 2002). The DOJ maintains these sites are misleading in the way they explain how to use the drugs makes readers feel as though they will be safe if they simply follow the appropriate directions (U.S. Department of Justice, 2002). The U.S. Department of Justice (2002) does admit that many of the Internet forums where drugs are sold are not indexed by the major search engines and thus must be accessed via word of mouth. Sites promoting drug use tend to use slang and drug terminology that the U.S. Department of Justice (2002) claims acclimates visitors to the "drug culture."

In the Erowid experience vaults, an archive of posts from various users, people post what it is like to use all kinds of experiences. The site offers a wealth of information about using drugs of all kinds—prescription, illicit, and over-the-counter, for example. In addition, Erowid offers images of all these types of drugs (pictures of the substances as well as users enjoying them), information on the chemical breakdown of each drug, "the basics" (dosage, effects, FAQs, drug testing, history, and slang), health information, legal status (including federally, broken down by state, and even international comparisons), a library, and miscellaneous links. Numerous sites are available to advocate the positives of marijuana and to mainstream its use. The site veryimportantpotheads.com offers a list of celebrities that currently smoke or have smoked pot, with a biography of each person. This is intended to affirm that use is OK.

At hipforums.com/forums/forumdisplay.php?f=15, one can find a variety of forums in which users describe their experiences with marijuana and psychedelic drugs. There is a marijuana photo gallery featuring all cannabis-related photos, a forum where users can post their experiences and stories about dealing with drug testing and law enforcement, discussion of growing tips, a place where people can "show off their piece" (demonstrate their pipe, bong, or other mechanism), a global price watch, a forum for people engaged in "cannabis activism" to change drug laws, and the more general "Stoner's Lounge," where stoners can discuss anything. The "psychedelics" thread features forums on psychedelic cacti, exotic psychedelic plants, magic mushrooms, LSD, methylenedioxymethamphetamine (MDMA), pharmaceuticals, synthetic (artificially made or designer) drugs, opiates, and S. *divinorum*. In addition, users can post and read about other people's psychedelic experiences, learn about drug testing and legal issues, and find out the technical details on preparing drugs.

A Google search for "how to smoke crack" revealed, in the top ten links, everything2.com, a site that teaches how to smoke crack like a pro, how to get a dealer, and what is needed to start up a crack-dealing enterprise. The list includes Brillo pads, lighters, and tire gauges to serve as pipes. You can also link to a forum, alt.drugs.hard, which allows users to share ideas on the best way to smoke crack. Certainly this would be useful to a crack-smoking novice, although it is hard to imagine a hardcore user consulting a Web site for this type of advice.

Although marijuana and marijuana-related information is the substance most commonly found on the Internet, a growing number of sites and chat features are devoted to the "club drugs" of ecstasy, LSD, Gamma hydroxy butyrate (GHB), and psilocybin mushrooms. GHB, also known as "Liquid E," "Everclear," and "G," is essentially the combination of a degreasing solvent and a drain cleaner (GHB, 2007). MDMA is often called "Adam" or "hug" on the street. It is similar to the stimulant methamphetamine and the hallucinogen mescaline. Both GHB and MDMA are often associated with date rape, as they allegedly loosen inhibitions and enhance feelings of sensuality (NIDA Infofactsheet, 2006). The U.N. International Drug Control Programme reported in 1997 that amphetamines were more popular than cocaine and heroin, due largely to recipes available on the Internet (Spinney, 1997). Because most of the precursor drugs to make MDMA are illegal, the Internet has been used to direct readers to suppliers and to recipes and instructions. The DEA recently arrested two chemistry doctoral students, one in Georgia and the other in Arizona, who produced MDMA, methamphetamine, and precursor drugs using directions they found online. The students also communicated via e-mail about their "work" (U.S. Department of Justice, 2002). Some sites simply point readers to raves, where these drugs are likely available, although they will frequently avoid using the word "rave," calling them techno parties or music festivals (U.S. Department of Justice, 2002).

In some chat rooms, bulletin boards, and newsgroups, users brag about their LSD use and share stories about "tripping." They also make sale arrangements and share information on how to ship and distribute LSD without detection (U.S. Department of Justice, 2002). Bluelight's users have been known to warn others of fraudulent sales, and to share information on where to purchase drugs like LSD in specific cities (Erard, 2004). Halpern and Pope (2001) found eighty-one hallucinogen-related sites offering information on obtaining, synthesizing, extracting, identifying, and ingesting hallucinogens.

Online instructions are available for converting powdered cocaine to crack, and one site even features a "Crack dealer locator service," which identified dealers in major cities. Readers can easily find charts about cocaine purity and price in most states (U.S. Department of Justice, 2002).

Information about steroids is readily available as well. Bodybuilders can ask peers for advice about using, can get information about where to purchase steroids, and can even order them online without concern about being judged by nonusing peers and little fear of being caught (Blake, 2005).

In addition to finding substances to purchase, someone trolling the Internet can easily find advice on doctoring pharmaceuticals and illicit drugs. A study published in June 2006 in *Drug and Alcohol Dependence* described the surge in people using the Internet to find information and exchange advice about how to tamper prescription drugs to get high. The study cited examples of Web sites where users share advice to crush and then snort time-released drugs like Ritalin or recommending that users chew pain-killing skin patches to slowly release fentanyl. Users also explain on the Web how to mix amphetamines with other chemicals in order to alter their pH, as well as which drugs should be mixed with tranquilizers (Muir, 2006). The author of the study, Edward Cone, a toxicologist at ConeChem Research in Maryland, explained that people obtain prescription drugs in a variety of ways, including buying them from rogue Internet pharmacies, using other people's prescriptions, and conning doctors into writing prescriptions for bogus ailments. Cone argued that Web sites detailing how to use prescription drugs recreationally, including recipes for how to get a better high, are the latest trend, and that these sites see tremendous traffic. One site featuring personal accounts of drug experiences, both illicit and prescription, receives an average of 420,000 hits per day.

One expert said he had previously been reluctant to discuss the issue publicly, for fear of giving users ideas. But now, claims toxicologist Bruce Goldberger, Professor and Director of Toxicology in the Department of Pathology, Immunology and Laboratory Medicine in the College of Medicine at the University of Florida in Gainesville, the information is so widespread anyone can access it through a simple Google search. Some companies are taking efforts to reduce tampering by making tablets that are harder to crush, and Novartis, makers of Ritalin, have released a one-a-day tablet that parents can give their children before school, which lessens the risk the drugs get into the wrong hands (Muir, 2006). Cone, however, maintained this will do little, claiming "I just touched the tip of the iceberg in my review" (Internet offers how-tos …, 2006). "This [the Internet] clearly is a way for illegal organizations to communicate. They use it to give directions to people working for them or to sell the product itself," said Jack Riley, assistant special agent in charge of the St. Louis office of the DEA (Ratcliffe & Kohler, 2006).

A simple search for "drug recipes" on Google reveals numerous sites where one can learn not only to make their own drugs but how to combine them in unique ways. Totse.com features a page called "Speedy Drugs" where one can find recipes for making methamphetamines, as well as cocaine pudding, "half-ass crank" (bad speed) and "how to make crack like a drug dealer." Online recipes for making methamphetamines are one of the main reasons for the spread of meth from the West to East Coasts (Sexton, 2006). Neonjointcom/drugreceipes.index.html offers users recipes for LSD, methamphetamines, crack, and Liquid E (Ecstasy). In addition, users of the site can learn how to get high from cough medicines and motion sickness pills, poppy seeds and nutmeg, as well as the ever-popular psychoactive toads. Also featured is advice on obtaining pharmaceuticals. A later check found the Web site not accessible. According to McHugh (2006), recipes for crystal meth, known as "Ice" or "Tina," can easily be found online.

Evidently, creative entrepreneurs have tried to capitalize on the nation's enjoyment of illicit substances by creating knockoffs. The DEA has cautioned retailers and consumers about candy bars packaged to resemble Snickers and Butterfinger candy bars named "Stoners" and "Buddafingers." These were found to contain 21.6 and 29.8 mg of THC, respectively, which the DEA warns is enough to have an impact. Another similar product is chronic candy, which can be found at chroniccandy.com. Unlike most drug-peddling sites, this one does have a disclaimer announcing that users must be 18 and must agree to enter the site. It is an elaborate site that, in the words of my graduate assistant, Erin, "looks like a Little John video, with fools dressed as pimps with their pimp juice cups and girls in bikinis who are enjoying their lollipops way too much." The site offers pot-flavored candy, with flavors named after specific marijuana hybrids. It does not actually contain tetrahydrocannabinol (THC). They also sell hemp lip balm and perfume, chronic clothing (clothes made of hemp, including thong underwear), and accessories like pocket scales, pot-leaf-shaped cookie cutters, pot leaf flip-flops, and an "orange chronic air freshener." Allegedly, rapper Snoop Dogg and party girl Paris Hilton are known to be fans, and in the "About Us" section of the chroniccandy.com Web site there is a video where Conan O'Brian is interviewing Snoop Dogg about the products. Prior to the interview, Snoop Dogg sent the studio a bunch of candy. In December 2006, someone could register to win a trip to Amsterdam from the site. Another candy site, cannabiscandy.com, is far less professional looking but features some interesting products. They advertise, "Hemp hogs—Milk Chocolate Truffles with Hemp Nut Cream Filling. This Chocolate is High on Omega 3 and 6, Mo=Betta! This Stuff Actually Makes You Healthy!" These drug knockoff products are important, as they are yet another way that drug use has been normalized on the Web.

MySpace, the social Website, claims more than 90 million members, surpassing Google, e-Bay, and AOL for number of page views (Kornblum, 2006). Founders Chris DeWolfe and Tom Anderson sold the company to Rupert Murdoch for $580 million (Newscorp is $580m..., 2005). MySpace has become a popular forum for users to describe their experiences with various drugs. "Kids are really open about it. I see posts from other people describing a night on acid or whatever. I think they think their parents are clueless. And I guess they are," said a 19-year-old about MySpace drug-related posts (Online teens openly chat ..., 2007). This system is so vast it is impossible to include even a partial description of what is available. For instance, the site myspace.com/chroniccandy had 37,533 "friends" as of early December 2006. It is full of photos of people with pot, bongs, and other devices. Myspace.com/myspacepotplace attempts to advocate for change in marijuana laws by including a chart describing the annual drug deaths in the U.S. This, however, is not cited. The site offer features recipes for marijuana butter, cannabis milk, banana bread with pot, pot pasta, and "magic pancakes." Another MySpace page called the "Pot Head Society" had 41,342 friends who are welcomed by the following message: "Welcome 'all' to a society unlike any other, the 'Pothead Society.' Where smoking Pot isn't looked down upon, but celebrated! Where the belief that the right dosage of marijuana mixed with any life style, will only improve it, is still held! Where we're trying to bridge the gap between tokers and non-smokers, with the vision that one day we can 'all' smoke in PEACE!!" It offers a thread for "The Truth about Marijuana" in which they provide and debunk thirteen so-called myths. Lucky O'Donnell, a 19-year-old who ended up in a hospital emergency room after taking advice he learned online to mix cocaine with Tylenol PM and alcohol. He said, "One site said it was fine, one site said it wasn't. I wasn't able to differentiate the information" (Online teens openly ..., 2007).

One MySpace member, a 14-year-old boy from New Jersey who claims he is 19, belongs to a number of MySpace groups, including "Pain pills," "The Drug club," and "I like lying on my bed for hours tripping on Benadryl." He wrote to Payne (2006), "My parents have not seen myspace but they do now [know] alot [sic] of the things ive [sic] done with my life but not to the full extent to which drugs ive [sic] take and how many times ... I don't show em, its that simple. In these groups we discuss the newest and easiest methods of ingestion ... we talk about legal highs and which pills are good and we also support those who made a change" (p. 9). In the "Druggie" group, users discuss which drug they like best. In the steroids group, users exchange prices and recommendations (Payne, 2006).

Videos, Web Cams and the Like

Not content just to describe their use online, some drug users enjoy videotaping it and sharing it with whoever they can. Brandon Vedas, 21, from Phoenix, Arizona, died in 2003 while he was online, the result of an overdose of prescription drugs he may have purchased on the Web, including Klonopin, methadone, Restoril, and Inderal combined with marijuana and 151-proof rum. Vedas had set up a Web cam in his bedroom, and at least a dozen chatters watched as he typed his last words, "I told u I was hardcore," then died.

The popular site YouTube features numerous short video clips, easily accessed via a site search for "drugs" or for a specific substance. By the end of 2006, YouTube claimed 100 million viewers. Google just purchased the company for $1.65 billion (What made 2006 memorable, 2006). One of the most popular videos is a two-minute clip of a burning marijuana joint posted by High Times magazine. In April 2007, news reports documented a surge of Internet activity by Mexican drug cartels. The cartels are using the Web to transmit threats, for recruiting, and to glorify the drug trafficking lifestyle. The cartels are even using YouTube to publicize their successes. Washington

Post Foreign Service reporter Manuel Roig-Franzia reported, "Drug raids in Mexico now routinely net cameras, computers and intricate computerized surveillance systems along with the usual piles of cash, cocaine and weapons. Hit men are just as likely to pack video cameras as 'goat horns'—the Mexican drug world's nickname for AK-47 assault rifles" (p. A1). Victor Clark-Alfaro, a Tijuana-based drug expert and director of the Binational Human Rights Center, explained, "The Internet has turned into a toy for Mexican organized crime. It's a toy, a toy to have fun with, a toy to scare people" (p. A1).

In September 2006, the ONDCP announced it was planning on posting antidrug videos to YouTube. A spokesperson for the ONDCP commented, "If just one teen sees this and decides illegal drug use is not the path for them, it will be a success." Others find the ideas laughable, and assert that the net-savvy users of YouTube will simply edit the ads into parodies (ONDCP posts ..., 2006). In December 2006, NIPC and CADCA asked their members to contact YouTube to protest their inclusion of unflagged "huffing" videos. One video, which is preceded by a message warning of inappropriate content, shows a young man squirting air freshener in his nose while another (with no warning) shows a young girl inhaling from a canned cleaning spray and saying, "I am Satan." NIPC leaders also placed public service announcements on YouTube, which has few restrictions, detailing the dangers of using inhalants like cleaning products and air fresheners. YouTube officials refused to be interviewed, but said YouTube does prohibit videos showing illegal or dangerous acts (Prevention groups criticize ..., 2006).

In Their Defense

Some people maintain that these sites are not a problem and that rather than promoting drug use, they are simply helping people who have already made the choice to use drugs do it more safely. Erard (2004) observed that, "Many of the drug sites appear to be offered in the spirit of harm reduction." John Robinson of Bluelight, another clearinghouse site, maintains they are performing a service in that this type of exchange allows users to be more informed and thus to make safer decisions (Erard, 2004). Shroomery.org features a welcome message proclaiming, "We help spread accurate information about magic mushrooms so people can make informed decisions about what they put in their bodies." This information, rather than being passed along slowly through an underground illegal drug network, can reach millions of people all over the world the moment it is posted. Shroomery.org provides links to sites in

Scotland, England, France, Brazil, Russia, and other countries. With a simple click, a user can also link to thirty-eight marijuana sites, six Ecstasy sites, and fourteen sites dealing with miscellaneous drugs (Erard, 2004). As technology journalist Jon Katz explained, "That's the power of the Net—it's really not for the government to be telling people whether they should be using marijuana or not, and the Internet makes it possible for people to make those judgments on their own. The Internet has killed off traditional notions of moral policing" (Goldberg, 1999).

Why the Web? Who Is Buying and Selling

The Pew Internet and American Life Project surveyed 2200 randomly selected adults aged 18 and older on their use of the Web to learn about and purchase prescription drugs. They found 45% of American adults, approximately 91 million people, take some type of prescription drug regularly. Just over one-quarter of Americans have researched prescription drugs online. This population tended to be older, more educated, have high-speed connections at home and work, and have been online for six or more years. Much of the population—62%—is concerned about online purchases, believing them to be less safe than making the same purchase at the local pharmacy. Still, 28% feel that online purchases are every bit as safe. Only 4% admitted to ever making an online purchase of prescription drugs. These people cited convenience as the number one reason for doing so. Three-quarters of the purchases were for chronic medical conditions, like arthritis or high blood pressure, while the remaining one-quarter were for some other purpose like weight loss or sexual performance. It is likely these numbers will grow, as 90% of the sample said they planned to fill a prescription online in the future (Fox, 2004). In fact, the *New York Times* reported an increase in the use of televised and Internet-based mental health counseling in June 2006, an appealing form of help for those living in rural communities (Telemedicine taking off ..., 2006).

One population of Internet buyers is those who are in search of accessible, cheap drugs that they actually need. Many who legitimately need certain drugs find it difficult to get them lawfully. In search of affordable access to what they need and want, many have turned to the Internet to shop. Online sales of pharmaceuticals from Canadian pharmacies grew from a total of $50 million in 2000 to $800 million in 2003 (Crowley, 2004). Cancer patients in England are trolling the Internet for modern cancer drugs they cannot get through the National Health System (Revill, 2006). One pharmaceutical expert has called the Internet "the Mall of America for prescription drugs" (Crowley, 2004). According to Boehm, et al. (2003), Medicare recipients in search of deals and diabetics looking for easy refills make many of the online prescription drug purchases. In October 2005, health watchdogs issued a lookout for an increase in online sales connected to the bird flu scare. Because of all the attention to a potential shortage of Tamiflu, experts were concerned that worried consumers would turn to the Web to make their purchases (Ingham, 2005).

The INCB, however, has said that the Internet does not necessarily offer cheaper drugs. It actually costs more and that most insurance companies and medical aid systems do not reimburse for the price of drugs purchased online. Hence, the INCB argues, the vast majority of Internet prescription drug purchases are made by people who do not have lawful prescriptions (Drug sales soaring ..., 2005). According to Hinkel (2000), one survey found a person could save as much as 29% by purchasing their prescription drugs online, whereas another person in the same year (1999) found that Viagra and Propecia cost 10% more than they did at a local pharmacy.

Another population who appears to be using the Web simply seek easy and low-danger ways to make their drug purchases. In particular, teenagers may be comforted by the fact that they can purchase drugs without having to deal with a traditional "drug dealer" (Cuomo, 2006). According to Joseph Califano of the Center for Addiction and Substance Abuse (CASA), a large part of the appeal is "You don't have to deal with a dirty drug dealers like they might have to with cocaine or marijuana or heroin," yet users can get a slowdown of the central nervous system much like an alcohol-induced high (Xanax often abused ..., 2002). In New Zealand, for instance, social service providers are expressing concern that teens are using the Internet to learn about drugs they wish to try. This most frequently involves some type of prescription drug, such as Ritalin (Tiffen, 2005).

Young people may have less fear of dabbling with prescription drugs than they do with other drugs. Carol Falkowski, Director of Research Communications for the Hazelden Foundation, a national nonprofit organization devoted to addiction, explained that prescription drugs are popular with young people because, in many social circles, they are viewed as more acceptable. Catherine Harnett, Demand Reduction Section Chief for the DEA, explains that teens often see prescription drug use as safe because it is "medicine," which seems sanitary and safe. Lawrence Diller (1998) explained why prescription drugs appeal to teens. Teens "think that since their younger brother takes it under a doctor's prescription, it must be safe" (p. 42). U.S. Representative

Ed Whitfield, R-KY, explained why teens are particularly susceptible to online dealers. "For young people in particular, online pharmacies seem especially seductive. For this generation, the Internet is a familiar medium and it feels safe. The seduction and convenience of the Internet coupled with the wide availability of controlled substances raises a disturbing prospect of many young people hooked on drugs with the ease of logging on to a computer" (Lyons, 2007).

Also, many teens begin using as a way of self-medicating for depression and anxiety (Leinwand, 2006). In 2006, the Chicago Tribune reported that young, healthy men were mixing stimulants like crystal meth and erectile-dysfunction drugs such as Viagra, Levitra, and Cialis to "last longer" (Young men mix Viagra ..., 2006). If the intent is to self-medicate, purchasing online makes a lot of sense—no potentially nasty interactions with a street dealer and greater (at least perceived) anonymity.

One 18-year-old explained that he used OxyContin, or "OCs" because they were easier to obtain than pot (Leinwand, 2006). Goldberg (1999) explained that in real life, if people do not have regular drug suppliers, they may need to spend weeks in search of a dealer. With the Internet, however, the next dealer is merely a click away. In addition, in contrast to the covert nature of traditional illegal drug sales, online dealers can advertise their product—not only to a local market but to a global one.

Simple curiosity drives some young people to experiment with drugs in general. When information about doing so is so plentiful on the Web, some adolescents may be even more enticed to try it out—why not? They have a how-to guide on the desk in their bedroom. In 2002, an Idaho teenager, Nick, was curious about marijuana and turned to an online encyclopedia for information. Nick is now 18 and in drug rehabilitation after becoming obsessed with the wealth of information he could find online. The encyclopedia he used receives 250,000 clicks each day and has thousands of posts from users detailing their experiences with various substances. Nick said, "I was so fascinated. The fear, the taboo of using ecstasy and crack—you really start to doubt that fear when someone tells you there's a healthier way. I would never have done a lot of the drugs I did if it wasn't for that Web site" (Khatri, 2006, p. A9).

Another 18-year-old, Jay, said, "For me, it was curiosity and wanting acceptance from others. I always said, 'I'll never use drugs.' But I tried it once, and the high was so great, it turned into a daily thing for me" (Khatri, 2006b). His mom said, "We all have perceptions about people who do drugs. My perception is that they wouldn't be able to function" (Khatri, 2006b).

In addition to access, misinformation about drugs is a concern. Brian Spitsbergen, director of youth assistance for Growth Works, a Plymouth, Michigan, agency for assistance with drug addiction, said, "To me, that's the bigger danger. You can find Web pages that tell you how to make ... name it, recipes for methamphetamine to hallucinogens to anything else. It's all over the place. But the recipes may be poison. You find a recipe for meth ... that may be instant death" (Khatri, 2006, p. A9).

Although there has been little research about the number of teens using the Web to become addicted to drugs, one study found all twelve teens in a rehabilitation program found information online that shaped their experimentation (Khatri, 2006). Other addicts who have been interviewed say it is easy to get a prescription for pain medication. Joe Leonetti told the Des Moines Register he would get Vicodin and Oxycontin when he told emergency room or clinical doctors he had back pain or other difficult to diagnose ailments. Fellow addicts also shared tips (Addict says its easy ..., 2006). The Waismann Method, an opiate dependency treatment, found that one-quarter of patients who had sought treatment for prescription painkiller addiction used the Web to find or obtain drugs (Survey indicates drug dependencies ..., 2005). One person I met doing this research explained that she started dabbling with prescription drugs when she was a nurse and thought she could manage her own use. Eventually, she was having huge shipments of assorted prescription drugs she bought online delivered to her home. This is not uncommon—there is a fairly lengthy line of research detailing pharmacists and other medical professionals as some of the people most likely to experiment with prescription drugs.

Outside the U.S., a U.K. National Audit Office survey in 2006 found as many as 600,000 Britons have purchased prescriptions drugs online (Lee, 2006). In the U.K, specialists are finding increasing numbers of patients using the Internet to purchase cancer drugs and other hide-to-find drugs, seeing it as worth the risk (Lee, 2006). Revill (2006) explained that these modern drugs are not available on the National Health Service, and some have not even been licensed by the National Institute for Health and Clinical Excellence (NICE). Many order from Canadian pharmacies. Karol Sikora, Professor of Cancer Medicine and honorary Consultant Oncologist at Imperial College School of Medicine, Hammersmith Hospital, London, explained that the younger generation is demanding the best treatments possible, and is technically savvy enough to make that happen (Revill, 2006). In 2006, the MHRA seized over GBP $2.3 million worth of prescription drugs sold illegally online, with the most popular being Viagra, and cancer drugs Avastin and Tarceva (Lee, 2006).

Part of the reason online drug sales have exploded is connected to marketing. Certainly anyone who has an e-mail account has received prescription drug spam. According to Internet security experts, almost one-quarter of all spam, approximately 15 billion messages per day, is spam advertising drugs (Grow, et al., 2006). In 2004, the top spam terms were related to pharmaceutical items, especially Vioxx and Viagra (Drugs, phishing top 2004 list ..., 2004). Journalist Catherine Holahan (2006) wrote, "There is a drug dealer in my e-mail inbox, and he really, really, wants to cure my erectile dysfunction" (p. F01). Evidently, this dealer knows about my problem too, as I receive his same e-mail offers. Indeed, direct-to-consumer advertising has certainly altered the landscape of American medicine as a whole. Sixty-three percent of Internet users said they received unsolicited e-mail advertising sexual health medications, 55% received unsolicited e-mail about prescription drugs, and 40% said they received unsolicited e-mail about an over-the-counter drug on the Pew Internet & American Life survey (Fox, 2004). Although the author had received drug-related spam prior to writing this paper, it has increased exponentially since she began. Each day, six to ten advertisements for prescription medications appear in my hotmail inbox, with approximately that same number landing promptly in my junk mail. Med Zone, AwesomeRx, Meds Delivered, Pharmacy Warehouse, Fantastic Meds, and Pharmacy Here all want me to buy from them, and Pharmacy Here tells me in their tag line I need no prescription to do so. In 2003, Virginia passed anti-spam legislation making it a felony to use fraudulent practices to send spam to or from Virginia. Included in the legislation is prohibition of forging the return address of an e-mail. Sending more than 10,000 of these deceptive e-mails in one day could result in a prison sentence of up to five years as well as forfeiture of assets and profits associated with the spam activity (Hansell, 2003).

Much like the profile of drug users provided by Hoffman (1987) in Chapter One, many of today's prescription drug users are older than the stereotypical drug user. *Psychiatric Times* reported in April 2006 that the average drug addict is in their mid-30s to mid-50s, with many of these middle-aged addicts ending up in emergency rooms for painkiller addictions (More middle-age Americans ..., 2006). Dr. Clifford Bernstein, a pain and addiction specialist at the Waismann Institute in California, explained "What we are seeing now are bright, aggressive people—some at the crest of their careers—who may start out on the drug for, say, a weekend sprained ankle, then find out how great it feels to be on it" (Critser, 2005, p. 160). Sara Simpson, supervisor of the Rx Task Force of the Pharmaceutical Narcotic Enforcement Team asserted, "The people who are addicted to these drugs are people that work just like you and me. We arrest police officers, nurses, airline pilots, school teachers" (U.S. unable to stop ..., 2004). Most of the new recreational users surveyed by the National Survey on Drug Use and Health admitted to previous use of illicit drugs. More than half the new users were female (Narcotic pain meds ..., 2006). Women and the elderly are two to three times more likely to become addicted to prescription drugs (Prescription drug abuse, n.d.). An executive friend of Greg Critser's, author of *Generation Rx*, described "Vicodin Fridays" to him. Each Friday, someone would dispense the prescription-only painkiller around the office. Critser (2005) commented: "There was no fun in Vicodin Fridays, no rebellion or even any major highly cool posing. The pills had simply become part of work" (p. 159). He goes on to explain, however, that these stories did not just happen with elite executives; instead, popping pills to confront life's daily challenges was widespread among middle- to upper-class suburbanites.

Today, more young people are using a variety of drugs as a tool. This is distinct from users who want to be more socially adept or want to lose consciousness because of horrible lives. For example, a study by Northeastern University found that many college students use ADD/ADHD medications as study aids, with Adderall the preferred substance. This study found more college students use these medications to help them study than to get high (Adderall preferred ..., 2006). The DEA is aware that college students are using the sleeping medicine Ambien for recreational purposes as well as to stay awake while studying. Recreationally, it is known as "A-minus" or "Zombie pills" (Sleep medicine ..., 2006). A 1997 study from the U.K. reported that the "typical" adolescent recreational drug user is "socially well-adjusted, knowledgeable about the substance he or she is using, cognizant of how drug use fits into his life, and is strongly disapproving of 'out of control' or 'problem' use behavior" (Holtorf, 1998, p. 38).

Young people are also experimenting with over-the-counter medicines to get high. In 2006, calls to the California poison center for misuse of dextromethorphan (DMX), rose 50 % between 1999 and 2004. DMX is in cough medicines like Robutussin and Vicks 44 (Calif. Reports rising DMX ..., 2006). This is why those products are behind the counter now. The DEA reported in 2006 that young people were mixing cough medicines with soft drinks or power drinks. Sometimes they add a Jolly Rancher candy and ice, a cocktail known as "Lean," "Sizzurp," "Purple Drank," among other names. A 2004 survey in Texas found that 8.3% of high school students reported using codeine-based cough medicines to get high. The issue gained national attention in September 2006 when San Diego Chargers defensive back Terrance Kiel was arrested for allegedly ordering cases of cough syrup that was shipped to his Texas home. Use of cough medicines has been popularized in rap songs and videos. Three 6 Mafia has a song called "Sippin' on the Syrup," and Houston disc jockey DJ Screw, who died from a drug overdose in 2000, advocated cough syrup mixes (DEA says misuse ..., 2006). In Texas, kids are reported to be mixing cold medicine with heroin, called "Cheese," and selling it at school for $2 dose (Texas kids mixing heroin, cold medicine, 2006). These products, too, can be found online.

When drug warriors have tried to adapt to the new class of users and dealer, the results have not been terrifically successful. For instance, Florida, Indiana, Ohio, Virginia, and West Virginia have all seen a surge in "pill mills" as well as addicts and dealers making "drug runs" because of the states' comparatively weak prescription drug monitoring. Florida does not track drug prescriptions. In one case, twenty-four people from Kentucky drove 2000 miles to purchase Oxycontin, Endocet, Percocet, methadone, and other painkillers (Florida drug tourism, 2006).

To date, little is known about online drug sellers. Sellers are not likely to be traditional drug dealers. The NDIC (2006) says there is little involvement by drug trafficking organizations (DTOs) in pharmaceutical trafficking. Most online sales to date are for small amounts. The National Drug Intelligence Center in Washington, DC (NDIC) does caution that DTOs could step up trafficking if access was limited. In particular, they argue limitations on access in the U.S. would increase the trafficking by Mexican DTOs (NDIC, 2006).

Unlike typical illicit drug sellers, online sellers may be actual doctors. Or, the seller may work with a doctor to provide online consultation or "prescriptions." The NDIC says doctors are paid up to $1500 per day for writing fake prescriptions online (Pharmaceutical drug threat assessment, 2004). Many sellers are doctors who have been in trouble and lost their credentials, or who went into a practice that wasn't as lucrative as they desired. Others are medical school wannabes.

In sum, two trends recently have altered the demographic of drug users and sellers from the traditional stereotype long held by drug warriors of young, largely minority males. First, prescription drugs and some of the new concoctions are far more likely to be used by females and older, more educated persons than are traditional street drugs. Additionally, sellers are more likely to be affluent and well educated. Second, Internet-based sales seem to be made by those who have more money and more education. To date, it looks as though Caucasians are more likely to sell drugs online, although this is an area in need of more research These changes offer a challenge to law enforcement, as they must adjust both their profile of suspects and the tactics for apprehending them. The next chapter delves into this and other challenges for policing the Web.

· 3 ·
POLICING THE WEB

Introduction

This chapter discusses in greater detail the challenges in policing the Web, both in general and specific to online drug deals. The difficulties in policing the Web begin with the concerns about applicable legislation and continue through discerning who has jurisdiction, how to apprehend offenders, and prosecuting those who have been caught.

Scope and Extent Issues

According to Casey (2000), cybercrime is any offense that involves a computer and a network. The degree to which the computer is a specific part of the crime varies. Clearly, this means anyone who has any role whatsoever in "policing" the Web will be dealing with a vast array of crimes. As noted in the Introduction, crimes of all sorts on or related to the Web present a number of challenges for law enforcement.

The sale of illegal drugs online is so prevalent it has overwhelmed law enforcement. Government agencies claim that, although they are aware of the problem, they can do little to control these sales without significantly more resources and funding. "The system we have in place has been overrun by the volume of illegal Internet drug sales," according to Richard Stana, Director of the Homeland Security and Justice General Accountability Office, the investigative arm of Congress (Sullivan, 2004). "These Internet pharmacies, these pill mills, have become a pain in our side. This is something that probably slipped through the cracks in the beginning. Now we're seeing a lot more of them, so we're starting to crack down," said Michael Sanders, a spokesperson for the New Orleans branch of the Drug Enforcement Agency (DEA) (Waller, 2006, p. 1). Part of the difficulty is knowing where to focus. Should the emphasis be on illicit drugs, on prescription drugs being sold in violation of trade or other laws, or steroids? If so, which law enforcement body should do the policing? What if the sale involves multiple countries?

Legal Issues

General Laws Addressing Cybercrime

Federal laws may not be specific enough to include the many cyber forms of traditional crimes. The American Bar Association (ABA) recognized the limitations of existing law early as the mid-1980s (Bequai, 1987). Some laws have been added recently to address this concern. For instance, Section 47 U.S.C. 223(h)(1) of Title 47 of the Communications Decency Act makes it a federal crime, punishable by a two-year prison sentence, to use the telephone or telecommunications devices to annoy, harass, abuse, or threaten another person; President Bill Clinton promoted Title 18 (Crimes and Criminal Procedure), Section U.S.C. 2425, in 1998, making it a federal crime to use any means of interstate or foreign commerce (including the telephone and Internet) to communicate with the intent to solicit or entice a child into unlawful sexual activity (De Angelis, 2000). Clearly, however, theses laws are directed at cyberstalking and solicitation, not online drug sales.

Also applicable to some, but not all, types of cybercrime are the Computer Fraud and Abuse Act, the Computer Abuse Amendments Act of 1994, parts of the Electronic Communications Privacy Act of 1986, the National Stolen Property Act, the Federally Protected Property Act, the Federal Trade Secrets Act, the amended Copyright Act of 1980, the No Electronic Theft Act of 1997, the Digital Millennium Copyright Act of 1998, and the Digital Theft Deterrence and Copyright Damages Improvement Act of 1999 (Judson, 2000; Schmalleger, 2005). None of these laws, however, are overtly directed at online drug sales. The 1998 Child Online Protection Act (COPA) prohibits anyone from knowingly using a commercial Web site to make communication that is "harmful to minors. Prohibited material includes pictures, writings, or recordings that are deemed obscene (Taylor, et al., 2001). Although it could be argued that sites offering drugs are harmful to minors, this application of the law has not been used to date. In 1998, Congress enacted the Protection of Children from Sexual Predators Act (PCSPA), which includes provisions related to transmitting information or obscene materials electronically (Taylor, et al., 2001). Again, this is not likely very useful for drug-related issues, as they have not been deemed obscene.

In 1996, President Clinton passed the Telecommunications Reform Act. The law contained a provision intended to impose controls on what was perceived to be a growing problem of Internet terrorism and pornography. The law made Internet Service Providers (ISPs) responsible for policing Web content. Those found in violation faced a maximum fine of $250,000 and two years in prison (Barrett, 1997). ISPs asserted that the law was impractical to ask them to police the huge volumes of data on the Internet and bulletin boards. They also partnered with civil liberties groups to protest the constitutionality of this provision. A federal appeals court declared the bill unlawful only months after its passage, focusing on the constitutionality arguments (Barrett, 1997). One judge asserted, "As the most participatory form of mass speech yet developed, the Internet deserves the highest protection from government intrusion" (Barrett, 1997, p. 128).

Laws Regarding Prescription Drugs

Regarding prescription drugs, some substances can lawfully be purchased for "research purpose." Any time a substance can be lawfully purchased, it is more difficult to control (Buying drugs online, 2004). The Food, Drug, and Cosmetic Act (FDCA) prohibits the manufacture and distribution of misbranded and adulterated drugs. A prescription drug may be considered misbranded if it is dispensed without a proper physician's prescription. In order to obtain a felony conviction of an FDCA violation, the federal government must demonstrate that an online pharmacy intended to defraud or mislead either the consumer or the government, or that the defendant is a repeat offender. The Department of Justice used the FDCA recently to prosecute doctors who were prescribing steroids for athletes and entertainers for nonmedical purposes and without an examination (Posner, 2000). Yet many of the sites, as noted in Chapter Two, offer online diagnoses and prescriptions. As each state regulates their own pharmacies, varying rules apply to Internet sites and to the issue of whether online diagnoses and prescriptions violate the FDCA (Posner, 2000). As of 2003, only California has a full-time investigator looking into doctors writing prescriptions for online sales (Gaul & Flaherty, 2003). State laws vary regarding whether some or all substances must be prescribed and dispensed after an actual examination. Florida and New York require a face-to-face exam before any prescription drugs may be prescribed or distributed, whereas Utah allows prescriptions for Viagra without an exam but does not allow controlled substances (Skoloff, 2007). In sum, "these laws were written long before the Internet, so they didn't envision the kind of drug trading we're seeing now," according to Susan Foster of the National Center on Addiction and Substance Abuse at Columbia University (Skoloff, 2007).

Racketeer Influences and Corrupt Organizations (RICO) laws might apply to large-scale online sellers (Levine, 1998). The Food and Drug Administration (FDA) has asked physicians and pharmacists for help, encouraging them to take action against those who prescribe online (Marwick, 1999), and the State Federation of Medical Boards has declared that the prescription of medications based on an electronic questionnaire alone is not an acceptable standard of care (Posner, 2000).

Since most sites purveying drugs operate by making certain claims to potential consumers, they might be regulated under the Federal Trade Commission Act (FTCA), which authorizes the Justice Department to investigate the claims made by Web sites and to bring civil proceedings if they are unfair or deceptive (Posner, 2000). If an online pharmacy defrauds consumers, it is also possible to enforce federal mail and wire fraud statutes, which might be civil or criminal (Posner, 2000).

Laws Applying to Cheating Drug Tests

The next two chapters address drug testing and the detoxification, or anti–drug testing, industry. A brief examination of relevant laws is provided here. Because many of the detox products are advertised and have been understood as health and herbal remedies, they are not subject to the same regulations as other food and drug products regulated by the FDA. In 1994, the Dietary Supplement and Health Education Act made manufacturers of dietary supplements responsible for ensuring that their products are safe before they are marketed. The FDA only takes action against those products for which there are safety claims. Essentially, "companies are free to claim nearly anything (other than disease treatment or prevention) about the efficacy of their products (Tunnell, 2004, p. 90).

In regard to cheating drug tests, although nine states prohibit the sale of urine or urine adulterants, only South Carolina has prosecuted someone for a violation (Cramer, 2005). Florida, Kentucky, and New Jersey prohibit the sale of any product designed to defraud or falsify a drug screen, and in Louisiana and Texas it is unlawful for someone knowingly or intentionally to deliver or manufacture substances designed to falsify or alter drug-tests. In the nine other states it is illegal to sell urine or adulterants for the purpose of passing drug tests. Only Illinois and Kentucky have made these offenses punishable as a felony (Cramer, 2005).

Laws Applicable to Illicit Drugs

As discussed in the previous chapter, there are a number of laws regarding production, distribution, and possession of illicit drugs. Most notable is the Controlled Substances Act of 1970. Certainly someone found distributing illicit drugs via the Web could be charged with a violation of the Controlled Substances Act (described in Chapter One).

The Controlled Substance Analogue Act of 1986 prohibits manufacture, sale, and possession of substances that are substantially similar to controlled substances and have an effect similar or greater to the controlled substance. The idea was to arrest chemists who were making minor changes to controlled substances.

Laws Regarding Paraphernalia

Laws regarding the sale of drug paraphernalia exist but are sometimes difficult to apply. There are two types of paraphernalia: user specific or dealer specific. User-specific paraphernalia include items marketed to users to assist in taking or concealing drugs, such as pipes, bongs, clips, and growing materials. Dealer-specific paraphernalia are items designed to help traffickers prepare their products for sale, such as scales, vials, and baggies. It is difficult to demonstrate clearly someone is using user-specific paraphernalia, as many of these things can be used for other legal endeavors. The drug paraphernalia statute is part of the Controlled Substances Act (full name: Comprehensive Drug Abuse Prevention and Control Act of 1970) and prohibits both types (Drug paraphernalia, n.d.). Violation of the federal paraphernalia law carries a sentence of up to three years in prison and a fine. Yet this law has never really been applied. As of 1999, forty-eight states plus the District of Columbia and the U.S. Virgin Islands have laws prohibiting the sale of drug paraphernalia. The federal law covers paraphernalia sales in Alaska and Iowa, the states that do not have their own antiparaphernalia laws (Van Sant, 2006).

In 2006, Pinellas County, Florida, approved a new drug paraphernalia law that makes it easier to go after people selling tools for drug use and trafficking. Florida state law requires proof that someone knew the product they sold would be used to ingest drugs. The county law does not require this proof—it allows for the prosecution of people who reasonably should have known what they sold, advertised, or manufactured would be used to take illegal drugs. A first time violation would result in a fine of $500 or sixty days in jail (Van Sant, 2006).

The Supreme Court has affirmed paraphernalia laws as constitutional. In *Posters 'N' Things Ltd., et al. v. U.S.*, 511 U.S. 513 (1994), the Supreme Court affirmed that the Mail Order Drug Paraphernalia Control Act (Anti-Drug Abuse Act of 1986) was not overly vague. In this case, officers searched the home and business and found clips, dilutants, and advertisements for various products. The U.S. Supreme Court had previously upheld the federal antiparaphernalia law in *Village of Hoffman Estates v. Flipside* 455 U.S. 489 (1982).

Laws Specific to Online Drug Sales

There are few laws that specifically address Internet drug sales. The 1999 proposed Methamphetamine Proliferation Act initially had an antispeech component that would have prohibited the publication of information relating to the manufacture of scheduled substances. It also made it illegal to advertise or link to a site that sells drug paraphernalia. These provisions were removed in committee. In 2001, New York Governor Pataki reformed the Rockefeller drug laws in that state to include greater penalties for online sales.

Congress is considering additional laws that would address online drug sales. In 2003, the House Energy and Commerce Subcommittee on Oversight and Investigations heard witnesses describe the rise in online prescription drug sales. Witnesses outlined numerous problems, including the fact that Miami's international mail facility alone receives some seven million packages of prescription and illegal drugs each year, that the FDA's interpretation of federal law means improper prescription drug imports cannot easily be destroyed, detained, or returned to their sender, and that criminals are increasingly involved in counterfeiting and adulterating drugs (Problems grow with drugs bought on Net, 2003).

Laws Outside the U.S.

Globally, most countries address cybercrime in some way. In a 1999 survey, author Ekaterina Drozdova (2001) found that 70% of the countries for which data were available had some computer crime laws or were in the process of creating them. Yet even these generally deal with unlawful access, tampering, and theft-related concerns and are thus not necessarily helpful to address drug-related cybercrime (Putnam & Elliott, 2001). Schmalleger (2005) reported that, of fifty-two countries, only the Philippines had adequate computer crime legislation to deal with transnational computer crimes. Sometimes, shipments of drugs purchased online take a circuitous route, as in the case of the steroid seller from Thailand who shipped from Shanghai to New York, then from New York to Lacrosse, Wisconsin, where the steroids were then distributed to several states (Doyle, 2005). In the U.K., it is illegal for unregistered companies to sell drugs online, but it is not illegal to purchase drugs online (Lee, 2006).

Canada also prohibits the sale of drug paraphernalia. Under the Criminal Code of Canada, it is illegal to import, export, manufacture, promote, or sell instruments or literature for illicit drug use. A court in Ontario deemed the portion of the code directed at drug literature unconstitutional. At present, the U.K. does not prohibit the sale of drug paraphernalia (Drug paraphernalia, 2006).

Jurisdiction Concerns

In the case of transnational computer-related crimes, the first question is which country has jurisdiction for policing the crime. Thus investigators must determine the location where the offense occurred, which is often quite murky in cases involving the cyber world (Grabosky & Smith, 2001). After that, it may be equally difficult to discern which police force or agency has jurisdiction (Barrett, 1997). Transnational efforts also require a convergence of values and priorities that is often unlikely (Grabosky & Smith, 2001). As Chapter Two briefly explained, some countries are far less prohibitive in their approach to drug control.

In the U.S.

Domestically, many agencies have played a role in policing cybercrime—perhaps too many. In addition to the FBI and the U.S. Secret Service, other agencies play a role in policing cyberspace. U.S. Customs has a special Cyber Smuggling Center devoted to developing leads and tips for law enforcement, receiving complaints through their Web site, and coordinating undercover operations (De Angelis, 2000). The U.S. Air Force Office of Special Investigations (OSI) is considered the only federal agency charged with computer security full time (De Angelis, 2000). The Federal Computer Investigations Committee (FCIC) operates from all over the country and had experts in all forms of cybercrime. They collaborate on a case-by-case basis (De Angelis, 2000). The Internet Crime Complaint Center, located on the Web at ic3.gov, is a partnership between the FBI and the National White Collar Crime Center (NW3C). They receive Internet-related criminal complaints, conduct research on Web-related crimes, and assist law enforcement with cyber-related crimes, such as property rights, hacking, economic espionage, online extortion, and identity theft. In 1996, the Justice Department created several the Fraud and Computer Crimes and Intellectual Property Sections of the Criminal Division (CCIPS) within their criminal division. These include divisions on intellectual property and trade secret violations, child exploitation and obscenity, fraud, illegal sale of pharmaceuticals, hate crimes, illegal gambling, and illegal drugs (Hitchcock, 2002). Each U.S. Attorney's Office has at least one computer crime prosecutor (De Angelis, 2000).

Federal agencies have assisted state and local law enforcement in some ways. In 2000, the Computer Crime Enforcement Act authorized the Justice Department to provide grants for training of state and local law enforcement and prosecutors regarding cybercrime (Schmalleger, 2005). Cyberlawenforcement.org is a Web site established by law enforcement officers who specialize in cybercrime investigations. They offer training to law enforcement and provide assistance to cybervictims. In 1999, the Department of Justice and the Information Technology Association of America Foundation (ITAA) collaborated to create a Cybercitizen Partnership intended to boost cooperation, expand public awareness, and provide the public with resources to address computer crimes (De Angelis, 2000). Cybersnitch.net debuted in 1997 and represents law enforcement from more than twenty-six states as well as officers in Canada and the U.K. It is intended to facilitate quick and aggressive investigation of all types of computer crimes, as well as to put victims of computer crimes in touch with law enforcement (Hitchcock, 2002). Samspade.org is a site used by law enforcement agencies as well as citizens to track computer criminals (Hitchcock, 2002). Since 1998, the National Infrastructure Protection Center (NIPC) articulated a plan in the U.S. for infrastructure protection that also includes the Internet (Wall, 2001b).

Statewide Efforts

Although most local police agencies have done little to address computer-related crimes, some have made more specific efforts. In Maine, the Main Computer Crimes Task Force is charged with taking care of online crimes. The Task Force is composed of detectives from state and local police as well as members of the Maine Department of the Attorney General. In addition to conducting investigations and performing computer forensic exams (testing evidence like hard drives, diskettes, etc.), the Task Force is also involved in public outreach and law enforcement training (Hitchcock, 2002). The High Technology and Computer Crimes Division of the Massachusetts Attorney General's Office was created in 1997. It generally provides support to local law enforcement (Hitchcock, 2002). In 2007, the Kentucky Bureau of Investigation (KBI) announced it would begin training officers on tactics to intercept online pharmaceutical sales. The training was developed in 2005 by the Attorney General's Internet Pharmacy Task Force. A new Senate bill in the state will require a face-to-face exam with a physician before any prescription drugs can be dispensed (Attorney General Greg Stumbo ..., 2007).

Most police agencies, however, have few, if any, officers devoted to online investigations (Moore, 2005). According to Moore (2005), law enforcement training academies are not spending much time on preparing future officers addressing computer-based crime and investigations involving computers. Furthermore, many manuals designed to assist law enforcement in understanding technology crime and techniques are not written with the novice in mind (Moore, 2005). This is logical in that the type of knowledge is indeed rather advanced for the average street-level drug patrol officer.

Outside the U.S.

Outside the U.S., law enforcement agencies have also begun to address the growing phenomenon of Internet crime. In the U.K., the Metropolitan Police Department has established a National High Tech Crime Unit devoted to dealing with technology-related crimes that require special skills and cross traditional police boundaries. Information about the unit is available on their Web site at met.police.uk/computercrime. Many local police agencies have specialists who monitor the Internet (Davies, 1998). Within the European Union, cross-border investigations involve Criminal Cases Mutual Legal Assistance in Criminal Matters Treaties between member states. These treaties ensure that each country will undertake investigations within their own country on behalf of others (Barrett, 1997).

Outside of Canada and Europe, however, law enforcement may not be so well prepared to deal with cyber offenses. In regard to Mexican drug cartels using YouTube to advertise their activities and make threats, Andrew Teekell, a private intelligence firm analyst (Stratfor, Austin, Texas), had this to say: "Mexican law enforcement is ill-equipped to deal with this. In the U.S., posting videos like that would be plain crazy—U.S. law enforcement has guys who do nothing but surf the Internet. But in Mexico, they can get away with it. It shows these cartels are untouchable" (Roig-Franzia, 2007, p. A01).

Finding the Offenders

Reporting Victimization

It is painfully obvious that some forms of crime are less likely to be reported than others. This seems to be the case with many types of cybercrimes. The public often perceives the only victims of cybercrime are corporations or the governments and thus may feel little sympathy (Bequai, 1987). Cyberstalking, for instance, may not be reported because victims do not see harassment on the Web as an actual crime. Others may not report cyberstalking or cyberharassment out of concern for the stigma associated with involvement in a chat room (Hitchcock, 2002). Some victims may not want to acknowledge they have been victimized or it may take them some time to realize victimization has happened, such as in cases of identity fraud (Wall, 2001a). It is unlikely that many people who are victimized by online drug dealers will call law enforcement, as their own activities may be questionable. For instance, the person who purchases a steroid online but gets one laced with cement is probably not going to call the police, as he would be informing them of his own purchase of a controlled substance. Clearly, underreporting of traditional "victimless" crimes has long been an issue, and the Web may simply exacerbate that concern.

Encryption and Concealing the Offense

Another concern in finding cyber drug dealers and buyers is that they may be highly skilled in using technology to not only commit their offense, but to conceal it as well. In addition to the fact that Web dealers can use encryption (discussed briefly in the Introduction), clever Web designers know how to misdirect and hide data. Information can also be hidden on remote hosts (Barrett, 1997). Illicit material can be embedded within a legitimate file, much like viruses are hidden (Barrett, 1997). Another trick used by Web designers is to provide what appears to be a Web "dead end." In these cases, the user sees an "Error 404" note or some other error message when they try to retrieve the page. Thinking it is dead, users typically look elsewhere. Yet some skilled Web designers can hide illicit material on these error pages (Barrett, 1997).

If officers are alerted to a site that is providing drugs illegally, the first step is often to identify who owns the Internet Protocol (IP) address. According to Moore (2005), the two most common ways to find who owns an IP address are via the Web on The American Registry of Internet Numbers (www.arin.net/whois) or the Sam Spade Web site (www.samspade.org).

Apprehending Offenders

Enforcement of Paraphernalia Laws

Drug paraphernalia laws are rarely enforced. For instance, Wren (1996) described how common it was to find marijuana pipes and other paraphernalia on the oceanfront of Myrtle Beach, South Carolina, a popular spring-break destination. Almost every tee-shirt shop was carrying paraphernalia. The city had a paraphernalia law they enforced sporadically in the 1980s, but it conflicts with a 1982 state law that decriminalized the sale of paraphernalia. It is still illegal to sell paraphernalia, but those who violate the law face only a fine and no criminal charges. Paraphernalia merchants generally claim their products are for legal use with tobacco and argue these products do not influence people to use illegal drugs (Wren, 1996). In March 2005, some neighborhoods in Missouri pressured local stores to stop selling materials that are used to smoke crack. Seemingly innocuous, the scouring pads and small glass vials combine to make a simple crack pipe. In Delaware, convenience stores were found selling miniature roses in glass tubes and small pieces of scouring paper (Delaware stores ..., 2005). Again, the difficulty for law enforcement is in discerning what is drug related and what is considered legitimate commerce (Innocuous drug paraphernalia ..., 2005).

Sometimes, enforcement of certain drug laws makes enforcement of others more difficult. Selkirk and Luse (2004) noted that paraphernalia laws in Ohio have posed a challenge to those advocating decriminalization of marijuana. There, possession of drug paraphernalia is a misdemeanor that carries a $750 fine and a 30-day jail sentence. This is harsher than most penalties for marijuana possession, and thus police and prosecutors have become masters at convincing judges that anything and everything is drug paraphernalia. In some places in Ohio, citizens found smoking a joint are more likely to be arrested for possession of paraphernalia (the rolling papers in their pocket) than actually be charged with marijuana possession (Selkirk & Luse, 2004, para. 4).

Online Stings and Entrapment Concerns

One way law enforcement has responded to online child pornography has been to employ specially trained officers who spend a good portion of their time online visiting sites and chat rooms. The officer will be given a screen name and will chat with others until a perpetrator initiates a conversation. Then the officer will hope the perpetrator transmits illegal material, or sets up a physical meeting in which he/she can be arrested. According to a handful of television programs, these stings have been highly successful. A challenge in any form of online investigation of this nature is that officers will need specialized training in use of the Web, as well as in Web "lingo." Additionally, officers need to be well schooled in what is and what is not considered entrapment. In one case, the verdict against a man convicted of intent to engage in sexual activity with a minor was overturned when the appeals court ruled the officer, through her communications, had planted the idea in the defendant's head (Moore, 2005). If undercover agents are used for sting operations of electronic bulletin boards, chat rooms, and the like, they are not required to identify themselves. They must, however, only partake in activities authorized for all users (*United States v. Aguilar*, 883 F. 2d 662, 705 (9th Cir. 1989). These same concerns are true if law enforcement use online stings for drug dealing.

In 2005, a sting operation shut down the online drug activities of Dr. David Stephenson. A New York investigator ordered steroids, Ritalin, and methadone via the Web. The investigator completed an online questionnaire in which he claimed to be a 4-foot-tall, alcoholic, heroin-addicted airline pilot who wanted "to get high to fly." Despite these ludicrous claims, Stephenson filled the order (Skoloff, 2007). Although this sting was a success, few people in law enforcement see this as the way to end online sales. "How do you, with millions upon millions of sites, look at every single one? You just can't," said DEA Agent Garrison Courtney. However, Albany (New York) district attorney and lead prosecutor for the case, Christopher Baynes, feels stings can still be a deterrent. "If we take down one pharmacy, then a couple of pharmacies and a couple of doctors, other people may very well decide this isn't worth it. You can very well change an industry. By taking a few people down, the rest of them may say, 'You know what, I'd rather sell Amway products'" (Skoloff, 2007).

Search and Seizure Online

Search and seizure is another challenge in investigating online crime. It is still not clear whether the Internet is considered public or private space (Drozdova, 2001). If it is considered public space, then law enforcement does not need a warrant to seize Web-based material. A federal court did determine that real-time, Internet conversations observed by an agent in a chat room were not protected by the Fourth Amendment, as the defendant did not have a reasonable expectation of privacy in a chat room (*U. S. v. Charbonneau*, 979 F. Supp. 1177 (S.D. Ohio 1997).

In the U.S., one court ruled that a warrant was overly broad because it did not list the specific digital evidence to be seized. Moore (2005) recommends listing as many items as possible and using the language "including but not limited to" (p. 142). Yet one court ruled that same language was not satisfactory (Moore, 2005).

Outside of cyberspace, one exception to the warrant rule is the Plain View doctrine, where an officer may seize evidence without a warrant if he or she is in a lawful position to view that evidence. To date, it is unclear whether the Plain View exception can be applied constitutionally to cyberspace (Drozdova, 2001).

Another exception to the warrant rule is consent. In many cases, the person using the Web for unlawful activity may not be the owner of the computer, which brings up the issue of whether a third party can consent to a search. In *United States v. Smith* 27 F. Supp. 2d 1111(C.D.IL 1998), the court upheld a search of a computer based on consent provided by the suspect's girlfriend. The court considered the fact that the two people shared a living space. They also considered the fact that the files were not password protected and thus accessible to anyone in the home (Moore, 2005). In another consent-related case, *U.S. v. Durham* Nos. 96-5107 and 96-5118 (1998), the court determined that a mother could not provide consent to search her son's computer. The court relied on two primary pieces of information: First, the son had taken steps to protect the files, and second, the son paid his mother a small amount in rent (Moore, 2005).

Prosecuting Online Drug Offenders

Although policing the Web is difficult, no doubt obtaining a conviction for a cyber drug offender is difficult as well. The introduction of complicated technology-based evidence is no easy task. First, police officers must collect the digital evidence. Casey (2000) explained that almost any activity on a computer can be tracked, which he called the "digital trail." This includes the trail of Web pages visited. In order to obtain this evidence, however, either officers must be skilled in computer forensics or the precinct must have someone they can consult for obtaining digital evidence (Moore, 2005). There is also a variety of computer forensic software packages available, including EnCase and the Forensic Tool Kit by AccessData, which aid law enforcement (Moore, 2005).

Courts are also not always up to speed regarding the introduction of computer-based evidence. Historically, hearsay rules, defined by Federal Rules of Evidence 801, prohibit the introduction of statements allegedly offered by a defendant. Hearsay is defined as, "a statement, other than one made by the defendant while testifying at the trial or hearing, offered in evidence to prove the truth of the matter asserted" (Moore, 2005, p. 206). Hearsay may be offered, however, to counter a defendant's assertion that she or he did not make the statements asserted in the case. Rule 801(d)(1) allows an exception to the hearsay rule for specific purposes (Moore, 2005).

Even if the evidence is admissible under hearsay exceptions, however, it might be inadmissible because of authentication requirements. The Federal Rules of Evidence require statements to be authenticated either by self-authentication or by a professional. Although there are ten methods by which a professional can authenticate evidence, Moore (2005) maintained there are only two that are applicable to digital evidence. Rules 901(b)(1) and 901(b)(3) allow authentication by a professional who has a combination of education and experience, in essence, an expert witness. It is still not clear, however, precisely what the courts will consider an expert witness when it comes to digital evidence.

The precedents for the introduction of scientific evidence come from *Daubert v. Merrell Dow Pharmaceuticals* 509 U.S. 579 (1993) and *Frye v. United States* 54 App. D.C. 46, 293 F. 1013 (1923), addressing the federal courts and various state courts, respectively. *Frye* set the precedent that scientific evidence must be accepted in the specific scientific community from which it was derived (i.e., DNA evidence is accepted in the genetics community). In *Daubert*, the Supreme Court ruled that scientific evidence must be scientifically valid and reliable rather than generally accepted (Moore, 2005). More recent cases dealing with digital evidence have centered on the qualifications of the person introducing the digital evidence.

Successes in Policing the Web

To date, there appears to be no centralized database of information about the number of people apprehended for online drug offenses. Thus, the following section offers a compilation gleaned from a search of news sources.

Prescription Drugs

There have been some successes in apprehending online prescription drug dealing. In 2004, the Louisiana Board of Pharmacy invalidated any prescriptions that came from online questionnaires and did not include a physical examination, and included fines, probation, suspension, and even revocation of licensure as a penalty (Waller, 2006). Malcolm Broussard, executive director of the Louisiana State Pharmacy Board, said, "It reminds me of stories from days before the federal government created the Food and Drug Administration, some of the snake-oil schemes, things you had in the wild, wild, west" (Waller, 2006, p. 1).

In April 2005, the DEA shut down an international drug trafficking network that included seventeen individuals operating from fourteen countries. The leaders were a graduate student at Temple University and his father in India. They have been charged with conspiring to import and distribute pharmaceuticals without a prescription in the U.S. They smuggled more than 11 million prescription pills to more than 60,000 American homes. Additionally, they were shipping steroids and the Ecstasy-like drug, Ketamine (Shiffman, 2006). Another sting, Operation Pipedream, included people in eighteen different countries and over $250 million in retail sales (Drug paraphernalia, n.d.).

In September 2006, eleven people in Georgia, North Carolina, South Dakota, and Belize were indicted for fraud. The indictment seeks to forfeit the properties, automobiles, and bank accounts of the defendants, who are accused of counterfeiting twenty-four drugs they marketed online (Shearer, 2006). The operation was based in Georgia, marketed the drugs as Canadian, and used pills made in Belize. The defendants are accused of making twenty-four different drugs they marketed with spam. They advertised the pills as authentic drugs like Viagra, Cialis, Lipitor, and Vioxx. They also marketed the steroids oxymethelone and stanazolol, and unapproved versions of Ambien, Valium, and Xanax (Shearer, 2006).

Steroids

Law enforcement crackdowns have also netted a few online steroid dealers. In October 2005, a judge ordered a three-year sentence plus two years of supervised release for a man who called himself "The Doc" or "Roiddoc" who was selling steroids and ketamine online (Judge exceeds sentencing guidelines …, 2005). In December 2005, DEA Administrator Karen Tandy announced the agency had targeted eight steroid manufacturers that used U.S.-based e-mail addresses to communicate with more than 2000 individuals to arrange the sale of steroids. Most of the drugs were produced in Mexico (DEA leads largest steroid bust …, 2005). In late October 2006, the DEA announced the arrest of five people in two cases involving illegal online sales of prescription drugs and steroids as part of Operation Cyber-Roid. The investigations, which included collaboration between the DEA, the FDA, and the IRS, began in 2005 when a Massachusetts man complained that his son used his credit card to buy steroids from Pmeds.com. Pmeds operated from Tinley Park, Illinois, but forwarded orders to Metepec, Mexico, Anabolic steroids and other controlled substances were then smuggled into the U.S. Another supplier of steroids was from Belize (Operation Cyber-Roid, 2006).

Illicit Drugs

There have even been a few successes in capturing online illicit drug deals. In 2002, 115 individuals in eighty-four cities in the U.S. and Canada were arrested for selling gamma hydroxy butyrate (GHB) online as the result of 200 separate investigations spanning two years (Internet drug dealers arrested in 84 cities, 2002). In 2005, authorities announced a crackdown on sales of narcotics and psychotropic drugs being exported from India to the U.S. via Internet pharmacies. Indian doctors were prescribing the drugs while U.S. citizens operated servers, Web sites, and e-mail communications. Vicodin, OxyContin, Ritalin, steroids, and Viagra were all being sold through this collaboration (Siddharth, 2005).

Paraphernalia

In 2003, then-Attorney General John Ashcroft announced that twenty-seven people in twelve states were being charged with violating the federal antiparaphernalia law. Ashcroft also asked the district court to shut down the sites, PipesForYou.com, OmniLounge.com, ColorChangingGlass.com, 420Now.com, AheadCase.com, and PuffPipes.Com, and to have them redirected to a DEA.gov page. Ashcroft said, "With the advent of the Internet, the illegal drug paraphernalia industry has exploded. The drug paraphernalia business now thrives not only in small shops but it is now accessible in anyone's home with a computer and Internet access ... Quite simply, the illegal drug paraphernalia industry has invaded the homes of families across the country without their knowledge" (McCullagh, 2003, para. 2).

Conclusions

According to Moore (2005), the best way to respond to high-technology crimes is to ensure that law enforcement agencies develop a basic understanding of this category or type of crime. Furthermore, law enforcement agencies should staff a specific team devoted to policing high-technology crimes. Although it would be the best way to respond, this would also be the most difficult way, according to Moore (2005) because of lack of funds and resources. In addition, Moore (2005) noted that some agencies have hesitated to train their staff in computer forensics because once they do, the individuals may leave the agency to work in the private sector and make a lot more money.

Another option follows the policing strategy referred to as "target hardening." This has been promoted as the best means to address online identity theft (Moore, 2005). The idea is that police may log lots of hours monitoring the Web and being trained in high-technology crime, only to apprehend a few individuals. Teaching would-be victims to be safe on the Web, or, in this case, of the dangers of purchasing drugs online, may be more cost efficient. Yet many people criticize target hardening in general, suggesting it puts far too much ownership for change on the would-be victim and not enough accountability on the part of the offender. Furthermore, target hardening related to the Web could easily end up becoming censorship—in order to protect potential victims from online drug traffickers, sites providing information about drugs get censored. This, of course, may elicit a host of civil liberties concerns. Indeed, the degree to which free speech, press, and basic privacy rights are available on the Web has already become a concern. These issues are addressed in Chapter Six.

· 4 ·

THE RISE OF DRUG TESTING

Introduction

One of the more popular vehicles for curtailing drug use (at least allegedly) is drug testing. Although this might seem the topic of a different book, increased drug testing is very much related to how Web-based drug sales are changing the War on Drugs. In essence, drug testing is a form of policing the body, even though it may not actually be traditional law enforcement doing so. Additionally, as additional agencies and organizations test their employees for drug use, more people are looking for ways to cheat the tests. All kinds of products and tips are available for those interested in fooling urinalysis tests, and the Web has, by some accounts, become the mall of choice for them. It is like a technology arms race, in that it was largely technological development that established drug testing as a tool of the drug war, then those committed to evading tests used technology to do so. This then prompted better and more tests, which only upped the ante for drug users to evade the testers. The issue of drug testing and evasion of drug testing represents another challenge for police and other agents is that it is not at all clear whether detoxification and adulterating products will remain lawful. If they are illegal, someone must enforce the law and apprehend those selling or buying the products. This chapter, then, sets the stage for the subsequent chapter, which examines the various products and tips available on the Web.

This chapter offers a brief history of the rise in drug testing. It discusses the key players involved in the expansion of drug testing to the workplace, schools, and elsewhere. It is also discusses significant court decisions regarding drug testing. Next, the chapter describes the various types of drug tests used and who is tested. The remainder of the chapter discusses concerns about drug testing.

A Brief History

Since the 1980s, drug testing for illicit drug use has expanded dramatically. Starting with the military and spreading to the workplace, to athletes, and to students in public schools, drug testing has been promulgated as a means of deterring drug abuse and ensuring a safe work or educational environment. Whether it actually does these things is doubtful, but hardly seems to matter to proponents. It is clear that it has been, like most drug war efforts, disproportionately used against vulnerable populations. Tunnell (2004) summed up how drug testing grew:

> The drug-testing industry, with obvious financial interests at stake, advanced its financial growth by working to expand drug testing to individuals occupying diverse settings who beforehand were exempt from such intrusions. The drug-testing industry grew nearly exponentially because of its aggressive marketing strategies and the simultaneous campaigns of politicians, office seekers, and moral entrepreneurs (p. 22).

The first drug testing programs started in the military in the 1960s and 1970s when the Department of Defense required urine screening of soldiers returning from Vietnam. In 1982, the U.S. Navy began drug testing all its personnel; in 1983 Greyhound Bus Corporation began testing all their bus drivers; and in 1984 the International Olympic Committee began developing testing for that year's Games. Workplace drug testing spread rapidly in the 1980s. By 1985, one-quarter of all Fortune 500 companies tested job applicants (Tunnell, 2004).

Key Players in the Drug-Testing Movement

Hoffman (1987) explained, "The urine test is as much a product of human persistence as technology" (p. 176). Dr. Robert DuPont, Jr. was a pioneer in advancing the urinalysis-testing industry. In 1971, DuPont was the first head of the National Institute on Drug Abuse (NIDA). Later he served as Director of the Special Action Office for Drug Abuse Prevention. In the mid 1970s, he took a moderate approach, advocating drug education. NIDA even sponsored research into beneficial usages of illicit substances. This was largely due to the slightly more relaxed national approach under President Jimmy Carter. DuPont even discussed the possibility of decriminalizing marijuana with National Organization for the Reform of Marijuana Laws (NORML) representatives, something Carter supported.

Contrary to these signs of a more humane approach to drug control, "DuPont, at heart a conservative, was preparing for a clampdown. While many states were decriminalizing possession of marijuana, NIDA quietly urged selected companies to improve methods of detecting individual drug use" (Hoffman, 1987, p. 176). One company, Syntex, had researched biochemical testing through its Syva division as early as 1966. They lost interest for a while, but testing was restarted when NIDA offered Syntex financial assistance. The immunoassay test was their first joint success. At first DuPont asserted that the test would be used to assist addicts, but when it became obvious Ronald Reagan would be the next president, DuPont shifted gears and advocated use with many different populations (Hoffman, 1987).

Other specific claimsmakers also took the lead with drug testing initiatives. Congressman Gerald Solomon (R-N.Y.), former Chairman of the House Rules Committee, introduced bills to equate refusal to submit to a federal drug test equivalent to a positive test result, to deny federal benefits to anyone convicted of a drug offense, to require pre-employment testing of applicants for all federal jobs, and many others (Holtorf, 1998). In the 1990s, Newt Gingrich proposed requiring drug testing of all U.S. newborns, an idea that, thankfully, went nowhere (Holtorf, 1998).

Industry Promotion

In addition to successful marketing, technological determinism was also key to expanding drug testing (Tunnell, 2004). That is, as more testing became available, it was assumed that this was the most appropriate way to address the problem (Gilliom, 1994). As new tests were developed, the federal government promoted drug testing as a means of expanding the War on Drugs and, allegedly, of protecting the economy. The drug testing industry quickly stepped in with self-promotion efforts as well (Tunnell, 2004).

More Drug Use = More Testing?

It is clear that drug problems were not the real reason per se for the rapid expansion of drug testing. Even surveys taken in the 1990s found only 0.3% of employers considered drug use in the workplace to be a major problem (Zeese, 1997). This demonstrated that the increased use of drug testing in the workplace is not driven by employers' concerns as much as it is due to, "public anxiety about drug use, aggressive marketing by drug testing companies, and government regulations and policies requiring testing" (Zeese, 1997, p. 12).

Drug Testing in the Workplace

The 1980s

This new social problem of workplace drug use did not emerge until the 1980s. Prior to that, various presidential councils and task forces found workplace drug use to be an insignificant problem (Tunnell, 2004).

In 1983, President Ronald Reagan established the President's Commission on Organized Crime. In 1986, that commission reported widespread drug abuse and recommended drug testing for all public and private sector employees. Reagan took that recommendation and issued Executive Order 12564, which requires drug testing for all federal employees. At the time, Reagan promised offenders would get help, not be fired or otherwise punished. In actuality, many places did dismiss employees, often after a first offense (Greenwood, 2003). Reagan claimed drug use to be a serious problem in the workplace, resulting in billions of dollars in lost productivity and less-reliable and more absent workers (Tunnell, 2004).

In 1988, Congress enacted the Drug-Free Workplace Act, which extended drug testing to some private employers. Under the Drug-Free Workplace Act, employers with federal contracts worth at least $100,000 and/or recipients of federal grants were required to employ a drug-free workplace program. Although the Act did not require drug testing, many interpreted it that way. Shortly after passage of the Act, the Department of Defense, the Department of Transportation, the Federal Highway Administration, the Federal Aviation Administration, the U.S. Coast Guard, the Urban Mass Transportation Administration, and the Nuclear Regulatory Commission implemented drug testing (Tunnell, 2004). At the same time, the Reagan and Bush administrations were scaling back money for drug treatment and rehabilitation (Tunnell, 2004). By 1986, the medical diagnostic market was a $2 billion industry, and urine-screening devices were estimated to cost over $100 million (Hoffman, 1987).

The 1990s

The Clinton administration supported drug testing in many ways. For instance, it endorsed testing of anyone receiving city, county, state or federal benefits, such as welfare recipients (Tunnell, 2004). It was during the Clinton administration that courts upheld drug testing in a variety of locations. The Substance Abuse and Mental Health Services Administration (SAMHSA) now requires that companies with people using commercial drivers licenses do some form of drug testing. Typically, companies test for what has been called the SAMHSA 5: Cannabinoids, amphetamines, opiates, phenyclidine, and cocaine. Some groups add to the list of substances they test for, typically three to four drugs. This might include some prescription drugs like benzodiazepines and club drugs like Ecstasy.

Today

Workplace drug use, it is now claimed, impacts the economy several ways. According to the Office of National Drug Control Policy (ONDCP), drug abuse costs the country $160.7 billion in 2002. ONDCP claimed that lost productivity comprised 69% of the total loss, totaling $110.5 billion (Tunnell, 2004). Early on in the campaign to expand the drug war to the workplace, corporations were told that drug use costs $33 billion in productivity per year. It was later discovered this figure came from a study that did not actually examine productivity; instead, the original research compared wages in homes with marijuana users to wages of those in homes with no marijuana users, failing to control for type of job, age, and numerous other critical factors (Morgan, 1988). In reality, it is not known precisely how much drug use on the job occurs, or the costs of it when it occurs (Nock, 1993).

Employers are now given a number of financial incentives to implement drug-free workplace programs, which many have interpreted to mean drug testing. The Drug Free Workplace Act of 1998 authorized funding for small businesses to implement drug testing (Schlosser, 2003). In fact, 53% of employers responding to an American Management Association survey indicated they implemented their drug testing program because of government requirements and incentives (Tunnell, 2004). In Nevada, the Senate passed Bill 371 (Section 26.2) mandating that insurance companies give employers performing drug testing a 5% discount on health insurance premiums (Holtorf, 1998).

According to Greenwood (2003), the drug testing industry grosses more than $673 million per year, giving them every incentive to continue and expand testing. Schlosser (2003) noted that two of the four companies on the Institute for a Drug Free Workplace board, one of the lead groups in promoting drug testing, are pharmaceutical companies that analyze drug tests.

Outside the U.S.

Outside the U.S., drug testing is not as popular, although it has expanded. Free-trade agreements expanded the use of drug testing for transportation workers in the later 1990s (Tunnell, 2004). The increase of trucks being used to transport of goods between Canada, the U.S., and Mexico meant more humans being required to pass a drug test. Elsewhere, in Australia, for instance, the National Rugby League has expanded testing of players to include midweek and off-season, and people driving in Queensland can be subject to a random drug test (Magnay, 2006). In 2005, Great Britain authorized mandatory drug tests for people arrested for "acquisitive crimes" such as burglary and mugging. Refusal to submit to the test is also a crime punishable with a fine or jail time (Europe: England to drug test ..., 2005). On the other hand, a judge in Alberta, Canada, ruled in June 2006 that pre-employment drug testing was discriminatory (Drug testing can be discriminatory ..., 2006).

Drug Testing in Schools

Who Is Tested?

High schools began testing students in the 1980s and 1990s. This is due to some court cases affirming the constitutionality of the practice, successful marketing, and, above all, rhetoric that students are drugged-out losers (Finley & Finley, 2005). Most frequently, schools have tested student athletes (Meyer, 2003). In the later 1990s and early in the 21st century, schools added testing for various subgroups of students. In 2000, a school in Arkansas required testing of students who wanted to attend field trips or the prom (Roberts & Fossey, 2002). After the 2002 *Earls* decision (discussed in detail below), more schools added testing policies. In a 2003 survey of 861 athletic directors,

13% indicated their schools test for drugs (Popke, 2003). An additional 17% of responding athletic directors indicated interest in implementing school drug testing (Popke, 2003). In September 2006, Retka (2006) reported in the *St. Louis Daily Record* that 14% of school districts across the nation use some form of drug testing. Although few schools currently randomly test their entire student body, The Bush administration, and in particular, current drug czar, John Walters, have recently advocated greater use of this search method (Lorenz, 2004).

The Bush Administration's Expansion

In his 2004 State of the Union address, President George W. Bush pledged $23 million in grant monies for schools wishing to conduct random testing (Bush's drug testing plan ..., 2004). In 2004–2005, the Bush administration gave 373 public school districts funding for random drug testing, an increase of almost 200 schools in two years. In fiscal year 2007, Bush asked Congress for $15 million in grants to support testing, a 45% increase (With courts' blessing ..., 2006). In total, estimates are that the drug-testing industry now has annual revenues of approximately $740 million (Schlosser, 2003).

Outside the U.S.

As noted elsewhere, former British Prime Minister Tony Blair has promoted drug testing in England's schools. In the U.K., groups like The Coalition Against Cannabis support student drug testing, calling it "A sound investment in our children's future" (The value of random student drug testing, n.d). In 2005, The Abbey School in Kent, England, began randomly selecting students for drug testing. Approximately twenty students per week were selected for mouth swabbing to check for cannabis, speed, Ecstasy, heroin, and cocaine. Echoing the rhetoric from the U.S., advocates claim the testing will deter students from using drugs (School starts random drug testing, 2005). In 2006, the Minister of Education in South Africa was pondering whether to implement random student drug testing there.

Legal issues Regarding Drug Testing

In general, "States typically allow testing if applicants are informed of the test at the time of application, if they are given a copy of the test results, and if testing complies with procedural safeguards" (Tunnell, 2004, p. 36). This was not always the case, however.

At one time, Armentano and Shea (2003) explained, lower and state courts in the U.S. regularly struck down drug testing policies as unreasonable search and seizure. In *Lovvorn v. Chattanooga* 647 FSupp. 875, 879 (E.D. Tenn. 1986)., the U.S. District Court of Tennessee ruled that individualized suspicion was required for testing firefighters. Also in 1986, a court struck down testing of probationary teachers (*Patchogue-Medford Congress of Teachers v. Board of Ed.*, 119 A.D.), and in 1987, for school bus drivers and attendants (*Jones v. McKenzie*, 628 F. Supp. 1500, D.D.C.).

According to Hoffman (1987), the case of *Shoemaker et al. v. Handel* 795 F. 2d 1136 (1986) established reasonable search without justifiable suspicion for specific individuals. Willie Shoemaker, a celebrated jockey, and four other jockeys, filed suit in 1985 to challenge the requirement of a breathalyzer test and a urinalysis made by the New Jersey Racing Commission. Their suit was dismissed, then upheld by the Third Circuit Court of Appeals. Following the decision in *Shoemaker*, courts began to approve so-called administrative searches of various populations, including prison guards (*McDonell v. Hunter*, 809 F. 2d 1302, 1307 [8th Cir. 1987]) and public school teachers (*Jones v. Jenkins*, No. 86-5198, 1989). A very significant case was *National Treasury Employees Union v. Von Raab*, 108 S. Ct. 1072 in 1988. In *Von Raab*, the Supreme Court ruled that people wishing to be employed in sensitive positions, such as public officials, have a reduced expectation of privacy (Armentano & Shea, 2003).

A landmark case in establishing lawfulness of drug testing was *Schmerber v. California* 384 U.S. 757 (1966). Schmerber was the driver in a serious car accident. When the police arrived on the scene, they smelled alcohol on his breath. They arrested Schmerber and, without a court order, took a blood sample. Schmerber objected to the taking of the sample. The blood test showed high levels of alcohol and was used in trial, where Schmerber was convicted. In contesting the case, his attorneys maintained that the involuntary withdrawal of Schmerber's blood violated the Fifth Amendment right against self-incrimination and that it was an unlawful search and seizure in violation of the Fourth Amendment. The Supreme Court agreed with the state, calling the blood sample physical evidence, not testimonial or communicative evidence, and thus saying it was not protected by the Fifth Amendment. They determined that the officer acted on fair, objective information in collecting the blood sample, and thus it was not an unlawful search and seizure.

Importantly, they did acknowledge the medical test as a form of search that could be subject to Fourth Amendment protections in some cases (Hoffman, 1987).

Court Cases Regarding Schools

There are three major cases that support testing in schools. The first, *New Jersey v. T. L.O.* 469 U.S. 325 (1985), was not specifically about drug testing. Instead, it affirmed a school administrator's right to search students based on reasonable suspicion, rather than the more stringent probable cause standard needed for a search by police (Finley & Finley, 2005). The court did not consider whether administrators needed individualized suspicion to search students. In leaving this question unanswered, as well as in their decision to affirm testing based on reasonable suspicion, the court set the stage for subsequent decisions allowing group-based drug testing policies.

Vernonia School District 47J v. Acton, 515 U.S. 646 (1995), the court upheld a drug-testing policy for students involved in after-school sports. A main factor in their decision, as is evidenced in the majority opinion written by Justice Antonin Scalia, was that students involved in sports have a significantly reduced expectation of privacy. Another critical factor was the fact that Vernonia schools could document at least some evidence of a drug problem, although it was not particularly clear if the population being tested was any more culpable than other student groups (Finley & Finley, 2005).

Board of Education of Independent School District No. 92 of Pottawatomie County v. Earls 536 U.S. 822, 122 S.Ct. 2559, 153 (2002), the court upheld drug testing for students involved in all extra curricular activities. The Drug and Alcohol testing Industry Association (DATIA) reported a 10% increase in the number of schools implementing student drug testing after the *Earls* decision (Keynes, 2003).

Types of Drug Testing

Employers use six kinds of drug tests. Almost every company uses pre-employment testing. The author been asked submit to urinalysis testing several times in order to get various jobs. Courts have typically upheld pre-employment testing in that future employees have less privacy than do current employees. Both an advantage and a disadvantage is that people are discouraged from applying if they are drug users. This is advantageous if it weeds out those who would not perform well, but a disadvantage if people who would be excellent employees do not apply. At least one study found that college students are less likely to apply to companies with drug-testing policies (Griffin, et al., 2001). Occupations in which safety is a concern often use random or unannounced testing. This form is also the fastest growing and most common form used with people already employed. When an employee's performance indicates some problem that could be due to drug use, employers may use reasonable cause or for cause testing. This is the second most common form of drug testing and the one most likely to yield positive test results. More specifically, when an employee has been involved in some type of on-the-job accident, employers may utilize postaccident testing. Just over one-quarter of employers use this type of testing (Tunnell, 2004).

Periodic testing is done on a regular schedule and is typically conducted in conjunction with other requirements, often a yearly physical examination. Because employees are given advance notice of the testing, few positive results are found. A small portion of employers use, rehabilitation testing, also called return-to-work testing, which involved repeated testing for people who have previously tested positive (Tunnell, 2004). Return-to-work testing is used when an employee comes back after some form of treatment for substance abuse. Random testing is controversial and not used much in the work world (Griffin, et al., 2001).

Regarding the specific type of test used, although testing methods vary, the vast majority of companies use urine testing. There are two methods of urine testing—immunoassay tests and chromatography. Both are screening tests in which a given urine sample is compared to a calibrator that contains a known quantity of the drug being tested. It is said that immunoassays are 95 to 99% accurate, but this still leaves tremendous leeway for adulterating, falsifying, and error (Tunnell, 2004). Chromatography is more sophisticated, hence more accurate but also more expensive (Tunnell, 2004). Hair follicle testing is more precise than urinalysis and is being used more frequently, despite concerns that it discriminates against African Americans because some substances seem to be more easily absorbed into dark, ethnic hair (Tunnell, 2004). In the last few years, the Food and Drug Administration (FDA) has approved saliva-testing products and sweat-patch testing (Tunnell, 2004).

Who is Tested?

Vulnerable Populations

Tunnell (2004) explained, "before drug testing swept through the American workplace, it was first applies to disparate classes of individuals for group-specific reasons" (p. 21). These groups include athletes being tested to ensure a fair playing field, inmates being tested to help provide substance abuse assistance, and soldiers being tested upon return from Vietnam in the hopes they would receive help. "Drug testing, on an immense scale, was first imposed on those who, at least theoretically, already had relinquished some of their personal liberties" (Tunnell, 2004, p. 21). These vulnerable groups continue to face testing—in 2000, Justice Department data indicate 71% of jails had testing policies and procedures, and almost half of all probationers are subjected to routine testing (Tunnell, 2004). In 1997, Oregon passed a law allowing landlords to demand urine samples from tenants and permitting them to evict tenants who tested positive (Holtorf, 1998). Louisiana requires testing of anyone receiving anything of economic value from the state, such as a scholarship, license, or some form of public assistance, with a positive urine test resulting in treatment and a second positive (or refusal to take the test) leading to termination of the benefit (Holtorf, 1998).

Workplace Testing

In employment testing, the larger the company, the more likely they are to test both applicants and existing employees for drugs. Companies with union employees are more likely to test than are those without unions, and blue-collar workers are more likely subject to drug testing than white-collar employees (Tunnell, 2004). Manufacturing sites, wholesale and retail trades, communications, utilities and transportation, and mining and construction industries are most likely to test, whereas finance, real estate, and insurance are least likely (Tunnell, 2004). Because so many corporations do testing, others seem to have resigned themselves to it as the only option for attaining and maintaining a drug-free workplace.

In Schools

In schools, as noted earlier, athletes are the most commonly tested group. In 2005, acting New Jersey Governor Richard J. Codey signed an executive order mandating steroid testing for all high school athletes who qualify for championship tournaments. This makes New Jersey the first state to require tests for performance-enhancing substances in all sports (N.J. orders steroid testing ..., 2005). New Jersey was the first state to enact a no-pass, no-play policy (Retka, 2006). However, some school districts have authorized testing for all students involved in after-school activities. In 2000, a Memphis, Tennessee, high school authorized random testing of the entire student body, with expulsion the consequence for refusal or failure to provide a test sample (Tunnell, 2004). Miami-Dade, Florida, public schools launched a "voluntary" testing program for all students, which required the consent of parents and students (Staples, 2000).

In 2006, the drug-prevention group notMYkid, cofounded by Steve Moak and his wife, Debbie, in 1999, announced they would expand their 7th grade programs throughout the country to include prescription drug abuse. Testing is the primary feature of the program, as Moak is an investor in First Check Diagnostics, of Lake Forest, California, a drug-test maker teaming with Moak, that has donated $2 million to notMYkid (Prevention group focuses ..., 2006). In September 2006, schools in El Dorado, Kansas, announced they would require middle and high school students to take random drug tests in order to participate in any extracurricular activity, including driver's education and school field trips. Students wishing to park a car on school grounds must also submit to testing (Broad drug testing ..., 2006). Illinois has considered requiring teens who wish to obtain a driver's license to pass a drug test (Drug tests for teen license, 2004).

Schools are also using new methods of testing. Palm Beach County, Florida, schools have trained administrators to use a new portable drug test when they have reasonable suspicion that a student is using illegal drugs. The portable test is a piece of sticky paper, similar to the kind of test used in airports, that is rubbed on a student's body or possessions, then sprayed with chemicals. If it turns a certain color, marijuana, heroin, ecstasy or other drugs may be present. Advocates maintain it is a nonintrusive means to search. The National Institute of Justice has funded the pilot program (Florida county evaluates ..., 2004). The schools in the author's home county, Broward County, Florida, also considered adopting a similar type of test (US FL: schools may use spray ..., 2004).

Some colleges require students to sign contracts that they will not be illicit drug users while enrolled. This is authorized by the Drug Free Schools and Communities Act of 1989. "Such a contract grants implicit permission for unannounced body fluid test, and violation of the contract can terminate financial aid or even enrollment. Virginia Governor L. Douglas Wilder went further, suggesting that all Virginia college students be tested for drug use" (Miller, 1996, p. 79).

It is not just students facing more drug tests; teachers, too, are subject in some areas. In Carroll County, Maryland, faculty and staff have to submit to drug tests based on reasonable suspicion (Maryland school district ..., 2004). The U.S. Court of Appeals for the Sixth Circuit upheld a policy testing teachers in *Knox v. Knox*, 158 F. 3d 361 (6th Cir. 1999), saying educators must keep students safe and, by extension, cannot do so if they themselves are using drugs (Finley & Finley, 2005).

Getting Creative

Drug testing is even being used on new and creative populations. In 2006, the Levy County Public Library System in Florida lost fifty-three of their fifty-five volunteers after a drug testing requirement was instituted. One volunteer explained, "It's not like we are a high-risk group for coming in drunk or high or stoned or whatever" (Oder, 2006, p. 15). Evidently, someone in the county read the risk management insurance to say volunteers must be treated the same as employees, who are required to submit a urine sample (Oder, 2006).

Even celebrities are not immune from urinalysis testing. Radio commentator Rush Limbaugh was required to provide urine samples for 18 months as a condition of his plea deal for "doctor shopping" for painkillers (Limbaugh faces random ..., 2006).

In the Home

Families are increasingly encouraged to use drug testing to check up on their kids' activities. *Newsweek* magazine reported in April 2006 that more than 200 Web sites offer drug tests marketed to parents of teenagers (More than 200 Websites ..., 2006). There are many different products targeted at the potential drug user in the family. The products tend to be the kind that can assess drug use without the knowledge of the person being tested. For instance, the wipes that you touch on the suspected users' skin or something they have touched and then spray with the product are marketed to families (Staples, 2000). A representative of Shertest Corp., which manufactures this type of product, was quoted as saying that the device is intended to enhance the love and care in the home:"'It's about breaking down barriers of denial between parent and child.' It is somewhat difficult to comprehend how sneaking a drug test on a child breaks down any kind of communication barrier. Barringer Technologies, Inc., a company that makes particle detection devices for law enforcement, created a consumer division in March of 1995 that has sold 'thousands' of similar $35 testing kits to parents" (Staples, 2000, pp. 98–99). Between 2003 and June 2005, sales of home drug test kits more than doubled, with annual sales reaching $20 million (Sales of drug-test kits ..., 2005).

Concerns About Drug Testing

Deterrence

Research seems to clearly demonstrate that drug testing is ineffective as a deterrent and for improving workplace productivity. There is some suggestion that workplace drug testing reduces injuries and Workmen's Compensation claims, although others dispute these findings. In 1994, the National Academy of Sciences reported that there was actually no evidence of negative effects of drugs on job performance. The only exception was alcohol (Maltby, 1999). Miller (1996) explained the problem:

> In 1989 President George Bush said drugs in the workplace cost our society $60 billion to $100 billion a year. But the White House extrapolated that claim from a single survey done in 1982, a survey reporting that daily marijuana users had incomes twenty-eight percent lower than non-daily users. The income differential might have explanations other than drug use. For example, losing a job is known to encourage drug abuse, and losing a job can reduce someone's income (Miller, 1996, p. 3)

Furthermore, the cost estimate compared very heavy users with the more normal light users, rather than the normal users with nonusers. In fact, research comparing users and nonusers on other measures has found regular light users to fare better. For instance, a study at Utah Power & Light found that illicit drug users have lower health benefit costs, and a study at Georgia Power Co. found that users had absentee rates 30% lower than nonusers (Miller, 1996).

What is most interesting is that, despite the widespread use of all forms of testing, few companies have evaluated whether it is a cost-effective practice. In 1996, only 8% of companies admitting they conducted some form of drug testing had conducted any analysis (Tunnell, 2004). Similarly, it seems that schools simply take proponents at their word when they say drug testing works.

Research in schools is mixed, but generally fails to support drug testing as a deterrent. In May 2003, the largest-ever national evaluation of the effectiveness of student drug testing found drug use to be just as prevalent in schools with testing as in those without. The study spanned several years and involved a sample of 76,000 students (Meyer, 2003). Another study found that students in schools with drug testing held more positive attitudes about drugs and overestimated the amount of drug use by their peers (Goldberg, et al., 2003). Currently, the U.S. Department of Education is conducting the first large-scale national evaluation of mandatory random testing that uses randomized controls. The Department plans to evaluate mandatory drug testing for students in extracurricular activities and for those not involved in extracurricular activities. The study will include surveys of up to 200 students from each of the participating schools. Participating schools will be randomly assigned to either conduct mandatory random student drug testing or not implement it at any time prior to spring 2008 (Industry comments sought ..., 2006). In the March 2007 issue of *Pediatrics*, the American Academy of Pediatrics criticized student drug testing as being ineffective and breeding suspicion and distrust.

Cost-Effectiveness

Drug testing is costly. During the time that the federal government spent $11.7 million on some 29,000 tests, 0.5% were positive. This means detecting one drug user cost the federal government almost $77,000 (Tunnell, 2004). Another study found that between 1993 and 1998 the federal government randomly tested 257,576 people. Of those, 1345 tested positive, a rate of 0.5%. These tests cost $31,791,811, or $23,637 per positive test (Greenwood, 2003).

Schools that test rarely "catch" students. Some say this means that students have been deterred from use, but that conclusion is far from clear. Perhaps they are not catching students because they are generally using the cheapest and least accurate tests. The cheapest type of drug test to detect marijuana, tobacco, cocaine, heroin, opiates, amphetamines, barbiturates, and tranquilizers costs between $14 and $30 per test, whereas a test for steroids runs more like $100 (Yamaguchi, et al., 2003). What is clear is that the cost-per-catch ratio is high. For example, one school district spent approximately $35,000 to test their middle and high school students. Four students tested positive, so the district spent just less than $9000 to catch each student (Hawkins, 1999). These figures generally only include the initial costs of testing, not the cost of testing additional samples to confirm the first result, nor the cost of multiple tests to check for various substances (Finley & Finley, 2005).

Some schools have gotten creative in trying to offset the costs (rather than abandon an ineffective and inefficient practice). At least one California school district has asked students to pay to submit their urine, at $26 apiece (Carpico, 2003). A Coca-Cola bottling company in Ohio has sponsored drug testing in their community in exchange for exclusive rights to sell their soda at the school for ten years (Hawkins, 1999). Of course, the drug-testing industry has every incentive to promote school-based testing. As reported elsewhere, Roche Diagnostic Systems contributed $100,000 toward drug testing in schools (Hawkins, 1999).

Despite consistent data that alcohol is more often associated with work-related accidents and problems, few companies test for alcohol (Tunnell, 2004). In fact, research has shown that being tired on the job is as damaging as small amounts of drug use. Similarly, students still use alcohol far more than any other substance, yet they are typically not assessed for it. Both substances are illegal for young people, so it is not clear why this is the case, although I would speculate the powerful alcohol and prodrug testing lobbies have something to do with it.

Detection Concerns

Another drawback to drug testing is that it cannot detect whether a person is actually being affected by the substance at the time of the test. Drug tests only check for drug metabolites, and individuals vary tremendously on the way and rate at which they metabolize specific substances (Tunnell, 2004). This has to do with an individual's weight and body fat, their metabolism, the strength of the substance they consumed, and numerous other factors. Nor can tests generally measure the amount of a drug present.

As many have heard, some substances create false positives. The cheaper immunoassay tests have falsely identified ibuprofen as marijuana, and research has indeed borne out that poppy-seed bagels can show up as illicit drug use (Holtorf, 1998). Holtorf (1998) maintained that scores of prescription medications can cause false positives, including diet pills, many asthma medications, many seizure medications, prescriptions for anxiety, migraines, insomnia, and Parkinson's disease, many antibiotics, diuretics, and most antidepressants. Additionally, phenylethylamine forms in unrefrigerated specimens, which can produce a false positive (Holtorf, 1998). Anti-inflammatory agents such as ibuprofen (in Advil and Motrin) and naproxen (Naprosyn) cause false positives for barbiturates, benzodiazepines, and marijuana in some types of drug tests (Holtorf, 1998). Liver problems, kidney problems, and diabetes have been misidentified as use of amphetamines, barbiturates, opiates, cocaine, ethanol, and benzodiazepines (Holtorf, 1998).

Human error is a significant problem when it comes to drug testing. This is true from the beginning phase of conducting the test all the way to the sample analysis. Although parents and school districts often ask physicians to drug test their children, many are unqualified to do so. Research from Harvard Medical School, in conjunction with Children's Hospital of Boston, surveyed 359 doctors who treat adolescents regularly. They found only 23% properly collected urine samples and only 7% checked samples for tampering. Many doctors did not know that certain foods would create false positives, and most were clueless that common drug tests do not address some drugs, including prescription drugs (Many docs not qualified ..., 2006).

In 1985, the *Journal of the American Medical Association* highlighted a Centers for Disease Control study in which they analyzed the testing programs of thirteen different labs between 1972 and 1981. They mailed drug-spiked samples to each lab, and in order to receive a "satisfactory" rating, the lab had to correctly detect the requested drugs 80% of the time. In some cases, false positives were at 100%, with false negatives ranging from 0% to 100% (Hoffman, 1987). The drug-testing industry denounced the study as unfair because it only assessed thirteen labs. Yet other studies found similar error rates. A study conducted by Northwestern University, Evanston, Illinois, found a national false positive rate of approximately 25% (Hoffman, 1987). In 1984, over 70,000 drug tests had to be reevaluated at taxpayer's expense when the Air Force testing lab in Texas found some grease that technicians had used to heat tacos had gotten into the screening equipment, leading to huge numbers of samples being diagnosed as positive for marijuana (Hoffman, 1987).

Bias in Testing

Another concern about drug testing is racial bias in the methods employed. More companies are beginning to use hair samples instead of urinalysis to test for drugs. The American Management Association says 67% of U.S. companies use some form of testing, with half conducting only urinalysis, 30% using saliva tests, and 20% using both hair and urine tests (More companies switching ..., 2003). Testing of hair samples is said to unfairly discriminate against blacks, as drug compounds bind better to hair with more melanin. A group of black police officers in Boston who were fired after hair tests found traces of drugs have sued. Many of the officers took follow-up tests showing no trace of drugs, and all contend they do not use drugs (Hair tests unfair ..., 2005).

Conceptual Concerns

A big problem with drug testing is that individuals using it may be ignoring more effective strategies of drug control, such as education and awareness. Similarly, by focusing on drug use as a problem in need of dire attention, employers and school officials may fail to address other, more important, social problems, including inadequate pay and health benefits for employees and the lack of educational resources in schools. A security guard for a St. Louis, Missouri, school district that is implementing mandatory testing for kids in sports or other extracurricular activities questioned the effectiveness of testing, asserting that the school's major "crime" problems lie elsewhere. He said, "Our biggest problems are adults that get drunk then want to play on playground equipment at elementary schools and people who want to break into the high school nurses office to steal drugs" (Retka, 2006, para. 7).

In fact, drug testing may be doing more damage than good. As noted, employees in companies that use drug testing report lower morale than those working in places without testing. Students complain they have to disclose personal information to testers so that they minimize the chance of false positives. This could be terribly embarrassing. Because it is relatively easy to purchase or concoct substances that might mask or adulterate the sample, some schools have even required students to strip prior to the drug test to ensure a clean sample. Amy Valdez was forced to strip to her underwear, lift her hair from her shoulders, and twirl around in front of her principal prior to emitting her sample. She said, "I felt like I was on display. It was devastating" (Hawkins, 1999, p. 72).

A major drawback to drug testing is that it reduces our understanding and expectation of basic human rights like privacy. Staples (2000) explained why so many people simply accept drug testing as a fact of life.

> Like other surveillance ceremonies, we are at first apprehensive, unsure, and uncomfortable. But, much like the way we march through metal detectors at the airport, the test becomes routine and repetitive. Therefore, drug testing acclimates clients to accepting their own subjugation and encourages their own docility. They may even find themselves wanting to take the test since this becomes the only way they can prove they are indeed 'clean' (p. 98).

Boire (2002) cautioned about the same problem with school-based testing. He wrote, "Raised with the ever-present specter of coercion and control where urine testing is as common as standardized testing, today's students will have little if any privacy expectations when they reach adulthood" (p. 40).

Holtorf (1998) explained that there is little recourse for innocent people wrongly found by drug tests to be drug users, as courts have held that testing does not need to be 100% accurate, only that they have a general scientific basis. Those who refuse to be tested in schools are often subject to ridicule and even overt threats, as in the case of the Tannahills. They supported their son in his refusal to submit a urine sample with the rest of his sixth-grade class. Their dog was shot with a paintball, and the local newspaper printed letters recommending they move (Fields-Meyer, 2000).

As we saw with the people making drug laws, employers and schools are often hypocritical in their use of drug testing. Historically,

> Employers have encouraged workers to use amphetamines, cocaine, opiates, marijuana, and nicotine *on the job* to improve productivity, and coffee breaks are still routinely provided to encourage employees to dose themselves with caffeine. Whether such policies have been wise is an issue we need not address here. The point is that until the war on drug users became popular, employers welcomed drug use by employees. Such employees were considered desirable and normal (Miller, 1996, p. 5).

Resistance to Drug Testing

Although drug testing spread rapidly in the 1980s and generally had widespread support, there was some resistance. In 1985, San Francisco became the first municipality to enact anti–drug testing legislation. It prohibited drug testing as a condition of employment as well as random or companywide testing but allowed drug testing for cause (Hoffman, 1987). In 1989, the state of Montana passed legislation restricting drug testing to only those situations in which objective fact implicated a person (Hoffman, 1987). Later that year, Vermont and Iowa passed similar legislation (Hoffman, 1987). On the other hand, Utah passed a law granting employers the right to test anyone for any reason without warning (Hoffman, 1987).

Not all parents favor drug testing of students. In 2004, the California State Parent Teachers Association, with a membership of one million, supported a ban on random, suspicionless testing (Kern, 2006). According to Holtorf

(1998), the American Medical Association opposes drug testing of doctors, and the American Academy of Pediatrics opposes drug testing of children and teenagers.

Some high school students have taken to the Web for activism about all kinds of issues, one being drug testing. In 1999, *The Nation* reported that high school students formed the Web-based International Student Activism Alliance after one found out that his school was considering drug testing all students seeking involvement in extracurricular activities (Featherstone, 1999).

Many drug users resist testing by cheating on or sabotaging the tests, which can be done in a number of ways. Many products and tips for cheating drug tests are available on the Web, the subject of Chapter Five. As noted, this drug testing arms race on the Web adds a whole new element for law enforcement. On one hand, law enforcement could use the sites listed in the next chapter and others as a vehicle to identify potential drug users and sellers. There is some evidence the Web has been policed in this fashion, as there have been reports of police in Florida checking out MySpace sites for discussion of drug activity. On the other hand, the amount of time and effort that would be needed to police the volumes of sites available for those interested in outsmarting law enforcement is overwhelming. Certainly one could argue that the few "catches" would be hardly worth the bother.

· 5 ·

MARKETING CHEATING ON THE WEB

Introduction

Paralleling the increase in drug testing has been an increase in sales of detoxification products and other goods intended to alter or mask drug use on tests. As testers have introduced more powerful tests as well as more surveillance of the testing process, adulteration has taken on new forms. Most significantly, users can purchase a vast array of adulterating agents, both in head shops and on the Web. According to Tunnell (2004), "The Internet apparently is the medium of choice for marketing products among the overt detox companies. It is at overt companies' Websites where one finds obvious and stated uses for the detox wares—to beat drug tests" (p. 61). Like the drug testing industry, the detoxification business is a multimillion dollar one (Tunnell, 2004). These multimillion dollar businesses pose difficulties for enforcing various drug laws.

This chapter begins by briefly overviewing methods used to cheat drug tests. It then provides a short history of drug test cheating. This is followed by an examination of the products available on the Web, as well as the information provided online regarding how to cheat a drug test.

Methods of Duping

There are many methods of duping drug tests. Flushing refers to drinking large amounts of liquids prior to a urine test to accelerate the excretion of drug metabolites. Some use over-the-counter diuretics, such as large quantities of caffeinated products like coffee and soda, whereas others simply ingest a great deal of water. Flushing has proven successful to a degree, and the National Institute on Drug Abuse now requires limitations on employee's water intake prior to a test. Additionally, many agencies now test samples for creatine levels, although this is a costly process (Tunnell, 2004). Because diuretics have worked in the past, the National Institute on Drug Abuse requires limits on an employee's water intake prior to submitting a sample. Some testers reject samples lacking color (an indication of flushing), but detoxification personnel have an answer for that, too: take B-complex vitamins two hours prior to providing the sample.

Masking involves ingesting some substance to cover up the presence of drug metabolites. Common over-the-counter forms of masking include aspirin, ibuprofen, Tums, and Rolaids. Several substances, including household items, can produce false negatives. Adding bleach, water, liquid Drano, salt, liquid soap, vinegar, or Visine to a sample, as well as ingesting large quantities of vitamin C, aspirin, and goldenseal, can mask some kinds of drug use (Holtorf, 1998). More sophisticated urine tests tend to discover these simplistic forms of masking agents, however (Tunnell, 2004).

Diluting involves adding water directly to the sample. Once widely used, and somewhat successfully, dilution has become more difficult since former Attorney General Edwin Meese ordered that all federal toilets be filled with blue dye. At the time, federal employees were using water from the toilet tank to dilute their samples. Additionally, most testing methods take the sample temperature, which would easily indicate if water had recently been added (Tunnell, 2004).

Substituting involves providing uncontaminated urine from another source, such as nonusing friends or from a purchased freeze-dried sample. Typically, the substituted urine is smuggled into the testing area via a special bag, called a bladder bag, although in some cases condoms or other holding devices have been used (Holtorf, 1998).

Users have been known to adjust their samples by adding various substances directly to them, called adulterating. Some adulterants are common household products, such as liquid soap, table salt, or cleansing agents like bleach or hydrogen peroxide (Hoffman, 1987).

A Brief History of Drug Test Cheating

Of course, innovative drug users have long found creative methods for concealing their use. For instance, a 1973 study by Lewis et al., found that 59% of heroin addicts used some flushing or substitution method to produce false negatives (Tunnell, 2004). Drinking a lot of water is the oldest, simplest, and cheapest method of flushing and, in some cases, has proven successful. Other diuretics, such as coffee, tea, soda, cranberry juice, and beer have long been recommended. Another factor to consider is never to use your first urine of the day for the sample, as it will have the highest level of metabolites (Hoffman, 1987).

Early in the history of testing, some people sabotaged the testing equipment by adding hydrochloric acid, sulfuric acid, or battery acid. Others have adulterated their sample by adding liquid soap, table salt, bleach, or hydrogen peroxide. Again, these were successful enough that the federal government noticed. At one time people could hide table salt under their fingernails to be added to the sample, but now pretty much everyone requires testees to wash their hands before urinating (Potter, 1999).

Another tactic recommended by drug test opponents was to subvert the screening process by changing the paperwork, the implements, or the test administrator. This might mean failing to fill in all the required information on the forms, thus allowing for testing at a later date (Hoffman, 1987).

In 1985, Jeffrey Nightbyrd, who had been a columnist for *The Daily Texan* in Austin, Texas, and then became involved with the underground news papers *The Rag* and *Rat Subterranean News*, founded one of the first urine sales industries. Nightbyrd became incensed after thirty construction workers at a Texas site were fired after their surprise urine test. He found that the test was a sham—the contractor had fallen behind schedule and had speeded up the work, resulting in errors and accidents that were said to be due to employee drug use. Nightbyrd named his business Byrd Laboratories and took out an ad offering pure urine samples for $45.95. He received 50 to 100 calls a day, and proceeded to advertise and build up his inventory of urine samples. These initially came from senior citizens homes, where he paid the residents for their urine. After several months of operation, Nightbyrd discovered the problems with selling liquid urine—it has a very short shelf life and is difficult to mail. He hired graduate chemistry students to work on freeze-drying urine. This initially failed, but his sister, a medical student, helped him find a way to dehydrate the urine so it could be packed in small vials. The powdered urine was a hit, and sales soared. Nightbyrd received national press coverage, where he hyped slogans such as, "Oil put Texas on top, urine will keep it there," and, "Test your government, not your urine" (Hoffman, 1987, p. 217). The local ACLU established a group called the Urine Defense Fund, and the group hosted a Urine Ball in which 1000 people called the White House and said, "We won't drop our zipper for the Gipper!" (Hoffman, 1987, p. 220). Byrd Laboratories is still in operation and has been joined by a number of companies offering similar and even expanded options for people's drug test needs.

Products Available Online

Tunnell (2004) described several Web sites devoted to overt detoxification sales. Passpee.com discusses "How to beat a drug test" and offers flushing teas. Tommy Chong's urineluck.com says users can "Pass Any Drug Test—Guaranteed!" Products include shampoos, carbohydrate drinks, carbohydrate teas, and quick-flush capsules. Cleanwhizz.com advertises "drug free urine" (as opposed to drugged urine?) that comes with a delivery hose, heat packs, and a thermometer. Passyourdrugtest.com offers urine, saliva and hair cleansers, as well as self-test kits and urine additives. Beatanydrugtest.com advertises products such as Clear Choice©, manufactured by Body-Flush USA with a double money-back guarantee if users are not completely satisfied. An innovator in the detox industry, 1stopdetox, offers a chewable tablet that (allegedly) blocks tetrahydrocannabinol (THC) (a psychoactive substance) from passing through to the urine.

In addition, Tunnell (2004) described three "clearing houses" for detoxification products. Detoxcentral.com, detoxking.com, and yahooka.com feature page after page of advertisements for products used in passing drug tests. Information can also be found at the Web site of *High Times* magazine.

Because some employers now test urine samples for adulterants, some sites sell these kits for home use. BioScan Screening System's Intect 6 is one test for adulterants and other masking forms. It is a stick that is dipped into the urine sample and, like a pregnancy test, it turns a different color nearly immediately if the sample indicates excessive fluids, do-it-yourself adulterants, and various commercially available cleansing products (Tunnell, 2004). It appears that evidence of some form of masking product shows up in approximately 2% of cases, and interestingly, more specimens test positive for adulterants than for opiates or amphetamines. Most of the items that are identified are common household cleaning agents, not the products available online or in head shops (Tunnell, 2004).

Building on the foundation initiated by Tunnell (2004), the author attempted to explore what is available on the Web as well. The sheer amount of sites devoted to selling products and/or providing information designed to help someone cheat a drug test is mind-blowing. A Google search for pass a drug test reveals more than 11 million hits. Another for detoxification products demonstrated the ease in which someone can purchase masking agents, fake urine, and other goods intended to help them pass a drug test. Whatever search words were used or search engine employed, advertisements offering to help pass any test were readily available. The following sections describe a small proportion of the sites, focusing on what is offered and the claims made. As a way to provide a snapshot of what is available, the information provided below is based on the first page of sites identified in a Google search for pass a drug test.

At tests-shop.com, users can learn a bit about the rise in drug testing, as well as purchase thirty-three different drug-testing products as well as tests for adulterants. Urineluck.com advertises "The World's best nicotine cleansing products since 1992." All of the language used on the site is directed at nicotine users, although the word "nicotine" appears to be a code for illicit drugs. The site discusses how common drug tests are, saying, "it is so poorly regulated that even nicotine-free workers taking over-the-counter medications can test positive falsely and lose their job." The motto of this company is "Live positive, test negative." The site features a drop-down calculator whereby users can select the type of test they will face (urine, hair, etc.), state how many times per week they use nicotine (one to four, more than five, etc.), whether they will be watched when providing the sample, whether they will have at least one hour notice to prepare for the test, and many other questions. After answering, users are told the best product to meet their needs. Again, given that it was obvious that nicotine was not truly the substance of discussion (since it is illogical to believe this type of testing would be given to assess someone's smoking), people who are searching for masking agents and detoxification products certainly will get it.

Dmoz.org/shopping/recreation/drugs/detox_products provides links to a number of other sites. This type of clearinghouse is very common. Ureasample. com advertises "Clean urine specimens and transport solutions." Users can purchase drug-free urine and "complete substitution kits." At the bottom of the home page are links, including translation services into eleven languages. Users purchase drug-testing products as they would making a purchase on amazon.com. Also provided is a wealth of information, including legal warnings that the government is mandating all laboratories perform specimen-integrity checks for additives, dilutions, and masking agents and a list of 250 medications that can cause false positives. The links are focused on marijuana, describing detection times, methods of drug testing, standards and accuracy of drug tests, and methods to beat testing. Above all, the site prompts users to continue using, just to do so in a way their use will not be detected. It claims, "Just think, you may have your clean urine sample and substitution kit waiting at your doorstep before you wake up tomorrow and be on your way to a new future the very same day. All of this with no lengthy detox or lifestyle changes."

Another link from dmoz is to alwaystestclean.com. Users can select the drug test type and learn about detection times, how to beat the test, and even "when to get a lawyer." Users can purchase a variety of drug test products, all with a 200% money-back guarantee, and orders placed by 5:30 p.m. on the East Coast arrive the same day. The site informs users concerned that their purchase will be detected that their products will be billed and shipped in a plain package, and that they are ordering through a secure and encrypted site.

Assured Testing Resources, through their Web site pretestedurine.com, offers a complete urine substitution system for $35 that is "so small it fits in the palm of your hand." The site also rails against the war on drugs, stating, "In America today, there is more emphasis on a person's ability to pass a drug test than on their actual ability to perform a task. As a result of the drug war, the pre-employment drug screen and random drug test has allowed an invasion into the privacy and confidentiality of people in ways hard to image [sic]." The company also promises to provide urine that is free of disease, pregnancy and other toxins or problems. The urine comes in a bag that is "less pliable" than other company's to avoid kinking.

Ipassedmydrugtest.com, in business since 1993, offers a "free online drug test:" a drop-down menu like other sites have to help users determine the right option for them to pass their test. This company offers a variety of cleaning products, including hair follicle cleaning, saliva cleaning, and cleaning specific to steroid use. The site is available in Spanish as well, and features a number of testimonials from those who have passed drug tests with no problems. They do make the disclaimer, "we do not condone the use of illegal substances," but qualify that by adding, "but we do understand your lifestyle and needs."

"Don't give up your civil liberties and bodily fluids to drug tests! Use ours!" is the claim made on 4cleanp.com. The site offers concealable urine substitution kits with overnight delivery. For $69, a user can order enough to pass two urine tests or get $300 back. Going on with their claims and commentary, the site states, "Give the piss police what they want—a clean urine sample at the proper temperature. We are just what the doctor ordered and won't let you get caught with your pants down." The site also provides users with details about state laws regarding sales of substitute urine and the punishments for doing so. Additionally, it provides information about more than 300 foods, drugs, and products that can create false positives. Lest they are misperceived, "We are not drug advocates, we are civil liberty advocates." Dr. John Morgan, listed as director of pharmacology at the City University of New York Medical School is quoted on the site: "Urine testing is a method for surveillance, not a tool for safety. Indeed, drug testing is not about safety or job performance; drug testing is a necessary feature of the surveillance state that is now being built around us to ensure total cradle-to-grave surveillance and control of workers."

Buying additives, urine substitutions or detox solutions from cleartest.com means a person would "never worry about a drug test again." Clear test products include various detoxification drinks, starting at $32, additives like Clear Choice©, which rings in at $31, various shampoos, and drug test kits and books. Perhaps their most innovative feature, however, is the "Pot smoker of the month" spotlight, which demonstrates that the diverse group of Montel Williams, Pancho Villa, Rodney Dangerfield, Oliver Stone, Melissa Etheridge, Bing Crosby, and Margaret Mead share(d) their use of the herb. It is not clear whether these claims can be substantiated. December 2006 featured former NFL player Ricky Williams, who says he smoked pot because it was better than prescription drugs for alleviating social anxiety disorder. In addition, the site offers Frequently Asked Questions and drug test news and allows users to sign up for a newsletter. Testimonials are also available to persuade users. One testimonial referred to how useful the "Test' in" hair kit was, especially when he shampooed his whole body with it multiple times.

According to The Detox Store, "Drug screen tests are a fact of life," but users can, "Take control of your body and your life!" They offer urine in capsules, chewable (!) and liquid forms, as well as "extreme products," which are cleaning liquids and capsules. They also offer detoxifying shampoos for people facing hair analysis, and permanent body cleansing for "complete inside out cleansing" at a price of $109.45.

Detoxify Brand Products offers "must read info" in a downloadable book from their site, passthatdrugtest.tripod.com. The Drug Testing Clearinghouse seems to be more of an information and blog-style site with its scathing anti-drug-warrior rant. An alternating title appears on the site suggesting users buy legal hydroponic buds (pure wild lettuce opium buds).

One of the most affordable products is available at passitkit.com, where a person can get "100 % undetectable urine" that is guaranteed reusable for $45. The site also features links to the 2005 Drug Testing Integrity Act of 2005, which was in subcommittee at the time of the post (July 2005) and would ban products designed to defraud a drug test. Interestingly, the site also features numerous Bible quotes.

Pass-any-drug-test.com attempts to appeal to the broad array of people now subject to drug tests. "Subject to random drug test, an athlete, starting a new job, on parole? One stop shopping for all your detox needs." This site also features a 24-hour hotline number in the event that users need immediate and personal assistance. Pbclear.netfirms.com tries to appeal to users by being "one of them." The site proclaims that users should, "Trust me. I have been on probation for 2 years due to a DWI. Its normal to relax after work. I am a registered nurse. I know what will clean your fatty tissues." Only one site, testingclean.com, specified that users must be 21 or older to enter.

NTDetox.com offers chemical strips for users to test their own urine prior to an official test. The site markets their products as health oriented, not specifically for detoxification purposes. For instance, they offer Vale's Solution, a "thin," premixed, easy to drink nutritional supplement specially formulated to aid your body's natural ability to eliminate unhealthy toxins, pollutants and unwanted substances." It is easy to drink and "tastes great," as well as including vitamins like B-2. Also available in fruit punch flavor, users are cautioned they should consult a health care practitioner before trying it if they are pregnant or nursing. Similarly, their Zydot Ultra Clean Shampoo is marketed as a way to purify and condition the hair. It is to be used "ONLY on the day you wish your hair to be clean and free of unwanted impurities," and heavy users are advised to use it twice back-to-back to "insure the purifying process."

Several sites offer prosthetic penises, most notably whizzinator.com. Gonumber1.com also has a urinating device for men and women that is, "Inexpensive, foolproof, undetectable, premixed, irradiated and guaranteed to pass every time." Gonumber1.com is a link from the whizzinator Web site. They offer a similar device but it seems to exclude the prosthesis. For $49.95, someone can purchase the device with heat packs and two packs of urine. Users can also see a photo guide on how to install the device. Cleartest.com offers a similar product and how-to video. In 2005, Minnesota Vikings running back Onterrio Smith was stopped at the Minneapolis-St. Paul, Minnesota, airport because security found a whizzinator in his luggage. The device is, as of now, legal in Minnesota, as are chemical forms of masking agents and freeze-dried urine (Athlete incidents centers on ..., 2005).

Learning Online How to Pass a Drug Test

Most prodrug sites feature information about passing drug tests. Ureasample.com offers information on over 250 medications that can cause false positives in drug tests and is available in eleven languages in addition to English. Alwaytestclean.com provides users with advice, detection times, and information on how to beat each type of drug test. Also featured is a discussion of "when to get a lawyer." Cleartest.com not only provides information about how to beat a variety of drug tests, it also features a Frequently Asked Questions link and the Pot Smoker of the Month profile, which describes pot use by celebrities. How-to-pass-a-drug-test.net includes a 24-hour hotline.

Neonjoint.com/passing_a_drug_test/index.html provides one of the most detailed overviews of how to pass a test, including specific information on detection times for different drugs, how to decrease detection times, drug test methods, standards, and accuracy, how testers detect countermeasures, drug screens that do and do not work, effective and ineffective substitution methods, what to do if you fail a test, and the politics and ethics of drug testing.

Totse.com/en/drugs/legal_issues_of_drug_use/drugtest.html provides the following nuggets of wisdom in their section on "How to beat drug tests." "NOTICE TO ALL CONCERNED: Certain text files and messages contained on this site deal with activities and devices which would be in violation of various Federal, State, and local laws is actually carried out or constructed. The Webmasters of this site do not advocate the breaking of any law. Our text files and message bases are for informational purposes only. *We recommend that you contact your local law enforcement officials before undertaking any project based upon any information obtained from this or any other Web site.* We do not guarantee that any of the information contained on this system is correct, workable, or factual. We are not responsible for, nor do we assume any liability for, damages resulting from the use of any information on this site" (emphasis added).

Additionally, the designers of totse.com's "how to beat drug tests" section clearly admire Abbie Hoffman and his work, as they recite it at length. Instead of reading the book (which can be found at most libraries), they can get the basics from the site. Advice is similar to other sites, but Hoffman also offers some unique tidbits. He recommends users say they have "Blushing kidneys"—the inability to urinate when somebody else is near. Furthermore, he recommends creativity in the bathroom. You can "Use your body to disrupt line-of-sight observance. Hand placement can conceal a lot of activity, but block with anything else that's available. Males might say they only urinate sitting down. Like a good magician, distract the observer. Ask them to run the faucet; say that the sound of running water coaxes your own activity. Hoffman also provides detailed instructions for urine substitution, and recommends drainage bags used by ambulant patients (the book was written prior to the advent of the Whizzinator and the like—perhaps Hoffman would plug those products were he alive today).

All kinds of forums where users exchange this type of information are also on the Web. For instance, the newsgroups of Erowid (a clearinghouse site for everything drug related) feature numerous posts about such questions as how to fake a test for Ecstasy, the detection times for various drugs, whether Adderall shows up on a drug test (yes), if a woman's period alters a test for cocaine (yes), and whether tests can detect Salvia (no).

At Erowid, one can read Justin Gombos' (1998) article, "Fooling the Bladder Cops," which offers a detailed, almost academic, rundown of cheating a drug test. Gombos makes several suggestions for the 15 million new job applicants being tested each year, some of who will try to beat the test. These start from the simple advice to call in sick on the day of the test (to allow yourself another day to excrete drug metabolites—providing you do not use again), to the more elaborate full-detoxification programs. Gombos' number one recommendation is that users increase their metabolism, either by physical activity or through a high-calorie diet, as this would help them store fewer metabolites in their bodies. A high-fiber diet is also recommended so users can excrete more of the THC metabolites before the test. He also cautions against using any calculators that allegedly determine how long THC will stay in the body, as these (which he says are available online) do not consider the potency of marijuana. If a hair follicle test is imminent, Gombos recommends Aloe Rid by Nexus, a shampoo designed for swimmers and available only at salons. Shaving your entire body and posing as a swimmer is not a bad idea, either, as hair samples may come from any place on the body, not just the head.

Gombos (1998) says there are more than 300 over-the-counter drugs that can create a false positive on a basic immunoassay test. If you are clean and are subject to a test, the least you can do for the cause is consume several of these and make the testers pay more for the higher-priced confirmation test. If dilution is the plan of choice, Gombos recommends eating a lot of red meat to raise creatine levels. If a user plans to purchase a detoxification product, Gombos recommends UrinAid by Byrd Laboratories, although he cautions that only masks pot and nicotine. Users wishing to substitute can get creative, although many of the methods that have been used are not terribly comfortable. Female users can hide clean urine inside a condom they insert into their vagina, then prick the condom with a sharp fingernail. Although it is possible to insert substituted urine into your bladder with a needle, as some athletes trying to hide steroid use have done, Gombos recommends catheterizing yourself instead. Another piece of wisdom is that you can make your own powdered urine, presumably at a time when you are confident the sample is clean. Simply urinate in a glass container and let the urine evaporate. Then scrape the inside of the jar for the residue and mix it with warm water when needed. Finally, Gombos says some people have had luck with substituting dog urine.

Gombos' article is hardly the only thing available at Erowid. Indeed, the site is a rich source of information for the would-be drug test cheater. Users simply need to select the substance they are using from a drop-down menu and they can read about detection times, how long metabolites generally stay in someone's system, and what substances can produce false positives. For instance, cocaine remains detectable through a urine test for 48 to 72 hours, and in a hair follicle test it can be detected up to 90 days later (for longer hair—users with shorter hair have a significant advantage. The antibiotic amoxicillin is noted as a false-positive producer. Single-time users can expect phencyclidine (PCP) to stay in their system 3 to 7 days, and regular users should expect detection up to 30 days later on a urine test. PCP is also easier to detect in longer hair. Unfortunately for PCP users, Erowid lists no substances producing a false positive.

Concluding Comments on Drug Test Cheating

There is no assurance that these products and tips are effective. Two stories learned in researching this book highlight how drug-test cheating can go awry. In one case, someone was in charge of moving urine samples collected from youth involved in juvenile drug court programs from a refrigerator to a different location. One day, she opened the refrigerator to find a tray of a dozen or so yellowish samples and one orange, congealed-looking one. She described it as akin to orange Jello, partially set. It turns out the testee had purchased some type of detoxification substance online that didn't do so well when it was refrigerated. In the other case, a testee was to be observed providing his urine sample. Evidently he didn't plan his cheating so well, as the Whizzinator he was using was clearly black although his skin was quite pale. Perhaps he bought it on e-Bay and forgot to check the skin color feature. No attempt was personally made to verify whether the claims made on these sites were true.

This chapter is by no means an exhaustive account of what is available on the Web, either in the way of products or advice. It was intended to highlight yet another complexity in the broader issue of policing the Web. As was discussed in Chapter Two, it is not clear to what extent the sale of these products is lawful. Nor is it clear whether the information posted to guide users in defrauding tests is considered free speech and free press, or whether it is illegal. As Chapter Three outlined, enforcement of existing laws regarding drugs on the Web is difficult, let alone if others directed at the content on Web sites providing detox products are added. Who would be charged with checking the sites? Who has jurisdiction if a possible offender is identified? These and other questions require significant attention.

· 6 ·

UNDERSTANDING AND PREDICTING THE FUTURE OF ONLINE DRUG SALES

Introduction

This chapter begins with an examination of one of the most difficult balances in controlling deviance and crime—how to enforce social control without infringing on people's civil liberties. Included is an assessment of speech, press, and privacy rights as they relate to Web-based drug sales and drug information. Next, this chapter draws together the main criminological theories used to explain drug dealing and using. Some appear to be more useful in explaining traditional forms of drug use and drug sales, whereas others seem to hold more promise in understanding the online drug phenomenon. Those that have traditionally been used to explain drug use and sales but do not appear to be very useful for understanding the online version are presented first. Theories that seem to offer more promise in regard to online sales are presented next.

Criminologists have not paid much attention to online drug sales specifically. Moore (2005) explained,

> Understanding the how is only one aspect of stemming the growing problem of high-technology crime. The other side that must be considered is the why. Why do people engage in high-technology crime? There are numerous studies to address why individuals engage in physical world crime. In the coming years there is a need to begin

testing these theories in an attempt to determine which, if any, help explain the actions of high-tech criminals (p. 232).

Readers should note that this chapter is by no means exhaustive of all criminological theory, nor is it a detailed description or evaluation of each. It is not based on empirical testing of the theories, either. Its goal is to show how these theories might connect to Web-based sales, and thus shed light on the direction needed for policing the Web. After presenting each category of theories, I have included how each can be applied to cyber drug dealing and the exchange of assorted drug-related information and detoxification products online. The goal is summarize not investigate in a detailed manner. Additionally, Chapter Six discusses theories that help explain the surveillance component of drug testing. Finally, the chapter offers some predictions and recommendations for the future of the war on online drug sales.

Civil Liberties Concerns

Free Speech and Press

Despite concerns about access to inappropriate material, in particular for young people, the U.S. has generally recognized the Internet as a tremendous source of free speech and free press. Thus, most have maintained it deserves the utmost constitutional protection. The Supreme Court has lauded the Internet for providing diverse thought and instant access, and Judge Stuart Dalzell of the U.S. District Court for the Eastern District of Pennsylvania has called it "the most participatory form of mass speech yet developed" (Cited in Corn-Revere, 2002, p. 2). Material on the Web has been protected as an important component of free speech in such cases as *Reno v. ACLU*, 521 U.S. 844, 850–52, 870 (1997) and *ACLU v. Reno*, 31 F. Supp. 2d 473, 476, 493 (E.D. Pa 1999). Although he recognized that inappropriate material is available on the Internet, Justice John Paul Stevens noted in the *Reno* case that users seldom come across this material accidentally (Senat, 1997). According to Kolbert (2001),

> The U.S. Supreme Court has long held that in most circumstances, free expression deserves the highest standard of constitutional protection. Thus, anytime the government wants to restrict speech, it must give a compelling reason for it and must then design the restriction carefully, to make sure it is "narrowly tailored"—that is, limiting *only* the particular speech that the government is concerned about, without spilling over onto other forms of speech (p. 7).

Anonymous Speech and Press

Jonathan D. Wallace of the CATO Institute agrees that limiting anonymous expression on the Web violates the First Amendment (Wallace, 1999). In *ACLU v. Miller* (N. D. Ga. 1997), a federal district court struck down a Georgia law criminalizing anonymous and pseudonymous speech on the Internet. In doing so, according to Wallace (1999), they affirmed an important American tradition and right. The Georgia law made it a misdemeanor to knowingly transmit data through a computer using a false name. The Supreme Court has repeatedly affirmed the right to anonymous and pseudonymous speech. In *McIntyre v. Ohio Campaign Commission* 514 U.S. 334 (1995), the Justices held that anonymity, "provides a way for a writer who may be personally unpopular to ensure that readers will not prejudge her message simply because they do not like its proponent" (cited in Wallace, 1999, p. 3).

E-Mail

In the case of e-mail correspondence, it is unclear what, precisely, is protected. In 1997, a federal district court threw out a Georgia law prohibiting anonymous and pseudonymous Internet communications (Wallace, 1999). H.B. 1630, enacted in 1996, made such communications a misdemeanor (Wallace, 1999). In previous cases, (see *Cubby v. CompuServe, Inc.* 776 F.Supp 135 (S.D.N.Y 1991)), courts have held that online services that edit, review, or reformulate material are liable for defamation, as are newspapers. They are not generally liable if they do not review or edit the material (Hiller & Cohen, 2002). Congress overruled the distinction between those that review and those that do not in Section 230 of the Communications Decency Act (CDA), granting Internet Service Providers (ISPs) statutory immunity in defamation claims (Hiller & Cohen, 2002).

Blogs

Free speech and press issues are also of concern with blogging. According to Stephen Baker of *Business Week Online*, there were some seven million bloggers in 2005, and the rate is growing at some 40,000 new members a day (Baker, 2005). The law is not clear regarding whether blogging is protected speech. Hudson (2006) maintained the true question is whether bloggers can be considered journalists. If they are, then they are covered by the First

Amendment's protection of the freedom of press. Senator John Cornyn (R-Tex), asserts that some bloggers have written about critical issues and can be considered the modern-day version of revolutionary pamphleteers (Hudson, 2006). Gregg Leslie, Legal Defense Director of the Reporters Committee for Freedom of the Press, which is a nonprofit organization dedicated to providing free legal assistance to journalists, argues that the more important question is the function of the blog (Hudson, 2006). In *Talley v. California* 362 U.S. 60 (1960), the Supreme Court did protect anonymous speech.

Dwyer (2005) documented the growth of confessional-style Web sites, in which people will detail their most intimate life experiences on the Web, basking in the perceived anonymity. Many of the postings are innocuous. For instance, users posted on the sites notproud.com and grouphug.us their gluttonous eating habits or unkind acts. Yet others are more graphic, detailing very destructive behavior or using vulgar language to describe sexual escapades. Some sites, such as e-admit.com, allow users to be interactive, providing opportunities for them to comment on others' confessions or cast a vote on someone's decisions. Now, anyone who realizes their sordid Internet past can "Google bomb," a procedure that involves having a number of sites include the anchor text—let's say, Paris Hilton—which would then make that search word appear higher in the list of links to come up on a Google search. If enough people do this on acceptable sites, the reference on unacceptable sites will be moved lower on the list of links. Thus employers or others interested in finding out about Paris Hilton via a Google search will have to scan through a long list to read the unacceptable or questionable material.

The case of Jake Baker provides an illustration of the complexity of online speech, press, and privacy issues. Baker, a student at the University of Michigan in the mid-1990s, wrote short stories about sexual torture and rape. He posted these on the Internet, which caught the eye of an alumnus, who contacted university officials. Baker also corresponded via e-mail with someone called "Arthur Gonda," and the two shared sexual fantasies involving abduction and rape. At one point, Baker wrote an e-mail stating, "Just thinking about it anymore doesn't do the trick. I need TO DO IT." He then described several women in Ann Arbor who might be targets. He was arrested in early 1995 and was the first person charged with making interstate threats via the Internet. A judge dismissed the case in January 1997, when he ruled that the e-mails were private, they were intended only for the eyes of "Arthur Gonda," and were not a real threat (De Angelis, 2000).

Outside the U.S.

Beyond U.S. borders, free speech and press are guaranteed human rights. According to the Universal Declaration of Human Rights of 1948, "everyone has the right to freedom of opinion and expression; this right includes freedom to hold opinions without interferences and to seek, receive, and impart information and ideas through any medium and regardless of frontiers." The Internet can make the ideal of this declaration closer to reality. As J. Dempsey of the Global Internet Liberty Campaign, a group of human rights and civil liberties organizations (2006), maintained, "The borderless nature of the Internet requires that the phrase 'regardless of frontiers,' which appears in the key international human rights instruments, be applied with a fresh eye. The concept of a right to 'impart' information takes on new meaning when anyone can be a publisher. Since censorship in one country may constitute direct infringement on the right of persons in other countries to 'impart' information 'without regard for frontiers,' the traditional deference given to local norms should be less relevant to the Internet." "Through any medium" allows this declaration the needed elasticity to reflect social and technological changes, including widespread use of the Internet to share and disseminate information. In addition, the Universal Declaration of Human Rights provides a broad affirmation of privacy rights that could be extended to privacy in one's Web-based information and interactions. Article 12 of the Declaration reads: "No one shall be subjected to arbitrary interference with his privacy, family, home or correspondence." Although this declaration is not a treaty, its provisions have been implemented in a variety of ways in many countries. In 1993, the position of Special Rapporteur, charged with the promotion and protection of freedom of opinion and expression, was created. In his 1998 report, the Special Rapporteur lauded new technologies like the Internet for being inherently democratic and cautioned governments of censoring the Web. He recognized censorship as paternalistic and as inconsistent with democratic principles and basic human rights (Dempsey, 2006).

The International Covenant on Civil and Political Rights (ICCPR), which took effect in 1976, reiterated and expanded on the rights of free expression and privacy guaranteed by the Universal Declaration of Human Rights. On a regional level, the European Convention of Human Rights of 1950 recognized a right to free expression. It included cross-border communications and thus is applicable to the Internet. In applying this right, European case law has recognized that protections vary for different forms of media, allowing that the Internet is a less immediate and less inflammatory medium and thus should be censored with less frequency and scope (Dempsey, 2006). A key part of European case law is that a form of censorship must be "necessary in a democratic society." The American Convention on Human Rights of 1969 provides for freedom of thought and expression, including "freedom to seek, receive and impart information and ideas of all kinds, regardless of frontiers, either orally, in writing, in print, in the form of art, or through any other medium of one's choice" (Dempsey, 2006). The African Charter on Human and Peoples' Rights, an international human rights instrument that seeks to promote and protect human rights and basic freedoms in the African continent, offers similar protections, albeit in less detail than the previous two (Dempsey, 2006).

Using Online Speech and Press to Prosecute

In the U.S., law enforcement has used online drug information to prosecute on a few occasions. Someone was convicted of aiding phencyclidine (PCP) manufacturing in the 1980s when they took out an ad offering information on producing the drug (Miller, 1996). Miller (1996) provided a more detailed example.

> A Drug Enforcement Administration agent described the marijuana information magazine *Sinsemilla Tips* as equivalent to child pornography, and accused the publisher of 'hiding behind the first Amendment.' Unable to close the magazine by fiat, the DEA raided and harassed the magazine's advertisers, cutting off revenue the magazine needed to stay in business. Eventually the DEA threatened the publisher with criminal prosecution, but said no charges would be filed if the publisher 'voluntarily' agreed to close the magazine. The publication folded. The marijuana information magazine *High Times* was victimized by the same tactic. Drug agents explicitly told the owner of a raided garden store, 'Your advertisement in *High Times* is what got you in trouble.' (p. 39).

The Global Internet Liberty Campaign (a privacy rights watchdog that focuses on the Web) cautioned that indirect methods of control, such as the speech and press regulations mentioned above, are just as harmful as direct governmental forms. Another way that governments have tried to indirectly control Internet expression is by controlling ISPs. In Germany, however, the 1997 Information and Communications Services Act held that providers are not responsible for the content third parties provide unless they "have knowledge of such content and are technically able and can reasonably be expected to block the use of such content" (Dempsey, 2006). In the U.S., Section 230 of the Communications Decency Act prohibits treating users or providers as publishers or speakers. Filtering, rating, and labeling systems also restrict freedom of expression and limit access to information (Dempsey, 2006).

Privacy Concerns

A Global Right to Privacy

In addition to issues of speech and press, there are important privacy issues related to monitoring the posts, blogs, and e-mails of Internet users. Privacy is a fundamental human right, following the 1948 U.N. Universal Declaration of Human Rights and the 1966 International Covenant on Civil and Political Rights. At the national level, almost every country recognizes a right to privacy. Over 100 nations do this via a constitution, and 55 others afford citizens privacy rights through other legal means, such as through judicial rulings, as in the U.S. (Drozdova, 2001). Some relatively new constitutions even specify the right to access and control of one's personal data (Drozdova, 2001). The U.S. Federal Trade Commission has found, however, that the privacy policies of many Web sites do not adequately protect the privacy of consumers (Drozdova, 2001).

Public versus Private

Many forms of online activity are clearly open to the public, thus there is no reasonable expectation of privacy. Following the Electronics Communications Privacy Act of 1986, it is not illegal to view or disclose a communication if it is "readily accessible to the public" (Privacy Rights Clearinghouse, 2007). Some services feature special access passwords, which appear to make the material private. Although these are initially only read by those with access; typically anyone can record the transactions and transmit them later, as in real-time "chatting." The Supreme Court has yet to hear an e-mail privacy cases (Staples, 2000). Public postings would include messages posted on a newsgroup or forum. Other online activities can be considered "semiprivate." These are generally communications in which there is some form of security or safeguards, such as restricted users with passwords. These may seem more private, but there is still nothing prohibiting a user from copying a communication and using it elsewhere (Privacy Rights Clearinghouse, 2007).

Some chat room rules specify that participants cannot discuss illegal drug use. America Online and Microsoft both prohibit discussion of drug use. As of now, no law requires ISPs to protect users' identities or even to warn users when they have been subpoenaed to identify them. It is, however, standard practice of many of the most widely known ISPs, including Earthlink, America Online, Microsoft, and Yahoo, to inform users their identity has been revealed (Internet and First Amendment, n.d.). The USA Patriot Act has affected the way ISPs operate, however, as several provisions contain a gag rule prohibiting them from warning users of a potential investigation.

According to *United States v. Charbonneau* 979 F. Supp. (S.D. Ohio 1997), postings on American Online chat rooms are not private (Moore, 2005). Seegler and Visconte (1997) coined the term "privlic" to describe the Web, as it contains elements of being a private and a public forum. In general, case precedent seems to suggest that individuals do have an expectation of privacy with their computers. Third-party consent for a search has been accepted in cases where the computer was shared and there was no evidence of password or other forms of protection. When it has been clear that someone took measures to protect their passwords and files, courts have ruled these are private (Moore, 2005).

In the U.S., the law already clearly protects some forms of Internet communications as private. The Electronics Communications Privacy ACT (ECPA) of 1986 has two provisions: Title I prohibits the unauthorized interception and disclosure of wire, oral, and electronic communications, and Title II applies to stored communication. There are four major exceptions to Title I. ISPs may intercept, disclose, or use an electronic communication when it is necessary to protect its property interests. The business extension rule allows employers to monitor communications, providing the employer had a clear policy, the employee was informed of the policy, and the monitoring was business related. As with any search, prior consent is an exception to the prohibition. Government and law enforcement agencies can intercept and disclose electronic communications when they have a warrant or in cases of immediate foreseeable threat (Ferrera et al., 2001).

Privacy Concerns with Web Surveillance and Monitoring

According to the Global Internet Liberty Campaign, "central to free expression and the protection of privacy is the right to express political beliefs without fear of retribution and to control the disclosure of personal identity. Protecting the right of anonymity is therefore an essential goal for the protection of personal freedoms in the online world." Although some countries, such as the Netherlands and Canada, are investigating means to extend Web anonymity, other governments are limiting anonymity protections. In December 1997, the Interior and Justice Ministers of the Group of 8 (G8), an international forum for the governments of Canada, France, Germany, Italy, Japan, Russia, the U.K., and the U.S., who represent 65% of the world's economy, offered their support for requiring Internet users to identify themselves (Dempsey, 2006).

Caspar Bowden of the U.K.'s Foundation for Information Policy Research, an independent body that studies the interaction between information technology and society, cautioned that new technology used by law enforcement to deter, detect, and prosecute cybercrime has great potential to violate citizens' privacy rights. He said, "If government was in the position to know which Websites you visit, what you buy online, the e-mail addresses of those who e-mail you and those you have e-mailed, and analyze and archive that information without hindrance, there is potential for an unprecedentedly serious abuse of power" (cited in Drozdova, 2001, p. 195). This type of intrusion has already occurred in a number of countries. In Russia, the Federal Security Bureau (FSB) has implemented a surveillance system that requires all ISPs to allow regular FSB monitoring. As of 2000, many of the nation's 350 ISPs had been forced to comply with the FSB's monitoring (Drozdova, 2001).

In the U.S., there is some concern about use of the Web to monitor legitimate activity. Although monitoring of Web activity occurs frequently, most notably of employees by their employers, there is great concern about the federal government monitoring the content of sites and e-mail exchanges. They have done so, although to what degree is unknown. In 2002, the Drug Reform Coalition, a Washington, D.C.–based nonprofit agency and a major national and global network including parents, educators, students, lawyers, health care professionals, academics, and others working for drug policy reform, submitted a Freedom of Information request and found that the DEA had monitored the Web site of seventy-five reform groups to date (Erard, 2004). The U.S. Federal Bureau of Investigations (FBI) has a wiretapping system that allows them to scan millions of e-mails in just one second. The system must be connected directly to the ISP's computer networks, allowing the FBI potential to access all customers' communications (Drozdova, 2001). In addition, a screening system called Echelon, a highly secretive worldwide signals intelligence and analysis network, links computers across the world to gather, sort, and analyze huge volumes of data. The American Civil Liberties Union (ACLU) has already filed a number of suits, alleging abuses (Drozdova, 2001). In 2000, the

National Organization for the Reform of Marijuana Laws (NORML) found that the Office of National Drug Control Policy (ONDCP) had been dropping "cookies" on the hard drive of visitors to the ONDCP's frevibe.com and theantidrug.com Web sites. Cookies are computer code, typically used marketers and advertisers, to track users' preferences (St. Pierre, 2000).

The Cable Communications Policy Act of 1984 prohibits the disclosure of cable subscribers' records to law enforcement without a court order and advance notice to the customer (De Angelis, 2000). Clearly, providing advance notice to someone that their Web activity is to be monitored gives them tremendous incentive to eliminate or hide any evidence of criminal activity. The USA Patriot Act made this type of monitoring far easier by requiring ISPs to provide investigators customer profiles and Web surfing habits without a warrant or court order (Taylor, et al., 2001). Recently, Google rebuffed an attempt by the Bush administration to make them provide search-engine data on millions of customers in their effort to crack down on Internet pornography. Yahoo! and MSN complied with the order (Swartz, 2006). Interestingly, Google claims this decision was not really about protecting privacy rights, but about their refusal to provide access to trade secrets. In the U.K., cooperation between ISPs and the Association of Chief Police Officers (ACPO) has been ongoing since 1997 (Akdeniz, 2001).

Young people are especially susceptible to various forms of speech, press, and privacy monitoring. Typically, the Supreme Court sides in favor of school-based monitoring, arguing it helps protect the educational environment. Sometimes courts favor students, however. In 2006, the Springfield (Ohio) School Board reinstated eighth-grader Jessica Schoch, who had been prohibited from attending school or participating in extracurricular activities after school officials found her parody of an administrator on MySpace.com. In other similar cases, judges have ruled that students may express themselves online, including comments about their school and school employees, as long as they do not do so during class hours or with school equipment (ACLU successfully defends ..., 2006).

Why Online Privacy Matters

Garfinkel (2000) explained why online privacy is so important.

> [A]s we move into the computerized world of the twenty-first century, privacy will be one of our most important civil rights. But this right of privacy isn't the right of people to close their doors and pull down their window shades—perhaps because

they want to engage in some sort of illicit or illegal activity. It's the right of people to control what details about their lives stay inside their own homes and what leaks to the outside (p. 4).

Controlling the Web

Filtering Devices

There have been a number of non-law enforcement attempts in the U.S. to control access to controversial material on the Internet. Platform for Internet Content Selection (PICS) is a filtering device that allows Web designers to create labels that steer viewers from inappropriate sites (Greenlaw & Hepp, 1999). Users can choose to block, block and record, or receive an alert when access to an inappropriate site is attempted when they use CYBERsitter (CYBERsitter, 2001). Net Nanny is another filtering device used to block inappropriate sites, including those encouraging illegal drug use (Net Nanny, 2001). The U.S. has even proposed creating an International Cyber Police force (Drozdova, 2001).

Some pioneering organizations are using the Web to out drug dealers. For instance, Dads and Moms Against Drug Dealers (DAMMAD) started a Web site in 2001 to take anonymous tips about people manufacturing and dealing drugs. They then pass those tips on to law enforcement (Website takes on drug dealers, 2001).

Outside the U.S., nations differ dramatically in regard to the filtering of information available online. The People's Republic of China severely restricts Internet use, prohibiting all forms of dissent. Private Web sites are not allowed to publish news information without prior approval from Communist Party officials (Corn-Revere, 2002). Furthermore, China prohibits what has been called the "Seven No's:" information that goes against the Communist Party or denounces Marxism, Leninism, Mao Zedong, or Deng Xiaoping, among others. Also barred is content that," "guides people in the wrong direction, is vulgar or low" (Corn-Revere, 2002, p. 6). Singapore also maintains tight control over the Internet. ISPs are required to install filtering devices to block material the government finds objectionable. This includes sites that undermine public security, national defense, racial and religious harmony, and public morals (Corn-Revere, 2002). Countries of the Middle East, including Syria and Saudi Arabia, have similar bans on information that the government deems threatening to national security. Citizens of Syria can even be jailed for sending overseas e-mail without the government's permission. The country only has one ISP, which is run by the government (Corn-Revere, 2002). In Israel, the Jerusalem Magistrate's court ruled in 2006 that ISPs have to identify people posting anonymous "talkback" posters on Web sites if there is a concern of libel with malicious intent (Yoaz, 2006). Australia has a classification system for Internet sites. X-rated sites are prohibited, and minors cannot access R-rated sites. Subjects deemed inappropriate for minors include "suicide, crime, corruption, marital problems, emotional trauma, drug and alcohol dependency, death and serious illness, racism, and religious issues" (Corn-Revere, 2002, p. 7). An English court, in *Godfrey v. Demon Internet, Ltd.* QBD [1999], determined in 1999 that ISPs can be held liable for defamatory postings when they make newsgroups that allow these postings available (Corn-Revere, 2002).

Parents can also police the net themselves through the use of blocking devices or filters on their explorer browser. Because the Net is so widely used by young people, many advocate blocking or filtering devices. Yet, according to Protectkids.org, a clearinghouse for information on protecting kids on the Internet, only one-third of the households in the U.S. with Internet access are proactively protecting their children with filtering or blocking software. According to Friedman (2000), the software screening services like Net Nanny and Cyber Patrol are inadequate to ensure the protection of children from undesirable material on the Web. None of these blocking devices would generally filter out prescription drugs.

Theories Used to Explain Traditional Forms of Drug Use and Sales

Anomie/Strain Theories

One school of theories used to explain drug use and sales in general are those that focus on strain. Robert Merton's (1938) discussion of anomie, derived from Emile Durkheim's concept of societal anomie, posits that society ultimately discourages deviant activities. Success is emphasized to people of all socioeconomic statuses, yet all do not have institutionalized and legitimate means to achieve success. Because it is difficult for people in the lower classes to achieve success legitimately, Merton maintained some would try to achieve it through deviant means. Merton explained that people respond to this goals-means disjunction in five key ways. Some continue to try to attain the goal using legitimate means; Merton called these people conformists. Ritualists use legitimate means, but reduce their aspirations. In doing so, many take on an almost ritualistic approach to obeying the rules. Merton maintained that this response is common in lower-middle-class people who work very hard and long hours—they may never attain financial success, but are often very proud of their hard work. These two groups are unlikely to use or sell drugs. Retreatists reject the goals as well as legitimate means to achieve them. In essence, they drop out. This is the group most likely to become hardcore drug addicts or alcoholics, although they are unlikely to be drug sellers. Rebels reject the current goal of success and the means to achieve it, but unlike retreatists, they want to overthrow the existing system and replace it with new goals and new ways to achieve them. Figueira-McDonough (1983) argued that retreatists are generally more involved in drug use and innovators are the people most likely to be drug dealers. According to Merton, retreatists believe in the goal of success; they simply reject legitimate means to achieve it. Innovators may deal drugs in order to experience financial success they see as being unlikely elsewhere.

Albert Cohen (1955), much like Merton maintained that there is a lack of fit between cultural goals and the means to achieve them for those in the lower classes. Instead of discussing the goal of financial success, however, Cohen said status is the real parameter. According to Cohen, strain is more interpersonal than structural, derived largely from group interaction. Additionally, Cohen focused on school-aged youth. Like their middle-class peers, Cohen asserted that lower-class boys wanted to achieve school success. This, he said, was difficult, because middle-class people set up the schools, and those institutions follow middle-class values, structures, and procedures. In essence, schools use a middle-class measuring rod to gauge student success. Because of the difficulties in constantly trying to measure up, lower-class boys will experience status frustration and will create their own delinquent subcultures. These would be in opposition to the "respectable" middle-class values. This delinquent subculture might include drug use and drug dealing.

Cloward and Ohlin (1960) accepted the basic ideas of Merton and Cohen. That is, they also believed that legitimate opportunities for success are limited for the lower classes. In their Differential Opportunity theory, they added the concept that illegitimate opportunities for success are limited as well. Their point is that, although all individuals in the lower class have limited opportunities, some have greater opportunity to commit deviant acts. The opportunities vary by community, hence there are different types of delinquencies found in different areas. Thus, some areas become riddled with violence, while in others property crime or drug dealing is more common.

Messner and Rosenfeld (2001) extended the concepts of Merton, Cohen, and Cloward and Ohlin by maintaining it is more than just lack of opportunity that causes people to use illegal or deviant means to attain success. It is, instead, the marketing of the American Dream, which tells people that success is so important and that any means of achieving it is acceptable. The U.S. capitalist system creates a cutthroat environment. Like the innovators Merton described, some people will find the best way for them to achieve the American Dream is to deal drugs. Or, similar to the retreatists, some may reject the idea that they can ever achieve the American Dream and use drugs to cope with their perceived failure. Messner and Rosenfeld's adaptation is far more applicable to deviant activity by the middle and upper classes than are some of the other strain theories. Thus it is not just the lower classes who might use and deal drugs. In a cutthroat environment, there is tremendous pressure on those who are achieving some degree of success—the middle and upper classes—to continue doing so. Some people will turn to drugs to alleviate these pressures.

According to Robert Agnew (1992), the primary problem with Merton's strain theory is that he posited only one source of strain—the failure to achieve economic success. In his General Strain theory, Agnew maintained there are other sources of strain that are not related to economics. The removal of positively valued stimuli and the presentation of negatively valued stimuli can also cause the strain that produces deviant activities. For instance, when a loved one passes away, a positively valued stimulus has been removed. Conversely, when a new stepfather begins abusing a young person, a negatively valued stimulus has been introduced. In essence, delinquency is the result of the emotional response to negative relationships. It is the anger or frustration of coping with these strains, then, that might prompt a person to begin experimenting with drugs as a means of coping (Agnew, 1992).

Elliott Currie (1993) attempted to explain drug abuse specifically. He concluded that drug abuse is due to economic deprivation. He argued that poor people use drugs because this is one of the few ways they can attain status. In poor communities, being in the drug culture might make someone feel and seem important. Some poor people also use drugs to cope with the daily hardships they endure. Drug use also helps reduce the monotony of life. Furthermore, drugs are simply easy to obtain in these communities.

Philippe Bourgois' (1995) *In search of Respect: Selling Crack in El Barrio* described the daily life of crack sellers in New York barrios from a strain and subcultural perspective. Bourgois highlighted how the Puerto Rican males he studied wanted legitimate employment, and even dabbled in it, but lacked the skills and opportunities to make it work. Instead of being a lucrative endeavor, their crack sales (and for some, use) merely kept them from abject poverty. Most of the dealers had, with their mother's permission, dropped out of high school in order to work. They had rotated between a series of low-paying jobs before landing in the illicit drug world. Wilson (1996) documented how the loss of nearly one million jobs in the 1970s and 1980s turned many young people in the inner cities to illicit drug markets as being virtually the only remaining source of income. Others have demonstrated how young people were pushed into the illicit drug market by adults, who attempted to avoid harsher adult sanctions. Baskin, Sommers, and Fagan (2000) explained that the loss of jobs in urban areas, coupled with the rise in female-led households, rapidly increased the number of females involved in illicit drug sales. Freeman (1992) documented a 22% increase in the number of youth who determined they would earn the greatest income dealing drugs in the 1980s. Youth acknowledged they could not make similar wages in the legitimate work world (Huff, 1996). Furthermore, Li and Fagelman (1994) found that youth felt they could achieve other external rewards through drug dealing, including possession of valued material goods and the perception of respect, which they could not obtain legitimately. Although these factors sound like cost-benefit analyses more consistent with the Rational Choice theory, a framework for understanding and often formally modeling social and economic behavior, they are indicative of strain in the lives of youth who are marketed the "American dream" of success and respect.

Anomie/strain theories would seem to suggest that those buying and selling drugs online do so to alleviate some form of strain. That strain might be financial, personal, or the result of living/working in a hypercompetitive environment. It would follow that surveys inquiring why people purchased drugs online would reveal these strains of some sort. There is some support for this notion, as presented in earlier chapters, although more so for those using the Web to purchase legal drugs. Online drug buyers say they do so because the Web offers cheaper versions of drugs they need, like those in England buying cancer drugs online, although there is some debate over whether drugs purchased online are indeed less expensive. There is nothing in the literature to date to suggest illicit drugs purchased online are cheaper than those purchased on the street, however. Thus strain theories do not seem to offer anything that specifically explains online drug dealing or sales.

People are turning to prescription drugs, some of which they purchase online, to deal with their workload at school or on the job, like Critser's (2005)

Vicodin Fridays and young people using Ritalin and Adderall as a study aid. Clearly, more research is needed on people who actually make purchases via the Web to investigate whether strain is truly their motivation.

Those peddling drugs online, according to these theories, also do so because of various strains. They would be Merton's innovators, since they are seeking new ways to make money and achieve success. Again, Bourgois' (1996) research generally supported strain as a key component in drug sales in the barrio. Messner and Rosenfeld's American Dream theory is most applicable to cyberdealers. In contrast to the descriptions of cocaine dealers provided by Bourgois (1996), online dealers seem to be at least middle class. They are not selling drugs online because they absolutely need the money to live; rather, they are selling because it is another way to get ahead in an ultracompetitive culture that values financial success above everything else. Traditional forms of strain are less evident with this population, and greed seems to be a motivating factor. People who sell drug paraphernalia and products designed to cheat drug tests are also innovators. They too have seized an opportunity to make a buck (or far more) in a capitalist culture.

Anomie/strain theories are less useful in explaining online drug information such as recipes, videos of tripping, and tips for consumption. Instead of being motivated by strain, these seem to be motivated by a shared resistance to drug legislation. In reference to drug use, a rebel might be someone who is a vocal critic of the war on drugs and who sees his use as part of his rebellion. He wishes to end the war on drugs and legalize currently prohibited substances. The Web activities of groups like NORML, the forums for "cannabis activism," and other examples of content posted on sites provided in Chapter Three indicate that many site sponsors see themselves as anti-drug-war activists.

Control Theories

Control theories are different than the others presented to date in that they essentially pose a different question. Instead of asking why some people are deviant, control theorists ask why do some conform? That is, control theories presume that we all have the capability to be deviant. The most widely used, and critiqued, control theory is Travis Hirschi's (1969) Social Bond theory. Hirschi explained there are four ways people are bonded to society, and that these bonds preclude people from becoming deviant: people (1) who are attached to conventional institutions and to people with conventional ideas,

(2) who are committed to conforming, (3) who are involved in conventional activities, and (4) who believe in the basic moral value of societal values are constrained from committing deviant acts. This theory suggests that those who are more attached, involved, have greater commitments, and believe in societal values are not prone to use or sell drugs. There is quite a bit of evidence to contradict this idea, particularly when prescription drug abuse is examined.

In 1990, Hirschi teamed with Michael Gottfredson to propose the General Theory of Crime. Here, self-control is the most important factor in explaining deviance. Self-control is learned. People who are inadequately socialized fail to develop self-control. They are impulsive and insensitive, and this may lead them to deviant activities (Hirschi & Gottfredson, 2000). Hence drug use and dealing are the result of inadequate self-control.

These theories seem to fall short in explaining cyber drug purchases and dealing. The Social Bond theory suggests that the people least likely to purchase or sell online are middle class, successful people because these people tend to have the most and strongest social bonds. Yet research is demonstrating that this is precisely the profile of most online buyers and dealers, as in the case of the father-son combination who sold a variety of drugs on the web. Furthermore, stings of high-profile athletes who obtained steroids online suggest that even those with many social bonds are using the Web as a vehicle for deviance and/or crime.

Labeling Theories

Derived from symbolic interactionism, labeling theories posit that deviance is a dynamic process. That is, individuals are given labels that push them toward deviance, and at the same time, they accept these labels as part of their personal identity. The basic idea is that once an individual receives a negative label, they will likely persist and even expand their deviant activity because they will already see themselves as a deviant. Deviance becomes a self-fulfilling prophecy. Labeling theorists explain that labels usually come from those in more powerful positions—lawmakers, police, educators, social workers, and the like. Thus, wealthy, white males have more ability to apply labels, as they are more likely to hold these positions (Becker, 1963). Applied to drug use and dealing, labeling theories might posit that these people have already received some type of negative label. They then turn to drugs because they feel they cannot reject the label. For instance, a youth who has experienced repeated failure in school and who has been labeled a delinquent by school authorities may turn to drugs because he already thinks everyone believes him to be "bad."

Like Social Bond theories, labeling theories don't seem to explain online drug dealing well. If the people making the purchases and sales were largely those with less power, these theories might work. But the research presented in this book about who is doing the buying and selling reveals a different profile—that of people who tend to have a higher socioeconomic status. Labeling theories also fall short in explaining the buying and selling of items and the exchange of information on how to defraud drug tests. One could argue that users are motivated to purchase or sell these products in order to avoid a label, rather than their use being a self-fulfilling prophecy. That is, perhaps they are purchasing online because they don't want others to know of their need or addiction. Maybe they are selling online to make a few bucks without being labeled a dealer.

In sum, although the three categories of theory presented in this section are often used to explain drug use and sales, they do not seem to offer much in helping to explain drug-related crime and deviance online. The next section highlights some of the theories that may be more promising to that end.

Theories with More Potential to Explain Online Sales

Neoclassical Theories

Derived from classical criminology, Rational Choice theory asserts that criminals make a rational, conscious and at least partially informed choice to offend. In doing so, they weigh the costs they perceive would be likely from committing the offense against the benefits they perceive they would obtain. If the benefits outweigh the costs, the individual would choose to offend. The implication is that punishments can deter offenders. Classical theorists like Cesare Beccaria and Jeremy Bentham maintained that in order to have a deterrent effect, punishments must be swift, certain, and proportionate to the offense.

In regard to drug use and drug sales, the Rational Choice theory would explain that offenders might weigh the chances of apprehension, the punishment they would likely receive, the impact on their families, and other factors against the benefit they would receive by buying, selling, or using the drug. Several studies have focused on Rational Choice theories as the key explanation for drug dealing. The relative economic benefits of selling, compared against the relative likelihood of apprehension, are key in the work of Fagan and Freeman (1999), Freeman (1996), and Nagin and Paternoster (1993). One factor in the cost-benefit analysis may be simple greed—that is, sellers may not be doing so to make a basic living, but rather to make more money. This may be particularly true of online sellers. As Chapter One explained, what we know to date is that Web-based sellers seem to be a different breed than street-based sellers. Many are even doctors peddling pharmaceuticals online, as the examples cited throughout this text demonstrate. As the author was completing the final revisions on this book in May 2007, the BBC reported that big-time traffickers are starting to use the Web as a vehicle for their sales. The radio broadcast stated that the Web has allowed a 100% increase in trafficking activity by gangs and organized groups. Although it is unclear how that figure was obtained, it suggests that not only is trafficking via the Web continuing to grow but that traffickers are making a rational choice to expand their sales via this medium.

Criminologist Jack Katz (1988) proposed that traditional rational choice theories do not go far enough in explaining the benefits people see in deviant or criminal activity. Crime is often pleasurable to those who do it, and this pleasure is the primary benefit they receive. In essence, crime feels good, which is why Katz called his theory "Seductions of Crime." Katz largely studied young people who shoplift or commit acts of vandalism, where he addressed the thrill, or "bloodlust," some feel when they commit homicides. Katz did not discuss drug use in great length, but his research does show how marijuana users derive sensual pleasure only after repeated use and "mastery of new practical tasks (such as sucking in smoke and holding it down), and then only after learning how to interpret the new experiences as pleasurable" (p. 57).

Neoclassical theories can be applied to online drug dealing, as one could argue both dealers and sellers think through the costs and benefits before they buy or sell. Clearly, the development of a Web Site takes some planning, a hallmark of these theories. And buyers must go through some type of logical process when they decide to go from viewing a site to actually making a purchase.

Rational Choice theory is also helpful in explaining the detoxification industry. Tunnell (2004) explained, "The detox industry in the United States (and elsewhere) operates within the logic of capitalism—a system that rewards cost-cutting, profit-making and false-need-creating practices" (p. 95). Given the information provided in this book, it seems logical to assert that these groups perceive little risk of their activities. The chances they will be apprehended are slim, given the sheer volume of activity on the Web, the lack of training and time restrictions on police, and other factors identified in Chapter Three.

Furthermore, although it may not be correct, people purchasing drugs online seem to perceive few other risks. Despite media attention in 2006 to cases in which people who made online purchases became very ill and even died (like the Scottish woman who lost her vision), there is no suggestion of a slowdown in Web-based sales. Thus, although people could have legitimate concerns about the safety and purity of the substances they order, they seem not to.

Katz's Seductions of Crime would explain that the people posting, reading, and viewing online tips, recipes, videos, and information get an almost sensual sort of pleasure from doing so. It is perhaps like the "badass" that Katz described, in that they feel pride in slipping one over "the man" and even the consumer, in some cases. More research is needed, but anecdotally this rings true. People who watch videos of stumbling crack addicts laugh uproariously. Others who have passed a drug test due to some tip they obtained online express perverse pleasure in doing so. The confessional culture that is growing on the Web suggests that many perceive it as a social network and, as such, are using YouTube, MySpace, and similar sites to brag about their exploits or share tips with their "friends." A quick glimpse of the most popular videos on YouTube on any given day suggests how many enjoy sharing their recordings of drug activity, as the top five often includes someone tripping on something.

Social Learning Theories

The world was a far different place when Edwin Sutherland authored the first social learning theory more than 65 years ago. Yet his Differential Association theory remains applicable to a wide range of deviant and criminal activity. Sutherland posited that crime, like any other behavior, is learned. People learn the motivation to commit deviant or criminal acts, as well as how to do so—the skills and strategies needed to burgle, for example. People don't just learn from anyone with whom they are in contact, however. Deviance is learned from those with whom we have frequent and intense relationships. Furthermore, relationships we give the most priority to are the most important in teaching deviant ideas. Thus likely sources are our families and our close peers (Sutherland, 1947).

The application to drug use and dealing is obvious: people learn both to use and to deal from those with whom they have intense, frequent, and prioritized relationships. They would learn the desire to use/deal, as well as the methods of doing so. As Neff and Waite (2007) explained, "adolescent alcohol and drug use results from positive definitions of substance use acquired within a youth's social circles" (p. 112). In their research with youth incarcerated with the Virginia Department of Juvenile Justice, Neff and Waite (2007) found peer groups to be the most influential factors in explaining substance abuse.

In 1956, Daniel Glaser proposed a somewhat different type of learning theory. What is really important in explaining deviance is that we identify with people holding deviant ideas. For Glaser, it does not matter if we associate with people holding deviant ideas as long as we do not identify with them. Glaser's theory helped adapt social learning concepts to changing technologies. It helped explain how some might identify with a criminal they read about or saw or heard in some form of media but had never physically met. People might, for instance, see a famous actor they admire using or dealing drugs in a popular film and identify with the character. Thus they may choose to use or deal drugs as well. It is not clear how often this occurs, although the body of literature detailing media's effects on people's behavior continues to grow (Glaser, 1956).

Burgess and Akers (1966) accepted the basic premises of the Differential Association theory but argued it did not adequately explain the specific process of how an individual learns to be deviant. Their Differential Association-Reinforcement theory, derived from operant conditioning theory, posits that, once a person tries out a particular behavior they have learned, he or she is motivated to continue using that behavior if he or she has been rewarded for it. Conversely, punishment would prompt the individual to discontinue the behavior. Applied to drug use and dealing, someone who initially experimented with these activities would persist if they were rewarded. A reward might be, for example, a good grade on a test after using a prescription stimulant to stay up all night studying. On the other hand, if that student was caught and criminally prosecuted for taking that substance without a prescription, he or she might never do so again.

These theories explain why people buy and sell drugs online—they have learned to do so. They also explain why people might post recipes, tips, and detoxification advice. The person posting has learned from others and is sharing that information with other like-minded people. As Tunnell (2004) documented, there are numerous conventions where people can meet to share tips and market their detoxification products as well. Because cybercriminals of all types are so difficult to apprehend, people buying, selling, and exchanging drug information online may experience no obvious punishment for their activities. Online buyers receive positive reinforcement in that they obtain the drugs they were seeking. Glaser's theory is very applicable to the cases when people post online videos, pictures, or descriptions of themselves using drugs. Others see and read these things and identify with the person who posted it. Online friends are helping each other with not just the motivation but the "how-to" of drug use. Again, it is not clear how frequently this occurs.

Other Sociological Theories

Graham Sykes and David Matza (1957) proposed a theory called Techniques of Neutralization to explain the mental processes offenders go through that allow them to overcome feelings of responsibility for their actions. The key idea proposed by neutralization theory is that, despite their involvement in offending, delinquents are still invested in social norms to some degree. Thus they must use "pre-emptive self-talk" to fend off the guilt they anticipate (Topalli, 2005). Sykes and Matza developed five types of justifications: denying responsibility, denying injury, denying the victim, condemning the condemners, and appealing to higher loyalties. These justifications are viewed as valid by the offender but are not considered legitimate by the legal system or other social institutions.

Building on Anderson's (1999) *Code of the Streets*, Copes (2003) argued that street criminals—in this case, car thieves—used techniques of neutralization, but did so differently than Sykes and Matza maintained. Copes argued that street criminals used neutralizations geared toward saving face with their street associates, not to deal with guilt because they had defied conventional norms. Topalli (2005) also found support for the idea of different types of neutralizations. He explained, "For those attached to conventional society, neutralizing allows them to engage in offending without relinquishing their image of themselves as good. For those dedicated to street culture, the process allows them to drift into a state in which the pressures of criminal life can be temporarily abandoned to allow for conventional behavior without sacrificing the intrinsically valued hardcore self-concepts" (p. 823).

Drug dealers might justify their actions by saying it is not their fault—there are no other opportunities for making money in their community. Users might maintain life is so depressing they have no other choices. They are also likely to deny the victim, arguing that drug use is a victimless crime and that dealers would be out of business if there were no demand for their products. Others condemn the condemners, arguing that neither use nor sales should be prohibited. Additionally, very few people are so addicted to drugs they are constantly using. Instead, most drug users do indeed drift in and out of this type of offending. Similarly, many dealers have other work as well.

Regarding online drug dealing, it is easy to see how all parties involved use Techniques of Neutralization to justify their actions. Those buying online tell themselves that they need or desire the substances and that they are hurting no one. Those selling justify it by saying they are not making anyone buy from them—that buyers are able to make their own choices. A market economy bears all kinds of small businesses. Purveyors of detox products seem to believe that there actions should not be prohibited; rather, it is drug testing that is the problem. As noted in Chapter Two, many of the sites overtly critique the war on drugs in general. People posting tips, recipes, and detox information also deny the victim, deny the injury, and condemn the condemners, often using language highly derogatory to the piss police. The reliance on Techniques of Neutralization was also clear in the interviews Tunnell (2004) conducted for *Pissing on demand*.

Conflict Theories

Coming from the work of Karl Marx, conflict theories posit that deviance has to do with the imbalances in society between the haves and have-nots. This imbalance is somewhat inherent in a capitalist system, depending on which specific conflict theorist one consults. Some make and apply laws, while others have little ability to do so. Thus those in more powerful positions are able to criminalize more of the activities of the lower classes while ignoring their activities that cause harm. When they are subject to application of laws, as in the case of a murder allegation (since even the wealthy supposedly cannot get away with murder without at least a trial), those with more power are able to use their resources to evade punishment or to receive minimal punishment. Conversely, those with less power lack these resources and generally must face the full punishment possible (Chambliss & Seidman, 1971).

Conflict theories are useful in explaining why application of drug laws has focused largely on poor minorities. Those in power can and do focus attention on use and sales by "the other" as another means of maintaining their power. When someone from the more affluent classes is caught violating these laws, conflict theory helps explain why their punishment tends to be far less. They have all the resources to assist them in the legal arena. Conflict theorists would explain that those with the power to make and enforce drug laws do so in a way that minimizes the kind of use and sales they are more likely involved in—that is, prescription drug abuse, doling out drugs with no prescription, etc.

Conflict theories help explain why online selling is such a huge business. If the people that are making and enforcing drug laws are some of the same ones who are buying and selling online, they have little incentive to really police it like they would a crack house in a poor neighborhood. As Tunnell (2004) noted, many of the purveyors of detox products see their job as somehow "fooling the man," a type of resistance of the status quo and the powers that be. The Web is a source of counter-hegemony.

Understanding Drug Testing

Outside the classics in criminology, there are other theories that help explain the rise in drug testing and, by extension, the responses to it.

The Panopticon and Surveillance

Jeremy Bentham's idea of the Panopticon also helps explain how drug testing is supposed to work. The Panopticon was a design for a prison in which prisoners could be constantly watched from a central tower. Yet another part of the design was the inclusion of blinds so that the prisoners would not actually know if they were being watched. The idea was that they would have to behave as if they were being watched at all times, as they did not know precisely when it would happen. Thus those in power were able to assert their power without force or resistance. Applied to drug testing, the idea is that people will not use drugs because they believe at any time they might have to submit a sample for testing. In essence, drug testing leads to self-control and obedience. The detoxification industry exists because not everyone will be so easily controlled or so obedient.

Weber and Bureaucracy

Max Weber proposed that modern society is increasingly rationalized. Rationalization involves reliance on science, rather than traditions and faith, to answer major questions. Furthermore, progress is seen as inevitable and, more importantly, a good thing. A major feature of rationalization is the rise of bureaucracy. Bureaucratic institutions are characterized by a division of labor, hierarchical power, impersonal relationships, and a focus on quantity, among other qualities. Activities are increasingly routinized. Drug testing is increasingly a part of these bureaucratic institutions. It is impersonal, routinized, and mandated by those highest in the hierarchy but often not expected of them. Invariably, some will resist the bureaucratization—in this case, these are the people who are cheating or deceiving the tests.

Foucault and Disciplinary Power

Michel Foucault (1979) posited that disciplinary power is a characteristic of the modern era. Unlike traditional power that is unidirectional in that it is used by some to control others, disciplinary power is bidirectional. Individuals may freely submit to this type of control, as in the case of employees who believe in drug testing, and are happy to submit their sample. This type of power is rarely physical. Instead, it involves control of knowledge and of the mind. Tunnell (2004) explained how Foucault's ideas apply to drug testing: "drug testing uses knowledge of the body to extract information about the body, which is then used to assess and, if need be, discipline the body (and in some cases mind, spirit, and livelihood)" (p. 109). Disciplinary power is applied through highly ritualized procedures. These help serve those with power because others within the hierarchy observe them, which Foucault called hierarchical observation. For instance, students can see the others who have been randomly selected to submit to a drug test and learn the importance of and how to submit their urine sample. Additionally, disciplinary power creates what Foucault called normalizing judgments. There is a continuum of acceptable behavior, and individuals are judged against this standard. Hence, the urine sample is judged against a dichotomy of being false or positive, and the positive result categories someone into the category of drug user.

Disciplinary power can be both repressive and productive. This, according to Foucault, is why it persists. If it was completely repressive, there would be more resistance. Again, individuals who are subject to drug testing may believe that drugs are bad and that use at work, in school, the military, and the like, is harmful, and thus they may submit to testing because they feel it furthers important social values.

Postmodern Surveillance

Staples (2000) explained that the current drug war is a form of postmodern surveillance. He identifies four qualities of postmodern surveillance: (1) it is largely technology-based, methodological, automatic, and sometimes anonymously applied, and they usually generate a permanent record of evidence, (2) it often targets and treats the body as an object that can be watched, assessed, and manipulated, (3) it is often local, operating in our everyday lives, and (4) local or not, it brings wide-ranging populations, not just the official "deviant," under control (p. 11). "The technique evokes the legitimacy of science and technical objectivity as it disassociates the client's surveillance from any particular individual. That is, it would appear that you are not really being tested by 'the boss,' supervisor, or your probation officer, but rather by the scientific 'magic' of the test kit and the laboratory" (Staples, 2000, p. 98).

His ideas about drug testing are summed up nicely in the following paragraph.

> I see drug testing, much like the electronic monitoring device, as an extraordinary example of a postmodern meticulous ritual of power ... Urine analyses can be administered effectively anywhere; an offender need not be institutionalized to be watched and monitored. It provides instant knowledge of an individual's behavior, and codes a complex set of activities into simple 'yes' and 'no' categories. The device is light-weight and efficient; there is little need to collect heavy dossiers or engage in long interrogations in search of evidence or a confession. And, again, since traces of most drugs (with the exception of marijuana) are present for only one to three days after use, random rather than scheduled testing is often justified. Random screening has the effect of making this form of surveillance operate 'panoptically,' since individuals never know when they might be tested (Staples, 2000, p. 97).

Conclusions and Predictions

In sum, there are numerous difficulties in understanding and policing online drug sales. Although some of the theories presented in this chapter hold promise for explaining the cyberdrug trade, none of them have been tested through research. Clearly, there is great opportunity for researchers. Policy has not kept pace with the volume of trade, and police training to deal with the issue is still inadequate. Global cooperation is hampered by differences in law and philosophy as well as sheer logistics. Texts devoted to global drug enforcement, such as Lee's (2004), barely include online sales. They tend to stress use of informants and surveillance. Although these things are applicable to the Web, they surely take on a different context. The section on electronic surveillance does not even discuss Internet-based surveillance. Lee (2004) even commented, "There is no substitute for traditional, hands-on surveillance" (p. 97). Censorship of the Web would help limit the amount of material available for sale, but at what price?

The Cyber War on Drugs

It should be clear by now that it is unlikely that the exchange of drugs, drug-related products, and prodrug information will end or even be reduced soon. Indeed, all forms of cybercrime seem to be on the rise. In late 2006, the *Miami Herald* reported an increase in cybercrime in general, dubbing it the "Year of the cyber crook." This, they say, is due to an unprecedented amount of spam. The volume of spam grew 60% in October and November of 2006 alone (Krebs, 2006). Although many people point to spam as a factor in cyberforms of deviance and crime, this has not been studied in any systematic sense.

It seems likely that buying drugs and finding information about drugs online will become even easier. As noted elsewhere, as this book was in the final stages of writing in summer of 2007, the DEA announced a dramatic increase of Web-based drug trafficking. More people are becoming regular Internet users, and even young people are designing Web Sites. Use of MySpace, Facebook, and YouTube has all exploded. There is no reason to believe that all of these people will avoid creating and visiting sites purveying drugs. As new technologies are developed, cyberentrepreneurs can more easily evade detection or at least apprehension. The disparity between the skills, knowledge, and confidence of the current generation and older -generations will also play a role. Law enforcement will always trail behind the rapidly growing ranks of young Web-savvy entrepreneurs, just as many academics lack any semblance of the skills possessed by their students. This is especially true given the nature of training for law enforcement. Police academy trainees laugh when asked if they received any training about cybercrime or online drug dealing. It simply is not, nor is it likely to be, a major feature of the academy. As was clear in Chapter Three, the vast majority of law enforcement officers receive little or no training about cybercrime ever, even beyond the academy. Clearly there are cyberunits in larger law enforcement agencies and at the state and federal levels, as described in this book, but they cannot possibly compete with the vastness of the Web.

There is no absence of agencies that could possibly deal with cyberdrug dealing in the U.S., but that is part of the problem. Too many cooks spoil the broth, as the saying goes. Lack of clarity in laws, jurisdiction, and strategies will surely hamper policing online drug sales. Furthermore, although there is grave danger that many Americans are willing to forego their civil liberties in the name of so-called homeland security, many are very protective of their right to free speech and press on the Web. This makes it unlikely that legislation restricting online sales, information, and videos will be a major issue. As noted in this book, the issue is far more complex because of the global nature of the Web. In an era in which the image of the U.S. is perhaps more negative than ever before, cooperation between nations is hardly a given.

Drug testing continues to expand. More employers, more schools, and more parents are doing some form of testing and are requiring samples from greater numbers of people. Because there will be more drug tests required, there will be more people posting tips on how to beat the tests, and more entrepreneurs offering shampoos, prosthetics, and other schemes to cheat the tests. In a free market economy, it must be expected that innovative entrepreneurs will seize new technologies to develop their niche. As the stakes increase and states make laws requiring testing for adulterants, these entrepreneurs will simply craft other products like the Whizzinator. It's a bladder cop arms race of sorts.

Because many online buyers are seeking prescription drugs, traditional mechanisms of the war on drugs are not very effective. These drugs cannot be prohibited per se, as they have legitimate functions (of course, many argue that all drugs do, but this is not the prevailing logic of lawmakers). Indeed, as Critser (2005) documented, the prescription drug industry is only growing. If more prescription drugs are out there, more people will look to all kinds of sources to make their purchases. Hotspot policing and other modern methods of policing drug sales, like weed and seed, are not terribly effective with prescription drugs. Many drug tests do not detect these substances (or do but are not included as part of the assessment).

Given that online sales are likely to continue if not expand, what should be done? Because law enforcement has essentially admitted that the Web is not policeable, one recommendation is that we believe them. Sure, they have had some small successes, like those described in Chapter Three. But these pale in comparison to the amount of illegal and material on the Web.

One option, the one supported here, is that little policing should be done that is specific to the Web. Nothing to do with policing the Web will address the demand people have to alter their consciousness. Policing the Web, if it is possible, would need to be a largely supply-side intervention. This is true in large part of the entire War on Drugs. In general, the U.S. has not done a particularly good job of figuring out what prompts some to so readily seek to escape their lives through drugs, whereas others have absolutely no interest in doing that. It is far more than a dichotomous moral issue, whereby those who use and sell drugs believe it is OK and nonusers pass judgment. Many are in favor of widespread decriminalization and even legalization of many substances yet have never and likely will never try.

A tremendous part of the so-called drug problem in this country is that we are, as Sullum (2003) pointed out, a drug culture. We are encouraged to drug ourselves (either literally or via druglike addictions to television, the Internet, consumption, and the like) virtually nonstop. How can we expect that people will resist drugs when they are pushed from every angle? The Web makes that push even greater, and it continues to normalize drug use and even abuse.

Furthermore, Americans want a quick fix for every ailment or issue in our lives. When we go to a doctor, we want a diagnosis and something—a pill, typically—to make it better. As Tunnell (2004) noted, "Myopic consumers like nothing more than bottled miracles" (p. 95). We want to make a quick dollar, not necessarily to wait it out for the long haul and eke out a profit. We seek immediate payoff and expect everything to happen fast. For instance, students have reported throwing out their home computers because they are "too slow." We want to be able to do all our shopping in one place and we want it cheap, too—we could call this the Wal-Mart effect. On the Web, perhaps it can be called the amazon.com effect. We want people to be able to find information and make purchases online with ease. Why would we believe people will not sell drugs or detoxification products online, when you could, until recently, buy a kidney or someone's virginity on e-Bay?

In sum, one could argue nothing should be done to police the Web for drug sales, drug information, and detoxification products. It is fair to continue enforcing existing laws when packages are intercepted, for instance at Customs, but we should not devote extra attention or manpower to that endeavor. Some argue stricter postal, airport, and border controls would significantly reduce drug trafficking, as the drugs (besides those produced domestically) must enter the country somehow. As this book has shown, however, the effort it would take, not to mention the potential for greater racial profiling and civil liberties violations, to up the number and quality of inspections at borders, airports, and post offices would be enormous.

It is also fair to punish doctors found violating laws involving prescription drugs, but again, we should not devote additional law enforcement resources to this. Instead, we could make better use of pharmacy boards and other organizations, allowing them to police themselves. Some organizations do this already, although more can. Sure, they may have a vested interest in prescription drugs, but one could argue law enforcement also have a vested interest in apprehending criminals—job security. We should leave the subjects of online paraphernalia, detoxification products, and information alone. These are only problematic if we believe in the tenets of the war on drugs and drug testing. If the U.S. scaled back drug testing significantly, fewer detoxification products and tips would be available because they would not be perceived as necessary. Perhaps then the creativity exemplified by the material in Chapter Five could be channeled elsewhere!

What is recommended is harm reduction. It is our responsibility as humans to share information with others and let them decide how to use it. Following Rational Choice theory, we can inform people about the dangers of online drug sales and the harms of drugs on their bodies. Tunnell (2004) argued this point as well. He said, "Rational Choice theory also highlights the importance of making informed decisions, meaning that decision makers should possess all the information necessary for making logical and rational choices" (p. 97). His point, however, was that most consumers know little about their own bodies or about the "hocus-pocus of detox products used for negating drug tests" (p. 97). Yet this does not mean we should prohibit those substances or the sites providing detoxification information. Instead, like the Google bombing described earlier, perhaps we should inundate the Web with all kinds of real and factual information so that it appears first in users' Internet searches. Then we could bank on the laziness of most of us, knowing that we would be most likely to read the first few, not the 800th, link that appears.

Along with helping to inform people's choices, we can work on reducing and even eliminating other social problems that contribute to excessive drug use. For instance, if we were to guarantee everyone the right to free healthcare, then perhaps people would not need to search the Web for assorted methods of self-medication. Following strain theory, if we were to alter social conditions such that fewer people felt the strains that prompted them to use and deal drugs, online sales would be a nonissue.

These conclusions may not be palatable to some, but that is OK. In fact, some may say that these conclusions render this book useless—if online sales don't really matter, why should people read this? Yet a lot can be gained from investigating new manifestations of an existing social problem. Like this author, perhaps others will learn about online sales and realize there are other ways we can handle them, as well as drugs in general, than strict prohibition. The time, manpower, and funds devoted to the War on Drugs should not be expanded but rather redirected to more underlying social problems, like poverty, racism, and inadequate education. It is the author's hope that this book prompts thought, dialogue, and action toward that end.

REFERENCES

Abuse of prescription drugs seen as global problem (2006, March 3). *Join Together Online.* Retrieved July 24, 2007 from www.jointogether.org

ACLU successfully defends student's free speech. (2006, April 27). Young girl who created fake MySpace profile will go back to school. ACLU of Ohio. Retrieved July 29, 2007 from www.acluohio.org/pressreleases/2006

Adderall preferred by college students who misuse prescription ADD meds. (2006, October). *Joint Together Online.* Retrieved October 30, 2006 from www.jointogether.org

Agnew, R. (1992). Foundation for a general strain theory of crime and delinquency. *Criminology,* 30, 47–87.

Akdeniz, Y. (2001). Controlling illegal and harmful content on the Internet. In Wall, D. (Ed.). *Crime and the Internet* (pp. 113–140). London: Routledge.

Albrecht, H. (2001). The international system of drug control: Developments and trends. In Gerber, J., & Jensen, E. (Eds.). *Drug war American style* (pp. 49–60). New York: Routledge.

American Bar Association. (1987). *Report on computer crime.* Chicago: American Bar Association.

Amon, M. (2003, August 14). Data show blacks pulled over at disproportionate rate. *Washington Post* [online version]. Retrieved September 8, 2007 from www.washingtonpost.com

Anderson, E. (1999). *Code of the streets.* Chicago: University of Chicago Press.

Andreas, P. (1995). U.S. policies at cross purposes in Latin America. *Third World Quarterly,* 16(1).

Armentano, P., & Shea, D. (2003, March 19). A look at the historical legal basis for urine testing. *NORML.* Retrieved December 19, 2006 from www.norml.org

Athlete Incident centers on drug-test cheat product. (2005, May 13). *Join Together Online.* Retrieved July 29, 2007 from www.jointogether.org

Attorney General Greg Stumbo announces KBI to train other law enforcement to fight Internet drug trafficking. (2007, February. 12). *States News Service.* Retrieved September 8, 2007 from LexisNexis Academic database.

Baker, S. (2005, February 17). Don't fear the blog and the fury. *Business Week* [online version]. Retrieved February 11, 2007 from www.businessweek.com

Barboza, D. (2006, March 8). 110 million surfers can buy sex and drugs, but reform isstill illicit. *The New York Times*, C1.

Barrett, N. (1997). *Digital crime: Policing the cybernation*. London: Kogan Page Ltd.

Baskin, D., Sommers, I., & Fagan. J. (2000). *Workin' hard for the money: The social and economic lives of women drug dealers*. Huntongton, NY, Nova Science Press.

Bawden, A. (May 15, 2000). Euphoria online. *Business Week* [online version]. Retrieved July 20, 2007 from www.businessweek.com/2000/00_20/

Bean, P. (2001). American influence on British drug policy. In Gerber, J., & Jensen, E. (Eds.). *Drug war American style* (pp. 79–96). New York: Routledge.

Becker, H. (1963). *Outsiders: Studies in the sociology of deviance*. New York: The Free Press.

Bequai, A. (1987). *Techno–crimes*. Lexington, MA: D.C. Heath and Co.

BlackBerrys "can damage thumb." (2005, January 31). *BBC News* [online version]. Retrieved September 8, 2007 from www.news.bbc.co.uk

Blake, L. (2005, September 22). Ordering online is the best way of getting steroids. *Ezine Articles*. Retrieved October 20, 2005 from www.ezinearticles.com

Boehm, E., Holmes, B., Bishop, L., & McAuley, S. (2003, January 13). Who buys prescription drugs online? Retrieved August 17, 2006 from www.forrester.com

Boire, R.G. (2002). *Sacred mushrooms & the law*. Berkeley, CA: Ronin.

Bouley, E. (2001). The drug war in Latin America: Ten years in a quagmire. In Gerber, J., & Jensen, E. (Eds.). *Drug war American style* (pp. 169–196). New York: Routledge.

Boyer, E., Shannon, M., & Hibberd, P. (2001). Web sites and misinformation about illicit drugs. *New England Journal of Medicine*, 345, 469–471.

Bourgois, P. (1995). *In search of respect: Selling crack in El Barrio*. New York: Cambridge University Press.

Breen, T. (2007, August 23). No prescription? No problem. *Forbes* [online version]. Retrieved September 8, 2007 from www.forbes.com

Broad drug testing adopted in Kansas town. (2006, September 13). Accessed July 27, 2007 from 4therapy.com

Brunker, M. (2005, January 20). Steroid dealers use ruse to sell wares on eBay. *MSNBC* [online version]. Retrieved September 8, 2007 from www.msnbc.com

Burgess, R., & Akers, R. (1966). A differential association-reinforcement theory of criminal behavior. *Social Problems*, 14, 128–147

Bush's drug-testing plan debated by schools. (2004, January 26). *Join Together Online*. Retrieved July 27, 2007 from www.jointogether.org

Buying Drugs Online. (2004). Retrieved October 28, 2005 from www.thesite.org/drinkanddrugs/drugsafety/thelaw/buyingdrugsonline.html

Calif. Reports rising DMX abuse among adolescents. (2006, December 6). *Join Together Online*. Retrieved December 8, 2006 from www.jointogether.org

Calman, B. (2006, October 27). This graduate died after inadvertently drinking the date rape drug GHB. *Daily Mail* (London) [Online edition], p. 42. Retrieved April 10, 2007.

Carpico, M. (2003, February 19). Boards considering revising drug testing proposal. *Pittsburgh Post-Gazette*, p. N6. Retrieved August 21, 2006 from LexisNexis Academic database.

Carpenter, T., & Vasquez, I. (2005). The international war on drugs. *CATO handbook for Congress*, 6th ed. Retrieved June 25, 2007 from www.cato.org/pubs/handbook/hb/109/hb_109.60.pdf

Carter, D., & Katz, A. (1998). Computer crime victimization: An assessment of criminality in cyberspace. *Police Research Quarterly*, 1(1).

REFERENCES

Casey, E. (2000). *Digital evidence and computer crime: Forensic science, computers, and the Internet.* New York: Academic Press.
CATO Institute. (2007). CATO Handbook for 108th U.S. Congress Washington, D.C.: CATO Institute.
Caulfield, S. (2000). Creating peaceable schools. *AAPS Annual,* 56, 170–185.
Chambliss, W., & Seidman, R. (1971). *Law, order, and power.* Reading, MA: Addison-Wesley.
Cloward, R., & Ohlin, L. (1960). *Delinquency and opportunity.* New York: The Free Press.
Cohen, A. (1955). *Delinquent boys: The culture of the gang.* Glencoe, IL: The Free Press.
Colvin, R. (1995). *Prescription drug abuse: The hidden epidemic.* Omaha, NE: Addicus Books.
Copes, H. (2003). Societal attachments, offending frequency, and techniques of neutralization. *Deviant Behavior,* 24, 101–127.
Corn-Revere, R. (2002, July 24). Caught in the seamless Web: Does the Internet's Global reach justify less freedom of speech? *CATO Institute Briefing Papers,* 71.
Court gives more latitude to drug dog searches (2005, April 4). *Join Together.* Retrieved July 23, 2007 from www.jointogether.org
Crackdown on online steroid sales. (2007). *4Therapy.* Retrieved September 10, 2007 from www.4therapy.com
Cramer, R. (2005, May 17). Drug tests: Products to defraud drug use screening tests are widely available. *GAO Report.* Retrieved December 15, 2006 from www.gao.gov/htext/d05653t.htm
Critser, G. (2005). *Generation Rx.* Boston, MA: Houghton-Mifflin.
Crowley, B. (2004). Lower prescription drug costs don't tell the whole story. Retrieved August 29, 2006 from www.aims.ca/library/prl1.pdf
Cuomo, C. (2006, March 9). Pharm country: Internet prescriptions. *Nightline—ABC News transcripts.* Retrieved March 22, 2006 from Lexis Nexis database.
Curley, B. (2005, September 9). Survey finds little change in U.S. drug use. *Join Together Online.* Retrieved September 8, 2007 from www.jointogether.org
Currie, E. (1993). *Reckoning: Drugs, the cities, and the American future.* New York: Hill & Wang.
Daley, W. (n.d.). Falling through the Web: Defining the digital divide. Retrieved December 27, 2007 from www.ntia.gov
Davies, D. (1998). Criminal law and the Internet: The investigator's perspective. In Walker, C. (Ed.). *Crime, criminal custice, and the Internet. Criminal Law Review,* special edition. London: Sweet and Maxwell.
Davis, H. (2003, November 13). One-click shopping for illegal drugs. *Penn Current Online.* Retrieved November 1, 2005 from www.upenn.edu/pennnews/current/2003/111303/research.html
Davis, T. (2005). *Anabolic steroids are easily purchased without a prescription and present significant challenges to law enforcement officials.* Washington, D.C.: U.S. Government Accountability Office.
DEA exhibit linking drugs and terrorism criticized (2006, August 14). Join Together Online. Retrieved July 23, 2007 from www.jointogether.org
DEA leads largest steroid bust in history. (2005, December 15). Retrieved July 27, 2007. from www.mesomorphosis.com/articles/government/dea-steroid-bust-of-mexican-steroid-makers.html
DEA says misuse of cough syrup/soft drink mix on rise. (2006, October 23). *Join Together Online.* Retrieved October 24, 2006 from www.jointogether.org
DEA steroid bust expands strategy of attacking trafficking via Internet. (2005, December 31). *Narcotics Enforcement & Prevention Digest,* 1–2.

De Angelis, G. (2000). *Cyber crimes*. Philadelphia, PA: Chelsea House.

DeKeiffer, D. (2006, June). The Internet and the globalization of counterfeit drugs. *Journal of Pharmacy Practice*, 19(3), 171–178.

Delaware stores found selling crack supplies. (2005, December 1). *Join Together Online*. Retrieved July 27, 2007 from www.jointogether.org

Dempsey, J. (2006). Freedom of expression on the Internet. *Human Rights Watch*. Retrieved September 8, 2007 from www.hrw.org

Diller, L. (1998). *Running on Ritalin*. New York: Bantam.

Dorschner, J. (2006, December 24). Click when sick. *Miami Herald*, E1-2.

Doyle, P. (2005, November 6). Journey to the underworld. Retrieved September 8, 2007 from www.ergogenics.com

Drozdova, E. (2001). Civil liberties and security in cyberspace. In Sofaer, A., & Goodman, S. (Eds.). *The transnational dimension of cyber crime and terrorism* (pp. 183–220). Stanford, CA: Hoover Institute Press.

Drug free workplace. (2002). Washington, D.C: Office of National Drug Control Policy.

Drug paraphernalia. (n.d.). *U.S. Drug Enforcement Agency*. Retrieved December 16, 2006 from www.dea.gov/concern/paraphernaliafact.html

Drug paraphernalia. (2006, June). *Wikipedia: The free encyclopedia*. Retrieved December 16, 2006 from www.wikipedia.org/wiki/Drug_paraphernalia

Drugs, phishing top 2004 list of spam terms. (2004, December 29). *Join Together Online*. Retrieved January 27, 2006 from www.jointogether.org

Drug sales soaring online. (2005, February 3). *Join Together Online*. Retrieved October 20, 2005 from www.jointogtheronline.com

Drug tampering guidance on the Internet: Hospital admissions are rising as details of prescription misuse are shared online. *Nursing Standard*, 20(50), 16.

Drug testing can be discriminatory, judge rules. (2006, June 30). CBC News. Accessed from www.cbc.ca/money/story/2006/06/30/ on July 27, 2007.

Drug tests for teen licenses. (2005, February 14). *Join Together Online*. Retrieved September 8, 2007 from www.jointogether.org

Duke, S., & Gross, A. (1993). *America's longest war: Rethinking our tragic crusade against drugs*. NY: G.P. Putnam's Sons.

Dwyer, M. (2005, October 24). Sinners in cyberspace. *MacLeans*, 118(43), 56–58.

Erard, M. (2004, October). How the government lost the drug war in cyberspace. *Reason* [Online edition]. Retrieved November 10, 2006 from www.reason.com/news/show/29264.html

Erickson, P., & Haans, D. (2001). Drug war, Canadian style. In Gerber, J., & Jensen, E. (Eds.). *Drug war American style* (pp. 121–148). New York: Routledge.

Europe: England to drug test arrested burglars and muggers. (2005, December 2). *Stop the Drug War*. Retrieved December 19, 2006 from www.stopthedrugwar.org/chronicle/413/ukdrugtests.shtml

Fagan, J., & Freeman, R. (1999). Crime and work. In Tonry, M. (Ed.). *Crime and justice: A review of research* (pp. 225–290). Chicago: University of Chicago Press.

Featherstone, L. (1999, June 21). Hot-wiring high school: Student activists across the country experiment with organizing by Internet. *The Nation*, 268(23), 15.

Ferrera, G., Lichtenstein, S., Reder, M., August, R., & Schiano, W. (2001). *Cyberlaw: Your rights in cyberspace*. Cincinnati, OH: Thompson Learning.

Fields-Meyer, T. (2000). He just said no. *People Weekly*, 54(8), 77–78.

Figueira-McDonough, J. (1983). On the usefulness of Merton's anomie theory: Academic failure and deviance among high school students. *Youth and Society*, 14, 259–279.

Finley, L.L., & Finley, P.S. (2005). *Piss off!: how drug testing and other privacy violations are alienating America's youth*. Monroe, ME: Common Courage Press.

Fish, M. (2007, March 27). Bonds lawyer acknowledges public perception. *ESPN* [Online version]. Retrieved September 8, 2007 from www.sports.espn.go.com/mlb/news

Florida county evaluates portable drug test for students. (2004, March 10). *Join Together Online*. Accessed July 27, 2007 from www.jointogether.org

Florida drug tourism. (2006, December 7). *Join Together Online*. Retrieved December 8, 2006 from www.jointogether.org

Foucault, M. (1979). *Discipline and punish*. New York: Vintage.

Fox, S. (2004, October 10). Prescription drugs online. *Pew Internet and American Life Project*. Retrieved June 26, 2006 from www.pewinternet.org

Freeman, V. (1996). Why do so many young men commit crimes and what might we do about it? *Journal of Economic Perspectives*, 10, 25–42.

Friedman, S. (2000). *Children and the World Wide Web: Tool or trap?* Lanham, MD: University Press of America.

Frith, M. (2006, April 18). My Pills.co.uk. *The Independent* (London), p. 36.

Garfinkel, S. (2000). *Database nation: The death of privacy in the 21st century*. Sebastopol, CA: O'Reilly and Associates.

Gaul, G., & Flaherty, M. (2003, October 20). Internet trafficking in narcotics has surged. *Washington Post* [Online version]. Retrieved April 10, 2007.

Gaylord, M. (2001). Hong Kong. In Gerber, J., & Jensen, E. (Eds.). *Drug war American style* (pp. 61–78). New York: Routledge.

Gerber, J., & Jensen, E. (2001). The internationalization of U.S. policy on illicit drug control. In Gerber, J., & Jensen, E. (Eds.). *Drug war American style* (pp. 1–18). New York: Routledge.

GHB. (2007, May 8). *Project GHB*. Retrieved May 8, 2007 from www.projectghb.org/what_is_ghb.html

Gillen, M., & Garrity, B. (2002). Industry's anti-priacy efforts 'doomed to fail,' says Forester. *Billboard*, 112(40), 9–11.

Gilliom J. (1994). *Surveillance, privacy, and the law*. Chicago: University of Chicago Press.

Girls arrested for pretending parsley was pot (2005, December 1). *Join Together Online*. Retrieved July 23, 2007 from www.jointogether.org

Glaser, D. (1956). Criminality theories and behavioral images. *American Journal of Sociology*, 61, 433–444.

Goldberg, L., et al. (2003). Drug testing athletes to prevent substance abuse: Background and pilot study results of the SATURN (Student athletes testing using random notification) study. *Journal of Adolescent Health*, 32, 16–25.

Goldberg, M. (1999, July 22–28). World wide weed. *Metro Active*. Retrieved November 1, 2005 from www.metroactive.com/papers/metro/07.22.99/cover/marijuana-9929.html

Gombos, J. (1998, March 15). Drug testing FAQ: Fooling the bladder cops. Retrieved September 8, 2007 from www.erowid.org

Gordon, S., Forman, R., & Siatkowski, C. (2006). Knowledge and use of the Internet as a source of controlled substances. *Journal of Substance Abuse Treatment*, 30(3), 271–271.

Grabosky, P., & Smith, R. (2001). Telecommunications fraud in the digital age. In Wall, D. (Ed.). *Crime and the Internet* (pp. 29–43). London: Routledge.

Green, L. (1996). *Policing places with drug problems*. Thousand Oaks, CA: Sage.

Greenlaw, R., & Hepp, E. (1999). *In-line/on-line: Fundamentals of the Internet and the World Wide Web*. McGraw-Hill: Boston, MA.

Greenwood, M. (2003, April 1). False positives. *Fire Chief*, *1*, p. 4. Retrieved July 28, 2003 from LexisNexis Academic database.
Griffin, S., Keller, A., & Cohn, A. (2001, Winter). Developing a drug testing policy at a public university: Participant perspectives. *Public Personnel Management*, 30(4), 467.
Grow, B., Elgin, B., & Weintraub, A. (2006, December 18). Bitter pills: More and more people are buying prescription drugs from shady online marketers. *BusinessWeek* [Online edition], p. 110.
Hair tests unfair, black officers say. (2005, August 25). *Join Together Online*. Retrieved July 27, 2007 from www.jointogether.org
Halpern, J., & Pope, H. (2001, March). Hallucinogens on the Internet: A vast new source of underground drug information. *American Journal of Psychiatry*, 158(3), 481.
Hansen, S. (2003, April 30). Virginia law spam, with fraud, a felony. *New York Times*.
Haney, C., & Zimbardo, P.G. (1998). The past and future of U.S. prison policy. Twenty-five years after the Stanford Prison Experiment. *American Psychologist*, 53(7), 709–727.
Hansell S. (2003, July 28). Diverging estimates of the costs of spam. *New York Times*. Accessed July 26, 2007 from http://www.nytimes.com/2003/07/28/technology/28SPAM.html
Harrison, P. M., & Beck, A. J. (2005). *Prisoners in 2004. Bureau of Justice Statistics Bulletin*. Washington, DC: US Department of Justice.
Hawkins, D. (1999, May 31). Trial by vial. *U.S. News and World Report*, 162(21), 70–73.
Health, E. (2004, March 1). Internet pharmacies targeted in crackdown of drug abuse. *CongressDaily*, 7–9.
Herper, M. (2005, May 23). Bad medicine. *Forbes*, 202.
Hickman, M. (2006, June 22). "Russian roulette" of buying prescription drugs on the Internet. *The Independent* [online version]. Retrieved June 26, 2006 from http://news.independent.co.uk/uk/health_medical/article1094701.ece
Hiller, J., & Cohen, R. (2002). *Internet law and policy*. Upper Saddle River, NJ: Prentice Hall.
Hinkel, J. (2000, January–February.). Buying drugs online: Convenient and private, but beware of "rogue sites." *U.S. Food and Drug Administration*. Available at www.fda.gov/fdac/features/200/100_online.html
Hirschi, T. (1969). *The causes of delinquency*. Berkeley, CA: University of California Press.
Hirschi, T., & Gottfredson, M. (2000). In defense of self-control. *Theoretical Criminology*, 4, 55–69.
Hitchcock, J. (2002). *Net Crimes and misdemeanors*. Medford, NJ: Information Today, Inc.
Hoffman, A. (1987). *Steal this urine test: Fighting drug hysteria in America*. New York: Penguin.
Holahan, C. (2006, April 23). Prescription for disaster; Illegal net drug dealers putting lives on the line. *The Record* (Bergen County, NJ), p. F01.
Holtorf, K. (1998). *Ur-ine trouble*. Scottsdale, AZ: Vandalay.
Hubbard, W. (2004, March 18). Statement before United States Food and Drug Administration. Retrieved October 28, 2005 from: www.fda.gov/ola/2004/internetdrugs0318.html
Hudson, D. (2006, January 5). Blogging: Overview. *First Amendment Center*. Retrieved March 7, 2006 from www.fac.org/speech/internet/topic
Huff, C. (1996). The criminal behavior of gang members and none-gang at-risk youth. In C. Huff (Ed.) *Gangs in America* (pp. 75–102). Thousand Oaks, CA: Sage.
Hutchinson, A. (2004). The war on drugs is succeeding. In Roleff, T. (Ed.). *The war on drugs: Opposing viewpoints* (pp. 17–25). San Diego, CA: Greenhaven Press.
Hyde, M. (1990). *Drug wars*. NY: Walker and Co.
Illicit internet prescription drug sales booming. (2003, October 21). *Join Together Online*. Retrieved September 8, 2007 from www.jointogether.org

Industry comments sought on student drug testing eligibility, requirements. (2006, June 6). *Workplace Substance Abuse Advisor*. Retrieved November 30, 2006 from the Lexis Nexis Academic database.

Ingham, R. (2005, October 18). Internet and Tamiflu: Bird flu scare exposes glaring loophole. *Agence France Presse*. Retrieved February 6, 2006 from Lexis Nexis academic database.

Innocuous drug paraphernalia targeted. (2005, March 17). *Join Together Online*. Retrieved July 27, 2007 from www.jointogether.org

Internet and First Amendment. (n.d.). *First Amendment Center*. Retrieved March 8, 2006 from www.fac.org

Internet Domain Survey, January 2001. (2001). Internet Software Consortium. Redwood City, CA.

Internet drug dealers arrested in 84 cities. (2002, September 20). *Out-Law*. Retrieved December 16, 2006 from www.out-law.com/page-2958

Internet offers how-to's for drug use. (2006, July 27). *Join Together Online*. Retrieved July 28, 2006 from: www.jointogether.org

Internet pharmaceutical operator receives 51 month prison sentence. (2005). U.S. Department of Justice. Retreived August 16, 2006 from www.doj.gov/opg/pr/2005/January/05

I-team 10 investigation: The hidden dangers of online drugs. (2005, November 14). Retrieved August 17, 2006 from www.buysafedrugs.info/reorts/nbsreport.html

Ja-Young, Y. (2006, May 11). Drug smuggling via Internet records dramatic increase. *The Korea Times* [online version]. Retrieved April 10, 2007.

Jensen, E. L., & Gerber, J. (1998). *The new war on drugs: Symbolic politics and criminal justice policy*. Cincinnati, OH: ACJS/Anderson.

Johnson, L., O'Malley, P., & Bachman, J. (2000). Monitoring the Future study. Ann Arbor, MI: University of Michigan News and Information Services of the University of Michigan.

Join Together Online. (2005, March 2). Most online drug sales illegal, UN says. *Join Together Online*. Received March 4, 2005 from www.jointogether.org/sa/news/summaries

Judge exceeds sentencing guidelines for Internet drug dealer. (2005, October 17). Retrieved July 27, 2007 from www.lawcore.com/legal-information/10-17-05.html

Judson, K. (2000). *Computer crime: Phreaks, spies, and salami slicers, Revised Edition*. Berkeley Heights, NJ: Enslow Publishers, Inc.

Katz, J. (1988). *Seductions of crime: Moral and sensual attractions in doing evil*. New York: Basic.

Kern, J. (2006). Random drug testing would meet fierce opposition. *Join Together Online*. Retrieved October 24, 2006 from www.jointogether.org

Kershaw, S. (2005, December 1). Hooked on the web: Help is on the way. *The New York Times—Late edition*, p. G1.

Keynes, A. (2003, January). More schools test for drugs after court ruling. *Inside School Safety*, 7(9), 5.

Khatri, S. (2006, September 11). Homemade hits a click away. *Detroit Free Press*. Retrieved November 20, 2006 from LexisNexis Academic database.

Khatri, S. (2006, September 22). Many teens turning to web as a drug encyclopedia. *Wisconsin State Journal*, p. A9. Retrieved November 30, 2006 from LexisNexis Academic database.

Kolbert, K. (2001). *Censoring the web* (also with Z. Mettger). New York: New Press.

Kornblum, J. (2006, January 9). Teens hang out at MySpace. *USA Today* [online version]. Retrieved September 8, 2007 from www.usatoday.com

Kraska, P., (Ed.). (2001). *Militarizing the American criminal justice system: The changing roles of the armed forces and the police*. Boston, MA: Northeastern University Press.

Krebs, B. (2006, December 22). Cybercrime hits the big-time in 2006. *Washington Post* [online version]. Retrieved September 8, 2007 from www.washingtonpost.com

Ksir, C., Hart, C.L., & Ray, O. (2006). *Drugs, Society, and Human Behavior, 11th ed.* New York: McGraw-Hill.

Law enforcement: Goose Creek agrees to pay up, change ways in settlement of notorious high school drug raid case. (2006, July 14). Stop the Drug War. Retrieved December 27, 2006 from www.stopthedrugwar.org/chronicle/444/goose_creek_drug_raid_settlement.shtml

Lee, A. (2006, November 14). Drugs for sale. *Express Newspapers.* Retrieved November 30, 2006 from LexisNexis Academic database.

Lee, G. (2004) *Global drug enforcement.* Boca Raton, FL: CRC Press.

Legal uses of coca touted. (2006, October 25). *Join Together Online.* Retrieved October 30, 2006 from www.jointogether.org

Leinwand. D. (2006, June 13). Prescription drugs find place in teen culture. *USA Today,* 1A.

Lenhart, A., Madden, M., & Hitlin, P. (2005, July 27). Teens and technology: Youth are leading the transition to a fully wired and mobile nation. *Pew Internet Surveys.* Retrieved November 1, 2005 from www.pew.internet.org/PPF/r/162/report_display.asp

Levine, H. (1998). *The drug problem.* Austin, TX: Raintree Steck-Vaughn.

Leviton, S., Schindler, M.A., & Orleans, R.S. (**1994**). African-American youth: Drug trafficking and the justice system. *Pediatrics,* 93, 1078–1084.

Li, X., & Fagelman, S. (1994). Recent and intended drug trafficking among male and female African-American early adolescents. *Pediatrics,* 93, pp. 1044–1099.

Limbaugh faces random drug testing. (2006, May 4). *Join Together Online.* Retrieved July 27, 2007 from www.jointogether.org

Littlejohn, C., Baldacchio, A., Schifaro, F., & Deluca, P. (2005, February). Internet pharmacies and online prescription drug sales: A cross-sectional study. *Drugs: Education, prevention, and Policy,* 12(11), 75–80.

Lopes, G. (2007, February 17). Patients get wrong drugs online; Anti-psychotic substituted for depression, insomnia medicine. *The Washington Times,* C11.*Observer* (England) [Online edition], p.1. Retrieved March 8, 2007.

Lorenz, B. (2004, June 4). Drug czar backs random drug testing at Pewaukee High School. *GM Today Online.* Retrieved June 5, 2004 from www.gmtoday.com

Lyons, B. (2007, March 4). Internet brings drug dealing into the home. *The Times Union* (Albany, NY) [Online edition]. Retrieved March 8, 2007.

Magnay, J. (2006, November 30). More drug testing for NRL but all under a veil of secrecy. *Morning Herald* (Australia). Retrieved December 10, 2006 from www.shm.com.au

Maltby, L. (1999). Drug testing: A bad investment. *American Civil Liberties Union.* Retrieved June 5, 2004 from www.aclu.org

Mander, J. (1992). *In the absence of the sacred: Failure of technology and the survival of Indian nations.* San Francisco, CA: Sierra Club Books.

Many docs not qualified to test for drug use. (2006, February 14). *Join Together Online.* Retrieved July 27, 2007 from www.jointogether.org

Marez, C. (2004). *Drug wars: The political economy of narcotics.* Minneapolis, MN: University of Minnesota Press.

Marwick, C. (1999). FDA has asked physicians and pharmacists for help. *Journal of the American Medical Association,* 281(100), 975–976.

Maryland school district toughens drug-testing policy. (2004, March 9). *Join Together Online.* Retrieved July 27, 2007 from www.jointogether.org

Marzilli, A. (2004). *Policing the Internet.* Philadelphia, PA: Chelsea House.

Mauer, M., & Keys, R. (2007, July). Uneven justice: State rates of incarceration by race and ethnicity. *The Sentencing Project*, Retrieved September 8, 2007 from www.sentencing project.org

McCandless, D. (2004, January 31). Cannabis online. *The Guardian*. Retrieved November 1, 2005 from www.cannabis.net/articles/commerce.html

McCullagh, D. (2003, February 24). Feds weed out drug paraphernalia sites. *News.com*. Retrieved December 19, 2006 from www.news.com/Feds+weed+out+drug+paraphernalia+sites/2100-1023_3-985785.html

McHugh, H. (2006, May 7). Recipes for danger sex drug found on Internet. *The People*, 31.

McLuhan, M. (2005). *The medium is the massage*. Corte Madeira, CA: Gingko Books.

McShane, L. (2006, May 16). Prescription drugs new preference of teens. *Miami Herald*, 8A.

Medical uses of psychedelic mushrooms explored. (2006, November 20). *Join Together Online*. Retrieved November 22, 2006 from www.jointogether.org

Merton, R. (1938). Social structure and anomie. *American Sociological Review*, 3, 672–682.

Messner, S., & Rosenfeld, R. (2001). *Crime and the American Dream*. Belmont, CA: Wadsworth.

Meth labs proliferate in Mexico. (2006, December 1). *Join Together Online*. Retrieved December 4, 2006 from www.jointogether.org

Meyer, P. (2003, May 19). Student drug testing not effective in reducing drug use. *University of Michigan News and Information Services*. Retrieved June 5, 2004 from LexisNexis Academic database.

Michigan court says trace of marijuana enough for DUI. (2006, June 27). *Join Together Online*. Retrieved June 30, 2006 from www.jointogether.org

Miller, R. (1996). *Drug warriors and their prey: From police power to police state*. Westport, CT: Praeger.

Misuse of pharmaceuticals sends half million to ER each year. (2006, May 10). Retrieved May 17, 2006 from: www.jointogether.org

Moore, R. (2005). *Cybercrime: Investigating high-technology computer crime*. New York: Anderson.

More blacks imprisoned for drugs, but reasons unclear (2003, August 20). *Join Together Online*. Retrieved July 23, 2007 from www.jointogether.org

More middle-age Americans dying from drug overdose. (2006, April 20). *Join Together Online*. Retrieved July 26, 2007 from www.jointogether.org

More than 200 Websites sell drug tests for teens. (2006, April 6). *Join Together Online*. Retrieved July 37, 2006 from www.jointogether.org

More web sites offer unfettered prescription drug sales, CASA says. (2006, July 14). *Join Together Online*. Retrieved July 17, 2006 from www.jointogether.org

Morgan, J. (1988). The scientific justification for urine drug testing. *University of Kansas Law Review*, 36, 683–697.

Most online drug sales illegal, UN says. (2005, March 2). *Join Together Online*. Retrieved March 4, 2005 from www.jointogether.org/sa/news/summaries

Muir, H. (2006, June 3). An epidemic of home-made hits. *New Scientist*, 190.

Musto, D. (Ed.). (2002a). *Drugs in America: A documentary history*. New York: New York University Press.

Musto, D. (2002b). *The quick fix drug control: Politics and policies in a period of increasing substance abuse, 1963–1981*. New York: New York University Press.

Narcotic pain meds become drug of choice. (2006, June 22). *Join Together Online*. Retrieved July 26, 2007 from www.jointogether.org

Nagin, D.S., & Paternoster, R. (1993). Enduring individual differences and rational choice theories of crime. *Law & Society Review, 27*, 467–496.

Neff, J., & Waite, D. (2007, March). Male versus female substance abuse patterns among incarcerated juvenile offenders. *Justice Quarterly,* 24(1), 106–132.

Neuspiel, D.R. (1996) Racism and perinatal addiction. *Ethnicity and Disease,* 6 (Winter/Spring), pp. 47-55.

News corp is $580m internet buy. (2005, July 19). *BBC News* [online version]. Retrieved September 8, 2007 from www.news.bbc.co.uk.

Nicklin, J. (2000, June 9). The latest trend: Mixing prescription drugs with other substances. *Chronicle of Higher Education* [Online version]. Retrieved January 5, 2007

NIDA Infofactsheet: MDMA. (2006, April). *National Institute on Drug Abuse.* Retrieved May 8, 2007 from www.nida.nih.gov/infofacts/ecstasy

N.J. orders steroid testing in all high school sports. (2005, December 22). *Join TogetherOnline.* Accessed July 27, 2007 from www.jointogether.org .

Nock, S. (1993). *The costs of privacy: Surveillance and republic in America.* New York: Aldine de Gruyter.

O' Connor, T. (2006). A history of the war on drugs. Retrieved September 8, 2007 from www.faculty.ncwc.edu/t_oconnor.

ONDCP releases prescription tracking strategy. (2006, July 20). *Join Together Online.* Available at www.jointogether.org

Oder, N. (2006, November 1). Drug test deters volunteers. *Library Journal,* 131(18), 15.

Office of National Drug Control Policy. (2002, October). Drugs, youth, and the Internet. *Department of Justice Information Bulletin.* Retrieved September 8, 2007 from www.usdoj.gov/ndic/pubs2/2161/index.html

ONCDP unveils strategy for methamphetamines, prescription drugs. *Join Together Online.* Retrieved June 5, 2006 from www.jointogether.org.

Online registries of drug offenders. (2006, December 7). *Join Together Online.* Retrieved December 8, 2006 from www.jointogether.org

Online teens openly chat about drug use. (2007, June 21). *Join Together Online.* Retrieved June 25, 2007 from www.jointogether.org

Operation Cyber-Roid snares illegal Internet pharmacy. (2006, Oct. 26). Retrieved July 27, 2007 from www.usdoj.gov/dea/pubs/states/newsrel/chicago102606a.html

Oregon weighs ban on Salvia. (2007, March 7). Retrieved April 25, 2007 from www.jointogether.org.

Parenti, C. (1999). *Lockdown America: Police and prisons in the age of crisis.* New York: Verso.

Pediatricians call for action on steroids (2005, April 5) *Join Together Online.* Retrieved July 23, 2007 from www.jointogether.org

Pharmaceutical drug threat assessment. (2004, November). National Drug Information Center. Retrieved August 16, 2006 from www.doj.gov/ndic

Pimentel, B. (2005, May 4). E-mail addles the mind. *San Francisco Chronicle* [online version]. Retrieved February 2, 2007

Pisik, B. (2001, April 16). Online traffickers feed "pill-popping culture." *Insight on The News,* 27.

Pollard, N. (2005, June 29). Illegal drug trade a world force. *Common Sense for Drug Policy.* Retrieved September 8, 2007 from www.commonsense.org.

Popke, K. (2003). *Lethal cure.* Dallas, TX : Durban House Publishing Co.

Posner, E. (2000, May 25). Statement of Ethan M. Posner before the Subcommittee on Oversight and Investigations Committee on Commerce. Retrieved November 1, 2005 from www.cybercrime.gov/posner.htm

Postman, N. (1996). *The end of education*. New York: Vintage.
Potter, B. (1999). *Pass the test: An employee guide to drug testing*. Berkeley, CA: Ronin.
Power, R. (2000). *Tangled web: Tales of digital crime from the shadows of cyberspace*. Indianapolis, Indiana: Que.
Prescription drug abuse. (n.d.). Medindia. Retrieved August 29, 2006 from www.medindia.net/patients/patientinfo/drugtoxicity-abuse.html
Prescription drug abuse, smoking higher among teen girls. (2006, February 9). *Join Together Online*. Retrieved February 11, 2006 from: www.jointogtheronline.org
Prescription meds Florida's top drug problem. (2005, October 31). *Join Together Online*. Retrieved November 2, 2005 from www.jointogetheronline.org
Prevention group focuses on prescription drugs, testing. (2006, February. 16). *Join Together Online*. Accessed July 27, 2007 from www.jointogether.org
Prevention groups criticize YouTube postings of huffing videos. (2006, December 11). *Join Together Online*. Retrieved December 12, 2006 from www.jointogether.org
Privacy Rights Clearinghouse. (2007). Privacy and the Internet: Traveling in cyberspace. Retrieved September 8, 2007 from www.privacyrights.org Problems grow with drugs bought on Net. (2003, June 25). *USA Today*, 5B
Putnam, T., & Elliott, D. (2001). International responses to cyber crime. In Sofaer, A., & Goodman, S. (Eds.). *The transnational dimension of cyber crime and terrorism* (pp. 35–68). Stanford, CA: Hoover Institute Press.
Ratcliffe, H., & Kohler, J. (2006, May 19). Using Internet for drug deals is not unusual, authorities say. *St. Louis Post-Dispatch*, C4.
Redden, J. (2000). *Snitch culture*. Los Angeles: Feral House.
Reaves, J. (2002, February 27). Clicking for fix: Drugs online. *Time* [Online version]. Retrieved October 18, 2006 from LexisNexis Academic database.
Retka, A. (2006, September 18). Drug testing offers school districts proactive appearance. *St. Louis (Missouri) Daily Record*. Retrieved September 8, 2007 from LexisNexis Academic database.
Revill, J. (2006, November 5). Cancer patients turn to Internet for cheap drugs. *The Observer* (England) [online edition], 1. Retrieved December 21, 2006
Roberts, N. & Fossey, R. (2002, April). Random drug testing of students: Where will the line be drawn? *Journal of Law and Education*, pp. 191–208.
Robinson, M., & Scherlen, R. (2007). *Lies, damned lies, and drug war statistics*. Albany, NY: State University of New York Press.
Roig-Franzia, M. (2007, April 9). Mexican drug cartels leave a bloody trail on YouTube. *Washington Post*, A01.
Roleff, T. (Ed.). (2004). *The war on drugs: Opposing viewpoints*. San Diego, CA: Greenhaven.
Ryan, K. (2001). Toward an explanation of the persistence of failed policy: Binding drug policy to foreign policy, 1930-1962. In Gerber, J., & Jensen, E. (Eds.). *Drug war American style* (pp. 19-48). New York: Routledge.
Rumbough, T. (2001). Controversial uses of the Internet by college students. Retrieved September 8, 2007 from www.educause.edu
Rydell, C.P., & Everingham, S.S. (1994). *Controlling cocaine supply versus demand programs*. Santa Monica, CA: RAND.
Sales of drug-test kits on rise. (2005, June 3). *Join Together Online*. Retrieved July 27, 2007 from www.jointogether.org
Salvia divinorum. (n.d.). *Salvianet*. Retrieved June 25, 2007 from www.salvianet.org
Sanders, W. (2006, August 11). Penethylemene use amongst young people. Paper presented at the Society for the Study of Social Problems annual conference, Montreal, Canada.

Schlosser, E. (2003). *Reefer madness*. Boston: Houghton-Miffline.
Schmalleger, F. (2005). *Criminal justice today*, 8th ed. Upper Saddle River, NJ: Prentice Hall.
School starts random drug testing. (2005, January 4). *BBC News* [online version]. Retrieved December 19, 2006 from www.newsvote.bbc.co.uk
Seeger, S., & Visconte, V. (1997). *Fourth Amendment ramifications of cyberspace surveillance*. Retrieved January 8, 2007 from http://wings.buffalo.edu/law/complaw.
Selkirk, R., & Luse, S. (2004, May 23). Marijuana legislation from decriminalization to recriminalization. Retrieved December 19, 2006 from www.freepress.org.
Senat, J. (1997, March 28). Extending First Amendment protections to the Internet. Retrieved March 8, 2006 rom www.cas.okstate.edu/jb/faculty/senat/jb3163/exterdrug.html.
Sessions, J. (2006, August 4). Sessions and Feinstein introduce online pharmacy bill. *Congressional Quarterly*. Retrieved August 15, 2006 from Lexis Nexis academic database.
Sexton, R. (2006, August 11). Impact of peudoephedrine legislation on illicit methamphetamines production ("cooking") in rural Kentucky and Arkansas. Paper presented at the Society for the Study of Social Problems annual conference, Montreal, Canada.
Shearer, E. (2006, September 20). 11 arrested for Internet drug sales. *Associated Press*. Retrieved November 30, 2006 from LexisNexis Academic database.
Shiffman, D. (2006, November 19). Drug Net, Ch. 1: Global hunt turns pushers into prey. *Philadelphia Inquirer* [online version]. Retrieved December 12, 2006 from www.philly.com
Siddharth, S. (2005, April 27). Illegal drug trade outsourced to India, too. *Asia Times* [Online version]. Retrieved October 28, 2005 from www.asiatimes.com
Sklar, H. (1995). Reinforcing racism with the war on drugs. *Zmagazine*. Retrieved September 11, 2006 from: www.zmag.org/Zmag/articles/dec95sklar.htm
Skoloff, B. (2007, March 17). Illicit Internet pharmacies called 21st century drug traffickers. *The Associated Press*.
Sleep medicine Ambien abused by teens. (2006, December 18). *Join Together Online*. Retrieved December 19, 2006 from www.jointogether.org.
Smith, J. (2005, September 19). For young doc, Internet drug case "is a nightmare." *Philadelphia Daily News*. Retrieved February 6, 2006 from Lexis Nexis academic database.
Sofaer, A., & Goodman, S. (2001). Cyber crime and security: The transnational dimension. In Sofaer, A., & Goodman, S. (Eds.). *The transnational dimension of cyber crime and terrorism* (pp. 1–34). Stanford, CA: Hoover Institute Press.
Some Internet drug sales put buyers at risk. (2004, June 18). *USA Today*, 3B.
Some states "out" methamphetamine dealers online. (2006, August 25). *Join TogetherOnline*. Retrieved August 28, 2006 from: www.jointogether.org
Spinney, L. (1997, June 28). Net recipes blamed for boom in uppers. *New Scientist*, 10.
Staples, W. (2000). *Everyday surveillance*. Lanham, MD: Rowman & Littlefield Publishers.
Stoppler, M. (2005, May 17). Buying prescription drugs online—are the risks worth it? Retrieved June 26, 2006 from www.medicinenet.com
Students turn to "smart pills" to boost performance. (2006, June 28). *Join Together Online*. Retrieved June 30, 2006 from: www.jointogether.org
Study finds significant financial benefits of providing substance abuse treatment. (2005, October 27). *Join Together Online*. Retrieved September 8, 2007 from www.jointogether.org.
Substance Abuse and Mental Health Services Administration. (2005). Drug Abuse Warning Network Report, 2005. Available at www.samhsa.gov
Suicide brings attention to teen prescription drug use. (2006, February 3). *Join Together Online*. Retrieved February 8, 2006 from: www.jointogether.org

Sullivan, M. (2004, August 4). Online drug sales targeted. *PC World* [Online Version]. Retrieved November 28, 2007.
Sullum, J. (2003) *Saying yes*. NY: Jeremy P. Tarcher/Putnam.
Survey indicates drug dependencies often supported via the Internet. (2005, April 29). *Drug Week*, p. 324.
Sutherland, E. (1947). *Principals of criminology* (4th ed.). Philadelphia, PA: J.B. Lippincott.
Swann, J. (2004). The FDA and the practice of pharmacy: Prescription drug regulation before 1968. In J. Erlen & J. Spillane, (Eds.). *Federal drug control: The evolution of policy and practice* (pp. 145–174). Binghampton, NY: Pharmaceutical Products Press.
Sykes, G., & Matza, D. (1957). Techniques of neutralization: A theory of delinquency. *American Journal of Sociology*, 22, 664–670.
Szasz, T. (1992). *Our right to drugs*. Westport, CT: Praeger.
Taylor, R., Caeti, T., Loper, D., Fritsch, E., & Liederbach, J. (2006). *Digital crime and digital terrorism*. Upper Saddle River, NJ: Prentice Hall.
Teens, technology, and drugs: An inside look. (2006, July 18). *PR Newswire*. Retrieved August 15, 2006 from Lexis Nexis Academic database.
Telemedicine taking off, especially in rural communities. (2006, June 28). *Join TogetherOnline*. Retrieved June 30, 2006 from: www.jointogether.org
Temin, P. (1980). *Taking your medicine*. Cambridge, MA: Harvard University Press.
Terkel, S. (1997). *The drug laws: A time for change?* New York: Franklin Watts.
Texas kids mixing heroin, cold medicine. (2006, November 20). *Join Together Online*. Retrieved November 22, 2006 from www.jointogether.org
School starts random drug testing. (n.d.). *Coalition Against Cannabis*. Retrieved December 19, 2006 from www.eurad.net/options/Student%20-drug%20testing.htm
Thompson, C. (2006, January 15). Internet experts testify about illegal drug sales *American Journal of Health System-Pharmacy*, 108, 110.
Tiffen, R. (2005, October 15). Teenagers research drugs on Internet. *The New Zealand Herald*. Retrieved October 15, 2005 from: www.nzherald.co.nz
Tinnin, A. (2005, October 19). Online pharmacies are new vehicle for raising some old legal issues. *Kansas City (Missouri) Daily Record* [online version]. Retrieved June 25, 2006
Topalli, V. (2005). When being good is bad: An expansion of neutralization theory. *Criminology*, 43(3), 797–835.
Tryon, T. (2005, October). Wife's death leads husband to sue Internet prescriptionpurveyors. *Sarasota Herald-Tribune*, F1.
Tunnell, K.D. (2004). *Pissing on demand*. New York: New York University Press.
UN gives upbeat assessment of global drug war. (2006, June 28). *Join Together Online*. Retrieved June 30, 2006 from: www.jointogether.org
U.S. arrests Internet merchants of designer drugs. (2005). *U.S. Drug Enforcement Agency*. Retrieved August 17, 2006 from www.dea.gov/pubs/stats/newrel/nyco72304.html
U.S. Department of Justice. (2002, October). Drugs, youth, and the Internet. *Information Bulletin*. U.S. Department of Justice, National Drug Intelligence Center.
US FL: schools may use spray. (2004, June 30). Accessed July 27, 2007 from www.mapinc.org/drugnews/v04
U.S. involved in discussions of Canadian drug strategy. (2006, December 14). *Join Together Online*. Retrieved December 19, 2006 from www.jointogether.org
U.S. unable to stop flow of prescription drugs from Mexico. (2004, October 28). *Join Together Online*. Retrieved March 4, 2006 from: www.jointogether.org

Van Sant, W. (2006, October 11). Paraphernalia law approved. *St. Petersburg Times* [online edition]. Retrieved May 12, 2006.

Veronin, M., & Youan, B. (2004, July 23). Magic bullet gone astray: Medications and the Internet. *Science*, 481.

Wall, D. (2001a). Cybercrimes and the Internet. In Wall, D. (Ed.). *Crime and the Internet* (pp. 1-17). London: Routledge.

Wall, D. (2001b). Maintaining order and law on the Internet. In Wall, D. (Ed.). *Crime and the Internet* (pp. 167-183). London: Routledge.

Wallace, J.D. (1999, Dec. 8). *Nameless in cyberspace: Anonymity on the Internet.* Cato Institute Briefing Papers.

Waller, M. (2006, October 16). Online drug sales are a growing concern. *New Orleans Times-Picayune*, p.1. Retrieved November 30, 2006 from LexisNexis Academic database.

Walmsley, R. (2003). World prison population list. London, England: Home Office Research, Development and Statistics. Retrieved April 29, 2003 from www.homeoffice.gov.uk/rds/pdfs2/r188.pdf

Wax, P. (2002, November 2). Just a click away: Recreational drug web sites on the Internet: *Pediatrics*, 109(6) [Online version]. Retrieved February 6, 2006 from: www.pediatrics.org/cgi/content/full/1096/e96

Website takes on drug dealers. (2001, July 31). *Join Together Online*. Retrieved December 16, 2001 from www.jointogether.org

What made 2006 memorable. (2006, December 31). *Parade*, 6-8.

Wilson, W. (1996). *When work disappears: The work of the new urban poor.* New York: Knopf.

Winnicoff, J., Houck, C., Roffman, E., & Bauchner, H. (2000). Verve and Jolt: Deadly new Internet drugs. *Pediatrics*, 106, pp. 829-830.

With Courts' blessing and federal funds, school drug testing grows. (2006, July 13). *Join Together Online*. Retrieved July 27, 2007 from www.jointogether.org World drug report. (2007). *United Nations Office on Drugs and Crime.* Retrieved September 10, 2007 from www.unodc.org.

World Internet users and population statistics. (2005, September 30). *Internetworldstats.com*. Retrieved November 1, 2005 from www.internetworldstats.com/stats.html

Wren, D. (1996, May 12). "Head shops" flourish on strand. *National Families*. Retrieved December 19, 2006 from www.nationalfamilies.org/publications/about_nfia/head_shops.htm

Xanax often abused for easy "high." (2002, January. 29). *MSNBC* Retrieved September 8, 2007 from www.msnbc.com.

Yamaguchi, R., Johnston, L., and O' Malley, P.M. (2003). *Journal of School Health*. 73(4), pp. 159-165.

Yoaz, Y. (2006, March 8). Internet suppliers may reveal identity of web posters. *Haaretz Daily* (Israel). Retrieved March 8, 2006 from www.haaretzdaily.com/hasen/spages/691793.html

Young, D. (2004). GAO reveals perils of Internet drug-buying. *American Journal of Health System Pharmacy*, 61, p. 1526.

Young men mix Viagra, other drugs. (2006, June 6). *Join Together Online*. Retrieved July 25, 2007 from www.jointogether.org

Zeese, K. (1997). The business of drug testing: Technological innovation and social control. *Contemporary Drug Problems*, 19, pp. 1-26.

Zirin, J. (2005, May 28). You've got drugs. *Forbes* [online version]. Retrieved September 8, 2007 from www.forbes.com.

INDEX

ACLU v. Miller, 133
ACLU v. Reno, 8, 132
Adderall, 57
adultering, 120
Agnew, Robert, 144
American dream, 144, 146
Anabolic Steroid Control Act of 2004, 40
anomie/strain theories, 142-146
anonymity, 21
anonymous speech and press, 133
Anslinger, Harry, 27-28
asset forfeiture, 32, 43-44, 48
athletes, 59

Bennett, William, 31, 33
Bentham, Jeremy, 154-155
blackberry thumb, 1
blogs, 3, 133-134
Board of Education of Independent School District No. 92 of Pottawatamie County v. Earls, 107
bodybuilders, 13, 58-59
Boggs Act of 1951, 28
Bourgois, Philippe, 144
Bureau of Narcotics, 27
Burgess, R., and Akers, R., 151-152
Bush, George, 33
Bush, George W., 38, 105

Canada, 36-37
Canadian online pharmacies, 54-55, 73-74
Carter, Jimmy, 31
Central Intelligence Agency (CIA), 31
cheating drug tests, 16, 118, 119
    history, 121-122
Chemical Diversion and Trafficking Act, 33
Child Online Protection Act of 1988 (COPA), 82-83
chromatography, 108
Clinton, Bill, 34
Cloward, R., & Ohlin, L., 143
club drugs, 18
coca cola, 25
cocaine, 14, 25
Cohen, Albert, 143
Communications Decency Act, 82
Comprehensive Crime Control Act of 1984, 32
Conflict theories, 153-154
Control theories, 146-147
Controlled Substances Act, 29-30, 85-86
Controlled Substances schedules, 13, 29-30, 58-59
costs of drug war, 41
crack cocaine, 33, 63-64, 67-68
    penalties, 32

Crime Bill of 1986, 32
Crime Control Act of 1990, 32
criminological theory, 142-154
criminologists, ix, 131
Currie, Elliott, 144
cybercrime, 4-6, 81-82
    costs of, 6-7
    difficulty for law enforcement, 7-8
    policing, 8-9, 18-21, 81-98, 156-160
    scope of, 5-6
    types of, 4-5
cybercriminals, 5
cyberdoctors, 5
CyberSitter, 141
cybersnitch, 181-182
cyberstalking, 90

Darvon, 56
date rape drugs, 63
deterrence, 19
Differential Association theory, 150-152
Differential Association-Reinforcement theory, 151-152
Differential Identification theory, 151-152
Differential Opportunity theory, 143-144
digital divide, 3
diluting, 120
Director of National Drug Control Policy (drug czar), 32
disciplinary power, 155-156
drug culture, 159
drug education, 33-34
Drug Enforcement Agency (DEA), 20, 32-33, 157-158
Drug-Free Workplace Act, 103
drug information on the web, 17-18, 65-66, 127-129
drug knockoffs, 69-70
drug paraphernalia, 16, 40-41, 97
drug recipes, 16, 69
drug-related spam, 77

Drug testing, 99-117
    bias, 115-116
    conceptual concerns, 116-117
    cost effectiveness, 113-114
    detection concerns, 114-115
    deterrence, 112-113
    history, 100-103
    in the home, 111-112
    in the workplace, 102-104, 109
    international efforts, 105
    legal issues, 105-107
    resistance, 117-118
    schools, 104-105, 109-111
    types of 107-108
    vulnerable populations, 108
dug war critics, 47-48
drug warriors, 46-47
Dupont, R., 100-101
Durkheim, Emile, 142

eBay, 13
Effectiveness of drug war, 41-42
Electronics Communication Privacy Act, 138
Email, 133, 134
Encryption, 91
Enforcement of laws, 91-92
Entrapment, 92-93
Erowid, 17, 62-63, 66, 128-129

Federal Bureau of Investigations (FBI), 88, 139
Federal Computer Investigations Committee (FCIC), 88
Federal Trade Commission (FTC), 84
filtering devices, 141-142
flushing, 120
Food and Drug Administration (FDA), 84-86
Food, Drug, and Cosmetic Act (FDCA), 83-84

for-cause drug testing, 108
Ford, Gerald, 31
Foucault, Michel, 155-156
free press, 132-137
free speech, 132-137

Glaser, Daniel, 151-152
Global Internet Liberty Campaign (GILC), 136-137, 138
global issues and the web, 20-21, 87
global policing efforts, 89-90
global speech and press, 135-136
Google, 1, 12, 55-57, 59-61, 62-63, 69, 140
Great Britain, 36

Hague Convention of 1912, 34
hair follicle testing, 108, 115-116
harm reduction, 72-73
Harrison Act of 1914, 26
hearsay rules, 94
heroin, 14. 64
Hirschi, Travis, 146-147
    with Michael Gottfredson, 147
Hong Kong, 36
Hutchinson, Asa, 46-47
hydrocodone, 56

illicit drugs, 14-16, 62-64
    global perspective, 15
    hallucinogens, 63
    marijuana, 14, 26-27, 39-40, 62-63, 67
    policing successes, 96-97
immunoassay tests, 108
In search of respect: Selling crack in El Barrio, 144-146
incarceration, 44-46
International Covenant on Civil and Political Rights (ICCPR), 135, 137
Internet
    history of, 2
    user profile, 2-3

Internet Service Providers (ISPs), 7, 140
Instant messaging (IM), 5

Jones-Miller Act, 27
jurisdiction, 87-89
Just Say No, 31

Katz, Jack, 149-150

Labeling theory, 147-148
Latin America, 37-38
laws relevant to web, 20, 82-87

man-made drugs, 38-39
mandatory sentencing, 29-31
Marijuana Tax Act of 1937, 27
masking, 120
medicalization, 43
Merton, Robert, 142-143
Mesner, S., and Rosenfeld, R., 144
methamphetamines, 39-40
methods of duping, 120
middle class measuring rod, 143
military involvement in drug war, 31-32
militarization, 43-44
moral panic, 40
Myspace, 70-71

Narcotic Drug Control Act of 1956, 28
National Association of Boards of Pharmacy (NABP), 11, 58
National Computer Crime Squad, 8
National Organization for the Reform of Marijuana Laws (NORML), 14, 140
National Survey on Drug Use and Health, 41-42
National White Collar Crime Center (NW3C), 88
Neoclassical theories, 148-150
Net Nanny, 141

new drugs, 64-65
New Jersey v. T. L.O, 107
Nightbyrd, Jeffrey, 121-122
Nixon, Richard, 24, 29, 30-31
nongovernmental agencies, 9
Noriega, Manuel, 33
North American Free Trade Agreement (NAFTA), 35
notMYKid, 110

Office of National Drug Control Policy (ONDCP), 39, 41, 72, 103, 140
Omnibus Drug Act of 1988, 32
online stings, 92-93
Online test cheating products, 122-127
    effectiveness, 129-130
online test cheating information, 127-129
Operation Pipedream, 95
Operation Cyber-Roid, 96
opium, 25
Oxycontin, 75

Panopticon, 154
periodic drug testing, 108
police, 7-8
policing successes, 95-97
pro-drug information, 65-66
polydrug use, 65
Posters 'N' Things Ltd., et al. v. U.S., 86
Postmodern surveillance, 156
pre-employment drug testing, 107-108
Prescription drugs, 8-13, 52-57
    counterfeits, 53-54
    global perspective, 12, 55
    impurities, 11, 53-54
    lawful sales, 9-10
    misuse, 53, 68-69
    no prescription required, 11-12, 52-53
    policing successes, 95-96
    user profile, 12-13, 55, 77-79
    usage rates, 38-39

privacy, 137-141
profile of web-based buyers, 73-79, 158
profile of web-based sellers, 79-80
prohibition, 27
prosecuting online offenders, 94-95
Pure Food and Drug Act of 1906, 26

racism, 24-26, 27-28, 43
Racketeering Influences and Corrupt Organizations (RICO) laws, 84
random drug testing, 108
Rational Choice theory, 148-150, 160
Reagan, Nancy, 31
Reagan, Ronald, 31-32, 102
Reefer madness, 27
Reno v. ACLU, 8, 132
reporting victimization, 90
Ritalin, 56-57
Rockefeller Laws, 30-31

Salvia Divinorum, 64-65
scope of drug war, 42-43
search and seizure, 93-94
Shmerber v. California, 106
Shoemaker et al. v. Handel, 106
Single Convention on Narcotics Drugs of 1961, 34
Social Bond theory, 146-147
Social Learning theories, 150-152
Staples, W., 156
state-wide policing efforts, 89
steroids, 13, 39-40, 58-61, 96
Substance Abuse and Mental Health Services Administration (SAMHSA), 103
substituting, 120
surveillance, 42-43, 154-156
Sutherland, Edwin, 150-152
SWAT teams, 44
Sykes, G., and Matza, D., 152-153
target hardening, 97-98

Techniques of Neutralization theory, 152-153
technological determinism, 101-102
Telecommunications Reform Act, 83
testosterone, 61
tripping, 68
tryptamines, 65
Tunnell, Kenneth, x, 100-119, 122, 149, 159-160

U.S. Customs Cyber-Smuggling Center, 88
U.S. Secret Service, 8, 88
U.S. Sentencing Commission, 32
U.S. v. Charbonneau, 93
U.S. v. Durham, 94
United Nations International Narcotics Board, (INCB), 11, 21, 36, 52, 74
United States Department of Justice, 6, 16, 88
United States v. Charbonneau, 138
United States v. Smith, 93
Universal Declaration of Human Rights, 135, 137
urinalysis, 107
USA Patriot Act, 140
use versus abuse debate, 24

Vernonia School District v. Acton, 107
Viagra, 56
Vicodin, 56
Vienna Convention of 1988, 34
Vietnam War veterans, 29

The Whizzinator, 16
Walters, John, 38
war mentality, 24
war on drugs, ix, x, xi, 23-50,
web cams, 71-72
Weber, Max, 154-155
widening the net, 42-43

Yahooka, 17, 62-63
YouTube, 71-72, 90

Jeffrey Ian Ross, *General Editor*

This book series is a forum for cutting-edge work that pushes the boundaries of the disciplines of criminology and criminal justice, with the aim of exploring eclectic, un- and under-explored issues, and imaginative approaches in terms of theory and methods. Although primarily designed for criminology and criminal justice audiences—including scholars, instructors, and students—books in the series function across disciplines, appealing to those with an interest in anthropology, cultural studies, sociology, political science, and law.

Books in the series include:

Hawking Hits on the Information Highway, by Laura Finley
Blood, Power and Bedlam: State Crimes and Crimes Against Humanity in Post-Colonial Africa, by Christopher W. Mullins and Dawn L. Rothe
Chinese Policing: History and Reform, by Kam C. Wong
Arrest Decisions: What Works for the Officer? by Edith Linn
Drug Court Justice: Experiences in a Juvenile Drug Court, by Kevin Whiteacre

Authors who would like to submit a proposal for a volume in the series, or a completed book manuscript please direct all inquiries to:

    Chris Myers, Peter Lang Publishing, 29 Broadway, New York, NY, 10006
    ChrisM@plang.com

To order other books in this series, please contact our Customer Service Department:

    800-770-LANG (within the U.S.)
    212-647-7706 (outside the U.S.)
    212-647-7707 FAX

    Or browse online by series at:
    www.peterlang.com